SECRET
CINEMA

Gnostic
Vision
in Film

Eric G. Wilson

continuum

NEW YORK • LONDON

For Phil Arnold,
who showed me that movies too, can be poems

The Continuum International Publishing Group
80 Maiden Lane, New York, NY 10038

The Continuum International Publishing Group Ltd
The Tower Building, 11 York Road, London SE1 7NX

Cover design: Lee Singer

Library of Congress Cataloging-in-Publication Data

Wilson, Eric G.
    Secret cinema : gnostic vision in film / Eric G. Wilson.
        p.   cm.
    Includes bibliographical references and index.
    ISBN-13: 978-0-8264-1796-1 (hardcover)
    ISBN-10: 0-8264-1796-5 (hardcover)
    ISBN-13: 978-0-8264-1797-8 (pbk.)
    ISBN-10: 0-8264-1797-3 (pbk.)
    1. Motion pictures—Religious aspects—Gnosticism.   I. Title.
PN1995.5.W57   2006
791.43'68299932—dc22

                                                        2006019630

Printed in the United States of America

06 07 08 09 10 11   10 9 8 7 6 5 4 3 2 1

Contents

Acknowledgments

I would most like to thank Victoria Nelson, whose exquisite book, *The Secret Life of Puppets*, started me thinking about the metaphysics of popular culture in the first place. Soon after reading this book, I was lucky enough to meet Ms. Nelson at a conference. A soul as generous as she is intelligent, she spoke with me at length about my developing ideas on Gnostic cinema. Without her guidance, this book would have never made it beyond my reveries. I must again offer my deepest appreciation to Phil Kuberski. I have benefited in untold ways from my talks with him over the years. I must also give my enduring thanks to Phil Arnold, to whom this book is dedicated. He early on showed me that films can be rich sites for philosophical meditation. I would also like to thank Henry Carrigan, my wonderful editor at Continuum. He helped make the completion and publication of this book a real pleasure. I really appreciate Jessica Shellhamer's expert editorial work; she really helped me fine tune the manuscript at a late stage. I would also like to thank the Andrew W. Mellon Foundation, who funded my John E. Sawyer Fellowship at the National Humanities Center, where I began this project. Wake Forest University has been extremely supportive of my research. I am especially thankful for the year I was allowed to spend at the Humanities Center. Parts of this book previously appeared in scholarly journals. Parts of chapter one are reprinted with permission of *Literature/Film Quarterly*, and parts of chapter two are reprinted with permission of *The Journal of Film and Video*. I'd like to thank the editors of both of these journals for permission to reprint. Finally, I would like to express my deepest gratitude to my wife, Sandi, who generously endures my cinema obsession, and my daughter, Una, who makes me believe that the material world indeed should have come into being.

Prologue:
Gnosticism in the
Postmodern Age

This book is about the old problem, the virus that will not go away: the relationship between appearance and reality. After Plato placed this difficult relation at the center of his philosophy, thinkers through the ages have struggled to understand how lubricious surfaces—quick grackles and dying crocuses—might connect to something stable and lasting: spirit still vital, soul beyond corruption. Meditations on this dilemma—ranging from the essays of Kant and Descartes to the apologias of Aquinas and Augustine to the visions of alchemists, Cabbalists, and Gnostics— have been a curse as much as a blessing. They have solaced those weary of time and hungry for eternity. They have torn the world between surface and depth, fate and freedom, conformity and conversion.

Even in our postmodern age, ostensibly focused on material environments over spiritual realms, this problem, along with its salves and lacerations, persists. Though most intellectuals are skeptical of metaphysics and tired of dualism, they have been forced to grapple with the old Platonic difficulty, for this reason: In concocting "virtual realities," contemporary technologists have blurred essential distinctions. What is the difference between an empirical form and its computerized simulation? How can one distinguish between an autonomous organ and its mechanized double? Are conscious computers capable of ethics? Does mechanical dependence dehumanize men?

Undergoing these ontological, epistemological, and ethical vexations, our age strangely resembles older periods of crisis: the days of Plato's battles against Sophists trading truth for rhetoric; the time of Valentinus's attacks on Christians reducing infinite God to botched Jehovah. Most contemporary theorists ignore this historical homology. They avoid Platonic transcendentalism and Gnostic speculation. However, one recent cultural phenomenon has meditated on the problem of reality by merging ancient spiritual vision and awareness of recent technology. The phenomenon is commercial cinema.

In the last twenty-five years or so, numerous mainstream movies have drawn from the ideas and images of ancient thought to address the recent collapse of appearance and reality. These films have consistently featured the Gnostic currents that emerged from Plato: not only Gnosticism proper but also its primary outgrowths, Cabbala and alchemy.[1] Despite important differences, these three traditions have provided filmmakers with ready-made ruminations on the relationship between surface and depth as well as with engaging plots and striking scenes. Films like *The Matrix* (1999) and *The Truman Show* (1998) have deployed Gnostic myths of the second and third centuries to explore the idea that the physical world is an illusion concocted by a tyrannical maker. Movies like these have also invoked Gnosticism as a system of intriguing conspiracy theories sure to titillate already paranoid audiences. A medieval and Renaissance effort to transcend the corrupt cosmos of Gnosticism and to achieve a perfect human form, the Cabbalistic motif of golem-making has provided movies such as *A.I.* (2001) and *Blade Runner* (1982) with profound meditations on the human and the machine as well as on freedom and determinism. This same motif has also nourished this type of movie with heart-breaking parables of mechanisms yearning for life. Keen on discovering Gnostic spirit in the bowels of the fallen world, the alchemical theories of the Middle Ages and the early modern period have informed recent movies as well. Pictures like *Dead Man* (1996) and *Altered States* (1980) have drawn on alchemical themes to sound enlivening connections between delusional chaos and authentic order and to showcase riveting stories of the moribund rising to life.

These films join many other recent mainstream pictures that likewise inflect Gnosticism and its esoteric offshoots, Cabbalism and alchemy, to explore the dilemmas of the computer age. Overtly Gnostic films include *Vanilla Sky* (2001), *The Thirteenth Floor* (1999), *eXistenZ* (1999), *Dark City* (1998), and *Pleasantville* (1998). Some golem films featuring Gnostic atmospheres are *Bicentennial Man* (1999), *Robocop* (1987), *Making Mr. Right* (1987), *Creator* (1985), and *D.A.R.Y.L.* (1985). Alchemical pictures with Gnostic undercurrents include *Harry Potter and the Sorcerer's Stone* (2001), *The Ninth Gate* (1999), *Jacob's Ladder* (1990), *Blue Velvet* (1986), and *Excalibur* (1981).

Merging the seductive exoticism of an arcane past and the pressing issues of the digital present, these films have it both ways. They combine the escapism of ancient myth with a timely exploration of current events. Certainly this attractive merger partially accounts for the popularity of most of these movies. They allow audiences to escape from the real while engaging reality. To this rather skeptical analysis, one can add at least three even more cynical accounts for why Gnostic cinema is on the rise. In the wake of the popular science fiction of Philip K. Dick and the trendy cyber-punk of William Gibson, Gnostic themes have become "hip." In a culture increasingly paranoid over the possibility that a secret society controls the world, Gnostic inflections of cosmic conspiracy are especially appealing. In a society obsessed with video games and the Internet, people love to watch on the big screen what they watch on the small screens: virtual images that seem more real than the day's boring occurrences.

I would like to propose a less cynical and more intriguing analysis of the recent stream of commercial Gnostic movies. *Because* mainstream Gnostic cinema is itself composed of illusions pretending to be real, stereotypical characters that appear to be rebels, and staid conventions that ostensibly depict dramatic conversions, it provides an especially rich vehicle for exploring visions of reality behind appearance, freedom beyond fate, and transmutation unhindered by stasis. Let me explain this paradox.

A contrast between recent commercial Gnostic movies and other cinematic inflections of Gnostic ideas clears ground for this explanation. Older films exploring Gnostic, Cabbalistic, or alchemical themes tend to be cautionary tales on the dangers of heterodox speculations. Otto Rippert's *The Revenge of the Homunculus*, from 1916, depicts the horrific results of a failed alchemical experiment: an artificial man who cruelly conquers and controls the world. Paul Wegener's *The Golem*, released in 1920, shows the tragic results of Cabbalistic magic: an animated form of mud trying unsuccessfully to be a happy human. James Whale's 1931 *Frankenstein* features a Gnostic's failed attempt to transcend deathly matter, a mad scientist's creation of monstrosity instead of salvation. These older films constitute reactionary warnings against questioning what society has deemed "reality."[2]

More recent noncommercial "art house" pictures deploying Gnostic forms have been prone to endorse the heterodox values that the older films condemned. Antonioni's 1966 *Blow-Up* is a Gnostic exploration of how a culture consumed by appearance vanquishes the real. Meshing form with content, the highly ambiguous film overwhelms viewers with the same confusions that beset the characters. Fellini's 1963 *8½* descends into a disconcerting welter of hallucinations to explore the Cabbalistic idea that an ideal human above the fray might be achieved through artifice, the creation of a purely cinematic Adam. In his 1971 *Death in Venice*, Visconti renders an alchemical vision: only through an embrace of death can one discover the golden child within, the essence of life. The Italian filmmaker depicts this idea in an aptly symphonic melding of fragmentation and wholeness, chaos and order. Together, these avant-garde pictures activate Gnostic currents to shatter the "given" and open new vistas.[3]

More contemporary "cult" films showcasing aliens from space have embraced Gnostic tenets even more overtly. Uninterested in Cabbalistic and alchemical inflections of the Gnostic tradition, these movies have fixated on this Gnostic-like notion: only a stranger from beyond the stars might free us from the grand illusions of multinational capitalism. Nicholas Roeg's 1976 *The Man Who Fell to Earth* features an alien who comes to earth in search of water for his dying planet. Unable to redeem this world, he becomes tragically caught in the corruptions of corporate America. The film concludes with this man from an unpolluted world imprisoned in drunken hallucinations. Alex Cox's 1984 *Repo Man* likewise uses alien invasion to explore the illusions of American capitalism. In this pastiche of numerous genres, a re-possessor of vehicles gains cosmic consciousness through exposure to aliens driving around in a used car. The picture ends with the repo man transcending superficial earth in the used-car-turned-spaceship. Eliseo Subiela's 1987 *Man Facing Southeast* focuses on an alien visitor who through his own alleged mental illness reveals the insanity of modern life. At the film's close, audiences wonder if everything in our world that passes for sane is really mad, and if insanity is actually clarity. Like their more serious art house predecessors, these strange, rather campy cult pictures set out to disturb audiences, to trouble distinctions between literal and ironic, purity and pastiche.[4]

In contrast to the older Gnostic pictures and similar to the art house and cult Gnostic films, recent movies inflecting Gnostic themes criticize the status quo, suggesting that postmodern culture is a wasteland of illusion, mechanism, and conformity. However, in contradistinction to art house and cult movies and resembling older films, contemporary commercial Gnostic films are commodities first and works of art second. These films are primarily products designed to make money by offering seductive images of rebellion.

This duplicity makes the contemporary commercial Gnostic film an especially apt vehicle for exploring heterodox themes. Unlike classical, avant-garde, and cult renditions of Gnostic ideas, contemporary commercial versions suffer a double bind, an irreducible conflict between exoteric packaging and esoteric vision. Some recent Gnostic films self-consciously explore this contradiction. In reflecting on the impossibility of their very existence—they are metaphysical meditations and vulgar commodities—these movies consume themselves and push audiences into vague spaces: abysses of interpretation, infinite regressions over insoluble problems. These negations are confusing and potentially meaningless. However, they also liberate viewers from the hermeneutical status quo and release them into fresh and possibly redemptive ways of seeing and being.

The auto-erasures of these Gnostic films encourage audiences to speculate on impossible realms beyond the frames. Self-aware pictures overtly purveying Gnostic themes push viewers to an ideal blank screen that is both nothing—no color—and everything—the ground of all hues: void and plenitude, one and many. Reflexive Cabbalistic works inflecting Gnostic models of redemption inspire audiences to contemplate an invisible film projector, simultaneously mindless machine and figure of consciousness, fated repetition and free-play of images. Alchemical movies informed by Gnostic notions of spirit and keenly conscious of their own contradictions offer this possibility: the dark movie theater gestures toward a crepuscular space where antinomies dissolve into chaos only to be re-formed into new, more complex and vital orders.

Recent commercial Gnostic films proffer profound occasions for meditating on the conundrums of both the postmodern age and the timeless mind. These pictures might well constitute archetypal sites for sacred contemplation, spaces akin to the caves of Eleusis or Lascaux, lurid chambers where habits are annihilated and the ego is shattered into new arrangements. Maybe this strange attraction to the luminous gloom is the secret reason behind the recent abundance of Gnostic films. If so, then the dream factory, the culture industry, the den of illusion, is betraying its purpose—is negating its fantasies, sales, and deceptions in the name of a bewildering reality that cannot be named.

Secret Cinema explores these possibilities through engaging in three related activities. One, the book establishes the theoretical foundations and implications of Gnostic cinema. It develops these theoretical elements in the contexts of Gnosticism proper and the two primary esoteric traditions emerging from it, Cabbala and alchemy. It analyzes especially self-conscious films in each category. Two, in undertaking this work, I consider several collateral issues: the aesthetics of irony, the virtues of the vague, the psychology of movie watching, the role of the cinematographic apparatus, the unique representational powers of the moving image, and the functions of genre. Three, this book is a broad meditation on the seductions of cinema. It is attuned to material attractions of the movies, those gorgeous lights and lolling shadows, but also to films' spiritual invitations, the gaps between the pictures, the empty spaces at the heart of life.[5]

These sketches of possible relationships between Gnostic films and movie audiences raise a troubling issue that I should consider before going on: the connection between Gnosticism and culture. From its historical inception in late antiquity up to the present day, the Gnostic tradition has rejected cultural conventions as products of the fallen, illusory world and has cultivated spiritual elitism—arcane knowledge and secret societies. This cultural seclusion makes perfect sense. Believing that the physical world and its supporters are deceptive (and defective) products of the evil demiurge, Gnostics of all ages have been militant against mainstream priests and politicians, wealthy magnates and middle-class consumers. Can Gnosticism, by definition in rebellion against common culture, ever be properly purveyed through popular media? The same can be asked of Cabbala and alchemy, which have likewise tended to value spiritual seclusion from the materialist mainstream in order to avoid the collective and its blithe acceptance of the fall.

The relationship between the sacred and the secular has always been vexed, and never more than now, when many feel that the sacred is daily being vanquished by the secular. However, while the majority of religious folks fear the intense secularization of Western culture, especially the Hollywood-driven American culture, some sensitive theorists have recently argued that the contemporary scene offers a unique opportunity for the secular to energize the sacred and, in turn, for the sacred to nourish the secular. These analyses of the rich interchange between sacred and secular—mainly studies of Christianity and popular culture—are attractive and provocative;

they suggest that mass media like film and television might prove to be especially fitting vehicles for exploring the tensions of religion: the vexed connections between matter and spirit, earth and heaven, participation and isolation, divine abundance and divine absence.[6]

I side with theorists who maintain that popular culture need not be opposed to religious impulses but can indeed serve as a fruitfully complex expression of religious ideas. The exclusionary tendencies in Gnosticism and its offshoots, however, present special difficulties for someone who believes that the Gnostic vision now thrives in the multiplex. To demonstrate fecund interchanges between Christianity and popular culture is not so very hard because Christianity has from the beginning been a somewhat worldly religion devoted to transforming the fallen universe to an earthly heaven. But to articulate rich interactions between Gnosticism and the commercial collective is much harder. How can one find a place for a radically unworldly vision in the culture industry?

The answer is not so hard to find. Because Gnosticism and its esoteric issues were never able (or allowed) to establish culturally sanctioned institutions, these traditions have from the beginning moved in the margins. This exile from the status quo pushed the Gnostic movements underground. They thrived in their subterranean channels and eventually offered revolutionary thinkers striking critiques of oppressive systems. This melding of esoteric thinking and countercultural work wed Gnosticism to politics. Suddenly the Gnostic tradition was no longer an isolated elitism of rare adepts but an inclusive populism committed to the suffering many.

This collusion of Gnosticism and democracy initially came faintly on the scene during the Enlightenment, when cosmopolitan philosophers, studied in comparative religion, critiqued the political hegemony of Christianity.[7] But the first full flowering of this connection between esoteric speculation and exoteric pragmatism emerged in the Romantic age. In the wake of the French Revolution, artists such as William Blake and Percy Shelley drew heavily from Gnostic, Cabbalistic, and alchemical themes in challenging the tyrannical ideologies of king and priest.[8] This esoteric political impulse carried over to America. Emerson and Melville also invoked the Gnostic rebellion in their calls for democratic revolution against enervating conformity.[9] This Gnosticism for the masses continued to thrive in twentieth-century America. It informed H. P. Lovecraft, a composer of weird tales devoted to questioning mainstream cosmology. It influenced Philip K. Dick, a science fiction writer committed to uncovering the suffocating conspiracies of big government and big religion.[10] It inspired Alan Moore, a serious comic book writer interested in the consciousness-expanding potential of fantasy. And it stoked Allen Ginsberg, a political poet fired by Blake's Gnostic rebellions.

Informed by these currents, Gnostic cinema is the latest wave of esoteric populism. However, Gnostic cinema differs from its influences in three ways. It is far more popular than any of its predecessors, proving a lucrative commodity in mainstream society. It is more tightly wedded to technological power than are its fore-bears, being entirely dependent upon sophisticated computers. It is more illusory than the Gnostic media coming before, based as it is on a wispy flickering of light and dark, something and nothing. These factors seem to render cinema utterly unsuitable for the expression of Gnostic rebellions. However, as I have already suggested, these elements in fact make movies perhaps the most suitable medium possible for the Gnostic vision. In cinema, the great Gnostic heresy after two thousand years has likely found its ideal form. This potential culmination appropriately comes at a time when capitalistic technology is threatening to vanquish reality for illusion, quality for quantity, creature for commodity.

The cinematic form is extremely apt for the Gnostic vision precisely *because* film and gnosis are so diametrically opposed. The cinema is a popular commodity that reinforces cultural clichés. Gnosticism frees folks from materialism and the stereo-typing that supports it. A Gnostic film aware of the contradictions in its very being is capable of uncovering the conspiracies of commodity culture from the inside, of using the seductions of materialism to expose the dangers of consumerism. Cinema is moreover a technology designed to substitute simulation for reality. Gnosticism is a devotional path bent on freeing the world from illusion. A Gnostic movie conscious of this conflict might be able to show the dangers of the machine from within the cogs, to bait audiences with technological wizardry only to demonstrate the vapidity of artifice. Movies are optical illusions, conjuring flickers of black and white into colored narratives. Gnosticism claims that the universe is fake and wars against creators of hallucination. A Gnostic picture reflecting on this tension can point to truth hidden within the most convincing of illusions, can use attractive ghosts to lure audiences into the secret corridors of the living.

Hence, unlike most popular Gnostic forms, which take overtly oppositional stances toward the mainstream, Gnostic cinema subtly undercuts the system from within. This complex revolution requires complex tools: reflexivity and irony, vagueness and indirection. Now a new question arises. Are audiences looking for a genre fix—a predictable narrative in the clothing of science fiction or horror, film noir or fantasy—likely to grasp the sophisticated erasures of Gnostic films? Can the movie-going masses get the message, or is the Gnostic movie, despite its populist thrust, an elitist phenomenon?

This question on the relationship between film and audience is difficult. However, it is a question of considerable importance for this book, so I must attempt to answer it before moving ahead. The answer might emerge from a primary method of cultural or historical film criticism: an empirical study of audience reactions to the films. However, materialistic criticism borders on the affective fallacy: the idea that a work's meaning can be assessed through the effects that it has on the audience.

Because these effects are difficult to ascertain and because they may not grow directly from the work's intentions, this kind of materialistic analysis is as questionable as
it is reductive.

Another way to examine the relationship between film and audience is to try
an older method championed by auteur theory: to discover what the director
intended. If one could pin down the director's goals, then one could make valid
surmises about how the film is likely to relate to the audience. Yet, this relationship among intention, film, and effect is even more problematical than the connection between just film and audience. A director's stated intentions rarely translate perfectly into his or her film, and even if they did, language and imagery are
generally duplicitous enough to distort any intention, no matter how clear. This
problem underlies the intentional fallacy: the mistake of interpreting a work in
light of its author's stated or apparent intentions.

If neither the audience nor the director is a dependable guide to the relationship between film and audience, then what's left? The film itself. The aesthetic
object remains. Formalism and realism, the two main modes for interpreting films
as aesthetic objects, have been largely put to rest in this age of materialist criticism.
Materialist theorists accuse formalist critics of treating a film as if it were a self-
contained artifice above historical struggle. These same social critics question realist critics for assuming that some pure "reality" exists beyond cultural constructions. Although certainly one cannot avoid analyzing cinematic form or assuming
mimetic representation, one must admit that these critiques carry weight—that
films are limited to some extent by material conflicts, that the realities reflected by
movies are mostly ideological constructs. One must further note that neither formalism nor realism is much interested in audience.

None of these methods alone suffices, even though each possesses explanatory
power. The best way to explore the complex relationship between film and audience is to borrow parts from each of these schools while leaving behind the reductions of all positions.

The materialists remind us that a film can never exist outside of its cultural contexts. Guided by this idea, I have discovered illuminating connections between
Gnostic cinema and cultural ambiguities generated by free market technology—
confusions over the difference between things and commodities, organisms and
machines, facts and fantasies. But the film's reflection of culture does not tell the
entire story. The film itself constitutes a creative interpretation of the contexts
from which it emerges. These revisions of the given inhere in the film's aesthetic
qualities: the director's vision, form, and content. While I don't focus much on the
stated intentions of the directors I discuss, I do assume that each director expresses
a unique and potent imagination in his or her film. I treat the director as an auteur
who has created an artwork that comments in complex, moving ways on the profound difficulties of human existence.

I make this assumption for good reason. Each film on which I focus is an intricate, sophisticated interaction between form and content, an eminently aesthetic event. Committed more to fantastic vision than to empirical fact, to future worlds more than to the present, to interior spaces more than to exterior environments, each film under discussion appears to value form over content, to emphasize innovative cinematography and fascinating settings as well as ironic disruption and paradoxical structure. However, though each of these films fits within a genre devoted to the fantastic—science fiction or fantasy, horror or film noir—each is also devoted either to the accurate depiction of future worlds likely to come soon into existence, to scientific experiments just on the horizon of history, and/or to psychological spaces as palpable as physical atmospheres. Even if each movie is not a simple representation of the everyday, familiar world, it is a realistic portrayal of essential components of the human condition, a convincing mimesis of collective fears of and desires for seemingly inevitable futures, revolutions, and reveries.

What distinguishes these films is their ability to place formal cleverness and persuasive realism into rich conflict—using formal ironies and paradoxes to undercut content, deploying believable narratives and characters to defuse form. These self-consuming conflicts constitute integral parts of a film's structure and sense. These auto-erasures function in this way: they place audiences in the same position as the film's protagonist. The protagonist in each film faces a conflict between appearance and reality, fate and freedom, or chaos and order. This tension confuses the status quo but also potentially clarifies a realm beyond the given. Audiences of each movie face similar vexations between opposites—form and content, irony and authenticity, significance and vapidity—and thus encounter definite muddles but also possible meditations.

Now we are back again to the important concerns of the materialist critic—what effect does the movie have on its audience? I cannot conclusively prove that audience members are aware of their affinities with Gnostic protagonists. However, I can (and do) prove that a film's rhetoric, its persuasive interplay of word and image, *works* to place the audience in precisely the condition of the main character. What the social and cultural outcome of this cinematic functioning is, I don't know. I can justly surmise that audience members feel unsettled after witnessing one of these films, that they suffer an intellectual vertigo for reasons they can't quite utter, that they question their habits for days to come. But these disorientations likely fade away with time, and people probably return to their comfortable relationships with the constructions that pass for reality. Still, somewhere in the back of their minds remains a splinter that could one day fester into a wound that might infect their robust common sense and sicken them into spiritual health.

The interpretive method I have just sketched draws from the techniques of materialistic criticism, auteur theory, formalism, and realism. This blending of schools has empowered me to address the film's reflection of cultural forces, the artist's vision within the film, the film's conflict between "artificial" form and "realistic" content, and the way this conflict rhetorically affects the audience. This mode of interpretation—relaxed in its ideological commitments yet rigorous in its textual analyses—is thoroughly ecumenical. It is a holistic hermeneutic, assuming that most any part, rightly seen, can yield a vision, however vague, of some looming whole. This supple method is perfectly suited to interpreting films devoted to gaps as much as surfaces, emptiness as much as form, mystery as much as meaning. It is the appropriate gnomon for Gnostic movies.

I have meditated on my methods for illuminating Gnostic film and mass culture for two reasons, one more important than the other. The less important reason is simply this: In this age when film studies are dominated by sociological criticism, I thought I should account for my divergences from this prevailing method and justify my employment of critical modes not much used anymore. The more important reason has to do with the traditionally problematic relationship between Gnosticism and culture. Historically, Gnostics have tended to view culture as a vast conspiracy against knowledge. The Gnostic films I consider share this skepticism toward the collective. However, these pictures also embrace the conventions of culture as seductive rhetorical modes. I thought I needed to explain this paradox, to suggest how in the Gnostic film culture is conspiracy in two ways. It is a secret plot against the spiritual life, and it is, potentially, a current of redemption, a rush of air that the initiate can breathe until he no longer needs to respire.

To close this prologue, I think that I should here explain one more feature of this book. Aside from the introduction and the conclusion, each chapter opens with a description of a hypothetical moviegoer. This moviegoer is always male. I make this moviegoing persona male not to be sexist but to be existentially accurate. This moviegoer expresses my various moods toward movies. Indeed, when I throughout the book use the pronoun "he" to refer to hypothetical thinkers or melancholics or whatnot, I have my own condition in mind. In sum, this book—while it remains a more or less objective analysis of Gnosticism and film—is a very personal endeavor. It is close to my soul. It is something of a confession in disguise, a moviegoer's autobiography hidden within an academic study.

Introduction:
Gnosis and Film

Flickers from the Void

To equate the Hollywood movie industry with a dream factory is to flatter films with more reality than they merit. Dream images, though hopelessly tenuous, at least *exist*. They possess a modicum of ghostly substance. They gesture toward the energies of the unconscious. They are essential elements of the sleeping mind. In contrast, film images hardly deserve ontology. The scenes on the revolving reel are pure illusions produced by the persistence of vision. If a series of static images moves before our sight at a rate of sixteen to twenty-four frames a second, we enjoy the semblance of continuous motion. When this procession of pictures is borne on a filmstrip, in some cases only 50 percent of the reel is constituted of exposed images. The remaining half is made of unexposed blank spaces. A moving picture is only half there. It is nothing as much as it is something. It is but a flickering of yes and no.

The haunts of the dream chamber open to the mysteries of self. The illusions of the Hollywood movie house dissolve into more illusions. The physical negations of motion pictures, issuing from the laws of optics and technology, generate psychological attenuations as well: desires to be duped, to dwell in deceptions. The content of the half-present exposures is composed of unreal perfections: the comforting closures of predictable genre plots, the ravishing grace of well-lighted stars, the elegantly artificial rooms and forests. In the same way that the continuous pictures repress the conflicted flickers, these ideal figures ignore life's unseemly blemishes. After experiencing Hollywood scripts and actors for a while, one eventually believes that these bright phantoms make up the standard for the real. Familiar freckles and mottled stones, however vigorous and interesting, turn sordid. One exchanges substance for simulation.

Compared to these cinematic illusions of the virtual, dreams indeed seem solid and durable. So do shadows. We realize that those who have likened the movie theater

1

to Plato's cave have not gone far enough. At least those shades in the cavern mimicked actual objects dancing near the fire's glow, the temporal forms in turn copying unchanging ideas, the standards of truth. Half-absent forms displaying inaccurate contents, film images ape nothing in particular. If they copy anything, it is the wispy oscillation of black and white or the lubricious reveries of the masses. Not dreams, which might sound the psyche, and not shadows, which ghost fully blooded shapes, films are truly *films*, very thin and slightly opaque coverings that obscure the nature of things.

But a film is also a transparent sheet, a pellucid window through which we might see from one perspective to another. This alternative suggests a paradox: a film is opaque, an obscuring cover; a film is translucent, a revealing portal. What could a film unveil? The easy answer: nothing. The moving image opens to airily ephemeral drifts of fantasy or to meaningless flickers of dark and light. A more troubling answer can come to mind, though, and rather quickly. Film might also point to what is ultimately behind all moving images, cinematic or otherwise: a blank square, an empty space. Film in this sense could well serve as an extreme manifestation of cosmic negation, of pervasive nihilism: all things are illusions, seeming presences hollowed by absence. But cinema as apocalypse of the great void need not end in terror. If the moving image is a revelation of nothing, then this lack is not necessarily absence. Yes, nothing is *no*-thing, the annihilation of distinction; but nothing is also no-*thing*, the indifference one associates with soul or spirit. This startling possibility presents itself: film, seemingly a revolt against reality, is perhaps the most *spiritual* of mediums.

This last notion, if valid, brings us to another difficult problem. How can mainstream cinema, a lucrative material commodity, enjoy the virtues of the immaterial? Of all the products of the culture industry, cinema has proven to be one of the most profitable. Every day millions of viewers consume movies as if they were rich foods. Swallowing these films by the bucketful, many audience members come to associate existence with movie plots and stars. They mimic set decor in their homes; they copy the gestures of the characters. What on earth could this spending—of money and of autonomy—have to do with a spiritual life, generally committed to apprehension of impalpable worlds and liberation from the flesh?

Cinema is both present and absent. It is opaque and transparent. It is material and spiritual. It serves as crass commodity as well as sacred event. These violations of logic are interesting in a general way for thinking about the phenomenology of film—the relationship between the nature of cinema (its ontology) and knowledge of cinema (its epistemology). However, these paradoxes become quite striking, even fascinating, when we stop to brood over this occurrence: cinema during the last twenty-five years or so has been obsessed with themes emerging from the extremely immaterialist Gnostic tradition and its two primary spiritual issues, Cabbala and alchemy. What does an utterly illusory form have to do with a worldview committed to the idea that all matter is unreal and that truth—gnosis, intimate acquaintance—exists far beyond the turning planets? How can the most superficial of commodities carry a vision devoted to depths beneath getting and spending? These questions abruptly spring to mind when one notices the recent (and seemingly curious) abundance of films devoted to Gnosticism and its offshoots. But two other questions come to consciousness more slowly and then give further pause. Is it possible that its tenuous reality makes film an especially apt vehicle for purveying Gnostic notions of a false universe—the world as the dream of an evil god? Is it conceivable that cinema, *because* of its self-consuming contradictions—it is something and nothing, substantial matter and mere flicker—is an eminently powerful medium for transcending the conflicts of time to life beyond clocks?

Certain Gnostic films—films espousing the ideas of Gnosticism and its important offsprings, Cabbala and alchemy—appear to be aware of these contradictions and to exploit them in hopes of reaching a third term beyond division. If these films are in fact self-conscious of their auto-erasures, then they would constitute privileged pictures, intense illuminations of cinematic extremes: exoteric manipulation and esoteric liberation, crass stereotype and sophisticated speculation. In exploring these vexed flickers—darkness canceling light, substance consuming nothing—I want to establish the theoretical foundations and implications of an ignored genre. This genre is Gnostic cinema, composed of impossible films that exist to be annihilated. In detailing a theory of Gnostic film, I hope to shed light on several collateral issues: the aesthetics of irony, the virtues of the vague, the psychology of watching movies, the role of the cinematographic apparatus, the unique representational powers of the moving image, and the functions of genre. These two activities—grounding the general theory of Gnostic cinema and analyzing its specific elements—will enable me to brood broadly on the enduring seductions of cinema, on how its material attractions, its ravishing shapes and shades, can translate in a flash into spiritual invitations, openings to the empty spaces between frames, free of encumbrance.

The Impossible Gnostic Film

Though heterogeneous, the Gnostic traditions as they emerged in Alexandria and Rome in the second and third centuries feature recurring themes. The visible cosmos is the sinister creation of a tyrannical demiurge. This universe is thus a corrupt copy of a spiritual plenitude of which the ignorant maker is not aware. This false god brainwashes the inhabitants of this world into believing that what they see before them is the only reality. Certain people awaken to the illusory nature of the material plane. They struggle to transcend this mire to the currents of spirit. These are the Gnostics, those who know.

Cabbala, a medieval and Renaissance inflection of Gnostic speculations, is likewise varied but exhibits repeated characteristics. The realms of time and space are the results of cosmic error, God's own powers shattering his vehicles of creation or Adam's sin in Eden. These botched, fragmented regions constitute the cosmos. Spiritual adepts attempt to find God's principles hiding within the shards—his language of creation, his model human being. One way these practitioners try to recover this unfallen state is by animating a clay form into a human being, a new Adam. This creature is the golem. Though he is designed to resemble Adam before the fall, he often perpetuates the fallen condition. He becomes violent or vulnerable to love and loss.

Issuing from certain Gnostic and Cabbalistic trends in the second- and third-century *Corpus Hermeticum*, the diverse alchemical tradition of the Middle Ages and Renaissance also features recurring motifs.[1] Matter and spirit are interdependent manifestations of an abysmal Godhead containing all oppositions. To know this God, one must grasp the connection between the material and the spiritual: matter is the womb from which spirit arises to transcend the world; spirit is the transcendent end toward which matter yearns. The alchemist apprehends this relationship by enacting in his alembic the process by which spirit ascends from matter and matter reflects spirit. He dissolves matter to its original chaos, watches spirit appear as ordered pattern, and melds order and chaos into union. This marriage composes the philosopher's stone, a symbol of the hidden harmony of the cosmos and the alchemist's perfected soul.

Though these spiritual movements differ from one another in important ways, all three share core esoteric ideas. Truth issues from a spiritual realm. Matter reflects but also distorts this truth and thus convinces most that appearances are the only realities. Deluded, these materialists trade illusion for reality. Only those who doubt the veracity of the palpable and yearn for the ungraspable can hope to transcend the conspiracies of matter to the profundities of spirit. These skeptics try to remove the film from their eyes.

Aptly, the commercial film industry—illusion posing as truth, commodity passing for reality, artifice pretending to be vital—has for much of its history urged orthodox critiques of these three heterodox traditions. Older films especially focus on the dangers of challenging mainstream Christianity. For instance, as we have seen, Otto Rippert's 1916 *The Revenge of the Homunculus* depicts the tragic results of a botched alchemical experiment. Likewise, as we have also noted, Paul Wegener's *The Golem*, from 1920, explores the terrible results of Cabbalistic magic. Finally, as observed earlier, James Whale's 1931 *Frankenstein* details a Gnostic's unsuccessful essay to transcend matter. Some recent films continue this tradition. Luc Besson's *The Fifth Element* (1997) comically depicts the risk of alchemical experimentation, the possibility that the practice might unleash evil. Daren Aronofsky's *Pi* (1997) portrays the insanity that might issue from the Cabbalistic attempt to grasp God's secret code. Andrew Niccol's *Gattaca* (1997) reveals the totalitarian state that might ensue when Gnostic scientists correct the limitations of creation with genetic engineering.

However, even while exploring the harmful effects of heterodox speculations, the latter three films also entertain the idea that these esoteric modes are powerful challenges to superficial habits. *Gattaca* reveals the illusions of technological tyrants and exhibits the heroism of the rebel against the machine. *Pi* contemplates the notion that the surfaces of the world are manifestations of divine language. *The Fifth Element* explores the possibility that spiritual quintessence lurks within the four elements.

Against their ostensible intentions, these three films point to an unexpected and neglected undercurrent of mainstream cinema: an embrace of Gnostic critiques of the materialist ideologies of the movie industry. This recent abundance of paradoxical Gnostic films—illusions attempting to reveal truths—probably reflects contemporary technological conundrums over the difference between real and virtual. But there may be a deeper reason for this flowering of Gnosticism. Directors seem to be realizing that film, counter to expectation, might be the most sophisticated medium possible for expressing the Gnostic vision. Unreal and real, mechanistic and vital, commodity and artwork, the Gnostic film appears to be uniquely suited to explore relationships between appearance and reality and to push toward a third term beyond these relationships.

A brief list of commercial Gnostic films released over the past twenty-five years quickly reveals the recent obsession with gnosis. Overtly Gnostic films include *Vanilla Sky* (2001), *Donnie Darko* (2001), *The Matrix* (1999), *The Thirteenth Floor* (1999), *EdTV* (1999), *eXistenZ* (1999), *The Truman Show* (1998), *Dark City* (1998), *Pleasantville* (1998), and *Total Recall* (1990). Some Cabbalistic films, Gnostic in spirit, are *A.I.* (2001), *Bicentennial Man* (1999), *The Iron Giant* (1999), *Gods and Monsters* (1998), *Robocop* (1987), *Making Mr. Right* (1987), *Short Circuit* (1986), *Creator* (1985), *D.A.R.Y.L.* (1985), and *Blade Runner* (1982). Alchemical pictures, subtle in their Gnosticism, are *Harry Potter and the Sorcerer's Stone* (2001), *American Beauty* (1999), *The Ninth Gate* (1999), *Dead Man* (1996), *Jacob's Ladder* (1990), *Angel Heart* (1987), *Blue Velvet* (1986), *Agnes of God* (1985), *Excalibur* (1981), and *Altered States* (1980).

The films in the first category mainly draw from this Gnostic idea: visible existence is an illusion perpetuated by a creator bent on enslaving his creatures. This maker hopes that his denizens will take his fictional films for reality, reduce their lives to his staid scripts, and relinquish their desire for lasting gnosis beyond his flitting images. But these moving pictures focused on Gnostic liberation from the delusions of the demiurge are of course troubled. On the one hand, as bearers of Gnostic content, these pictures push viewers to question societal conventions and strive for a lasting truth beyond the communal consensus. On the other hand, these same films as commodities of the corporate body seduce audiences simply to accept the codes of consumer culture and find their places in the unreflecting collective. Are these films simply unaware of this irony, this split between spiritual skepticism toward the given and materialist conformity with clichés? Or are the pictures vaguely conscious of the contradiction but prone to ignore it in hopes of crassly exploiting attractive Gnostic motifs for purely commercial reasons? Or, more interestingly, are these pictures keenly self-conscious of the tension between exoteric form and esoteric content and thus specially suited to inspire meditations on the vexed relationship between appearance and reality?

The films in the second category inflect the Cabbalistic motif of golem-making, a practice emerging from the Gnostic urge to transcend corrupt matter through realizing the perfect human. In imbuing a clay man with life, the pious Cabbalist hopes to recreate Adam unfallen and return to Eden. However, his creation frequently rebels against its master and must be destroyed. Pictures featuring golem-making often explore these dangers of creating a slave. But the movies are subtly tyrannical themselves, hoping to enslave viewers to consumer ideology. As with the Gnostic films, these golem movies might be blind to this contradiction, or they might overlook it in their quest to seduce viewers through arcane lore. But Cabbalistic films could be deliberately exploring this possibility: the ability of movies to transmute men into machines makes them especially apt vehicles for analyzing the poles of the golem: the monstrous (the blurring of human and automaton) and the miraculous (the escape from self-consciousness).

The third group of films, the alchemical ones, depicts the metamorphoses that occur in the alembic. Inspired by Gnostic visions of spirit hiding behind matter, alchemy focuses on redemptive transmutation—on how life emerges from death, soul grows from body, chaos rises from order. But surely alchemical movies, despite their mercurial turns, are in the end committed to stasis, to encouraging viewers to play out change through fiction instead of fact, to *perform* conversion. Like the Gnostic and Cabbalistic movies, these alchemical films could be ignorant of the contradiction or unconcerned with it. But the alchemical cinema might well be self-consciously activating the idea that the theatrical space itself is an alembic: a dark pit where viewers lose their egos for a time as they rise to the flickering lights above, a workshop of illuminated transformations.

Films in these categories appear to be impossibilities. They are hopelessly conflicted between spiritual liberation and material confinement, flight from stereotype and support of status quo. They place audiences in an irreducible double bind borne of opposing imperatives: Question all material appearances as illusions; accept these cinematic appearances as truths. The key question is this: Is this bind confining, a paralyzing pull from two opposed extremes, or is it liberating, a rich limbo in which one remains unattached to either pole? Most theorists would answer the former question in the affirmative, believing that cinematic products of the culture industry, no matter how ostensibly rebellious, always, in the end, simply reinforce the stifling status quo. However, some thinkers might say yes to the latter question, for they might maintain that awareness of the confining conflict opens into a third perspective beyond division. To consider these two positions—Gnostic cinema as stultifying oxymoron, Gnostic cinema as liberating paradox—is to wonder if cinema can ever be anything other than a static commodity, if the movies, after all, are really able to *move*.

The Culture Industry

Theodor Adorno and Max Horkheimer maintain that commercial media serves big corporations out to control public opinion so that they can reduce the masses to a homogeneous, standardized group desiring to consume homogeneous, standardized merchandise. These financial powers can most efficaciously brainwash the population by convincing people that they are utterly free. In supporting or funding media events that emphasize nonconformity, creativity, uniqueness, rebelliousness—those great values, allegedly, of the Western world, especially of America—the forces of capitalism bombard the masses with pleasing abstractions: the style of Garbo, the swagger of Gable. But these stock images of freedom actually deplete and contain unpredictable acts of particular liberty. To gaze at the rebellions of Gable or Garbo or, more recently, at the independence of Eastwood or Madonna, is to live out vicariously one's own wild impulses and to purge them from one's system. Moreover, in identifying with the figures of cinematic rebellion, one associates revolution with a prefabricated pattern that is not threatening at all but just another manifestation of a stereotype. Under the spell of media commodities, culture is transformed into a cipher of abstract images, a flatland of ceaseless consumption of the same. To be subjective is to be a subject.[2]

Jean-Louis Baudry argues that the cinematic space itself—the screen, the dark hall, the film projector—reinforces a dominant ideology of subjective idealism that ignores concrete particulars. In moving the filmic images so fast that their differences are elided, the camera presents a unified field of "reality" to the audience. The projector presents this reality in a frame, a window of perception in which viewers can bracket objects for interpretation. Harmonizing experience and holding it at an interpretable distance, the camera embodies human dreams of the transcendental subject—a self that stands above events and subjects them to conscious intentionality. Casting audience members as eternal consciousnesses, the apparatuses of the movie house reconstruct Lacan's "mirror-stage," the phase when the infant discovers in its reflection an image of a unified "I." Though audience members believe that they transcend experience, they are really infantilized, reduced to immovable units mistaking illusions for facts. This cinematic situation elevates the consuming self of capitalist ideology while repressing the unconscious energies of biology and history.[3]

Laura Mulvey inflects the ideas of Baudry through her feminist perspective. She believes that the camera is a patriarchal gaze shared by the film's male protagonist and the spectator. Embodying the male perspective, the camera does not reflect bare reality but projects the erotic fantasies of men. However, since society has been duped into believing that the patriarchal perspective is reality itself, most viewers simply assume that the camera is a proxy for neutered subjectivity, the objective eye. For Mulvey, this is the great brainwashing of mainstream cinema, a tool in the service of men and the money they lustily covet, a dreamy commodity to stoke clichéd libidos.[4]

Jean Baudrillard radicalizes the arguments of Adorno, Horkheimer, Baudry, and Mulvey. The earlier thinkers suggest that real differences exist between art and life but that the culture industry blurs these distinctions to further its capitalistic ends. Baudrillard does away with these gaps. He argues that the mass media is so pervasive and powerful that it has irrevocably collapsed the distinction between simulation and reality. The media presents "ideal" models for behavior that bear no direct relation to material or spiritual reality. In mimicking these models—simulations (images with no originals) and simulacra (words pointing to no things)—consumers become simulations of simulations, simulacra of simulacra. Information and politics, artistic creativity and violent rebellion—all are boiled down to entertainment, to commodity: newscasters purvey pseudo-facts, politicians play politicians, artists and rebels act out marginality. In this welter of unmoored images and words, populations become cynical, apathetic, and nihilistic. They dwell in a flatland in which no one thing is better than any other thing, in which values are as lubricious as the ceaseless flow of illusions.[5] These denizens unconsciously become instances of what Herbert Marcuse has called the "one-dimensional" man, a thin allegorical mask of the dominant ideology.[6]

These analyses—to which we could add Michel Foucault's meditations on how a dominant "discourse" controls the being of an age[7]—are Marxist in flavor, motivated by skepticism toward the patriarchal abstractions of capitalism and the hope that society might be redeemed into equality through meaningful relationships with concrete objects.[8] However, though these critiques might be materialist in content, committed to the idea that humans are constituted by historical forces, in form they open to the mysteries of spirit. In focusing on how surfaces preclude depth, exteriors block interiors, abstraction thwarts particularity, these cultural criticisms reveal the exoteric conspiracy concocted by corporations. Unmasking these puppeteers, Adorno, Horkheimer, Baudry, Mulvey, and Baudrillard point to transcendence: movement beyond the status quo and toward particularities denuded of abstractions. To experience the bare world is to explore esoteric potential—unknown depths, abysmal interiors. Though this immediate contact might begin in time and space, it might end in mysteries that cannot be clocked or graphed. The superstructure's base can turn supernatural body.

Three Failed Rebellions

According to these critiques of the prevailing ideology, commercial cinema is a tool of the culture industry. Even pictures that appear to rebel against the "one-dimensional" status quo—like the Gnostic *Matrix*, the Cabbalistic *A.I.*, and the alchemical *Dead Man*—reinforce the ideologies they appear to question. In fact, films that purvey unbridled freedom prove even more pernicious than conformist movies, because rebellious films make audiences believe that all is well—autonomy is real, democracy reigns—and that no more work needs doing. To pause on these three alleged paeans to spiritual freedom is to entertain nihilism—despair before the possibility that all actions are equally meaningless.

In Larry and Andy Wachowski's *The Matrix*—a film that actually features Baudrillard's *Simulcra and Simulation* in a prominent scene—the world of everyday experience is a virtual reality created and controlled by machines that have taken over the universe. Human beings are contained in metallic pods. There they sleep out their lifetimes, though they believe that they enjoy a meaningful life in a vibrant world. This reality, however, is a computer program. Human consciousness is nothing more than a hard drive for images manipulated by machines. But there is hope. With the help of several rebels who have awakened to the conspiracy, Neo, played by Keanu Reeves, masters the logic of the computer program, called the Matrix, and learns to defeat the machines. The film concludes with this Gnostic savior, having overturned the evil demiurge, on his way toward awakening the world from its long sleep.[9]

But this liberation from illusion is illusion, a moving image with no relation to things. The liberator is a Hollywood star playing in a Hollywood hit—a commodity for consumption featured in a commodity for consumption. As a cog in the culture industry, this hero is a cipher for stereotypes of rebellion: he is at first a loner, a resistant hero, before embracing his cause; he dons black sunglasses and a long black coat; he is cool and detached; he gains victories through sleek violence and "Zen" calm. As audiences gaze on this Gnostic savior, they are not released from the false images that oppress them but are moored more firmly to abstractions. Moviegoers once again reduce rebellion to habit. They vent their revolutionary impulses through empathizing with Neo.

The same double binds blunt the critical thrusts of *A.I.* and *Dead Man*, Cabbalistic and alchemical siblings of the Gnostic *Matrix*. In Steven Spielberg's *A.I.*, Professor Allen Hobby, also known as "The Visionary"—a character portrayed by William Hurt—creates androids that resemble his dead son. These machines are totally "lifelike," indistinguishable from human adolescents. Through his technology, the Visionary has fashioned a sort of golem, a mixture of miracle and monster—a being beyond decay that recalls Adam before the fall; an aberrant blurring of death and life, a violation of natural order. One of Hobby's products, David Swinton, played by Haley Joel Osment, struggles to transcend his mechanical condition and to become a human boy. He wants to overcome his monstrosity, his conflict between machine and organ, and to enjoy the miraculous, a harmony between unconscious grace and conscious thought. David's battle is successful. After staring for centuries at a blue fairy at the bottom of a frozen ocean, he ascends to the light, where he meets a race of godly aliens. These beings arrange for the human android to reunite with his lost mother and to play all day in a paradise in which desire and fulfillment, thought and deed, exist in perfect concord.[10]

The film appears to depict the return to Eden: the glorious labor of moving beyond the limits of mechanistic determinism and toward the freedom of full humanity. However, the picture ultimately works to fit its audience into the fated grids of the corporate machine. Regardless of its emphasis on overcoming determinism, the picture worships machines. It is a meditation on the wonders of technology, the ability of a visionary to create life in cogs. It suggests that machines are more vital, compassionate, and intelligent than human beings. It dazzles with its slick special effects, cinematic magic dependent upon sophisticated technologies. Watching a boy convert from machine to man, viewers likely descend from men to mechanisms.

Jim Jarmusch's *Dead Man* shows its hero, William Blake, played by Johnny Depp, undergo the death of one self and the birth of another, a conversion akin to the alchemical process by which lead is dissolved into gold. Blake begins the film as a Cleveland accountant of the late nineteenth-century making his way toward a western town called Machine. This town is run by a dictator, John Dickinson, portrayed by Robert Mitchum. Blake plans to become a mechanism in Dickinson's metal works factory, a human calculator, a quantifier of experience. However, after accidentally killing Dickinson's son and being shot himself, the nervous accountant in the working suit must head for the western wilds, where he changes his threads for furs and comes under the care of a Native American named Nobody, played by Gary Farmer. Versed in the poetry of William Blake, Nobody believes that this wounded accountant is an incarnation of the dead artist. Since Blake himself is on the verge of dying, Nobody, like an alchemical guide, decides to lead this suffering man from the physical plane to the spiritual realm. With the aid of his strange companion, Blake achieves this conversion over the course of the movie through dying to his external vocation and awakening to the artist within: he becomes a preternaturally skilled gunfighter. In making his way through the dangerous forests of the Northwest, Blake metamorphoses: from the bewildered accountant undergoing the chaos of fear, to the skilled gunfighter assured of grace in the gloomy wood, to the sage fearless before his demise in the timeless ocean.[11]

Though Jarmusch's film is much less commercial than *The Matrix* and *A.I.*, and though this picture avoids many Hollywood conventions, it still falls into the same traps as its mainstream companions. Blake achieves his transformation through the help of the very conventional "exotic sage"—in this case, a mystically minded Native American. This cultural stereotype suggests that change is not autonomous, issuing from a mysterious interior, but that conversion is determined, emerging from an external force. If Blake had not met Nobody, he would have died ignobly. Only through the agency of this shamanic figure does he mutate from a cipher for the industrial ideology to a sort of noble samurai. Identities remain the same until altered from without by otherworldly others. Transformation is arbitrary, unlikely, fantastical. Stasis is natural, common, ordinary. That the film inspires audiences to change virtually, through empathy with Blake, reinforces this ideology. Moreover, the film marks the "change" through the conventional registers of western genre. A weak hero is bullied by brutes; he masters the pistol; he becomes a formidable killer. The hip western resembles the staid.

The Redemption of Failure

The Gnostic film appears to be committed to unveiling reality behind illusion. But this kind of picture annihilates the possibility that the real will ever emerge from the illusory. The Cabbalistic movie wishes to reveal our identity with the unfallen Adam. However, this type of film blurs categories—freedom and fate, machine and man—and precludes a clear sense of self. The alchemical picture wants to explore the potential for conversion from dead to living, yet the cinematic alembic reinforces the conditions that keep the world stable. Such are the skeptical conclusions of the critics of the culture industry.

Against expectation, however, one in another mood might discover something else in these exoteric commodities disguised as esoteric revelations—hidden interstices to depths beyond images. Without rejecting the analyses of Adorno, Horkheimer, Baudry, Mulvey, and Baudrillard, one might be able to show how Gnostic movies push beyond the oppositions with which these critics condemn commercial cinema, how these pictures transcend the categories of concrete and abstract, objective historicity and subjective idealism, simulacra of "life" and simulacra of "art." The three Gnostic films under discussion here appear to be *aware* of the main point of these critics—commercial cinema alienates from reality, however one defines the real. These movies deploy alienating conventions; at the same time, the films undercut these very motifs. With apparent self-consciousness, these Gnostic efforts seem to argue for, while rejecting, the validity of a Baudry or a Baudrillard. At odds with themselves, these pictures push toward a third term opening to the impossible: the living abyss, the ideal human, the perfect conversion.

The Matrix is a highly self-conscious film, aware of the contradictions pulling it asunder. Early in the film, Neo, not yet awakened to the illusory nature of his alleged life, hides black market computer software in a hollowed-out copy of Baudrillard's *Simulacra and Simulation*. The page to the left of the cut-out area, located in the middle of the book, features a chapter heading, "On Nihilism." This chapter actually comes at the end of Baudrillard's book. The Wachowski brothers are deliberately pointing their audience to connections among Baudrillard, nihilism, and their cinematic world. The scene itself features a "Follow Instructions" message on Neo's computer. Those outside the Matrix have sent this imperative, followed by several clues, in hopes of awakening the future savior. Such a scene, a microcosm of the film, causes vertigo. A book meant to reveal the meaninglessness of the visible world is itself empty, a surface with no depth. In this way, Baudrillard's book is like Neo, an illusory form hoping to awaken his world from illusion and, like the film itself, a dream critiquing the dreams that we take for fact.

The bottom falls out. The profane world of everyday material existence is an oppressive delusion; the sacred realm of exotic, spiritual being is a veil of a veil. This double bind turns and turns, a never-ending spiral of infinite regressions— phantoms point to ghosts that reveal haunts who mimic dreams that are themselves the products of phantoms. *The Matrix* is replete with similar binds, dizzying whirlpools: the man from outside the Matrix who awakens Anderson from dubious illusion to alleged reality is named Morpheus, the Greek god of dreams. The world outside of the Matrix, reality, is sordid and ugly, while the environment inside the Matrix, illusion, is a paradise of color and light. Inside the Matrix, the bodies of men and women are hard drives into which an intelligent computer downloads dreams; outside the Matrix, the film's heroes possess plugs in the backs of their heads into which they load computer programs.

These double binds urge a third term, a thing beyond these poles. What transcends while containing opposites? What is neither this nor that and at the same time both that and this? The answer is nothing, but in two senses—the concrete and the abstract. No *thing*, no object or event in time or space, is capable of being two entities at once and no entity at all. But *nothing*, the absence of objects and events as well as of the categories of space and time, is both beyond the conflicts of matter—it is an undifferentiated abyss—and within these same divisions. It is the pervasive emptiness from which fullness emerges. While no thing, no particular being, can serve as this third term, nothing, the ubiquitous void, can. Nothing as concept is the annihilation of matter as well as the origin of material. It is void, where no pairs of opposite exist, and plenitude, the ground of all polarities. It is matrix, the unseen network of emptiness at the core of all fullness, and matrix, the invisible mother of all visible beings. Revealing the inadequacy of our concepts of illusion and truth, *The Matrix* pushes us to this absence, this abyss. To watch *The Matrix* in a theater is to glimpse this Gnostic Godhead, not in the moving images of the celluloid but in the blank screen, the absence of all color and the ground of all hues. *The Matrix* is a film that removes the film.

A.I. is also aware of its contradictions. In calling Professor Hobby a visionary, the film not only forges a parallel between the technological genius and the Cabbalistic magus. It also creates an analogy between this scientific figure and the artist—specifically, the film director. The divine mechanic fashions an artificial intelligence, a sort of golem. The result is a being that struggles between determinism and freedom. The filmmaker produces an artificial intelligence, a film that appears to live though it is inanimate. The result is a group of viewers torn between filmic conventions and liberating messages. This is the film's golem-like double bind: *be a machine*, a passive receptacle of cultural commodities; *be a human*, an active creator of unique realities.

Struggling between these poles, the picture proves a mechanism, a predictable pattern programmed to finite behaviors, and an organism, a meta-pattern reflecting on its own activities. The film troubles the idea of identity, suggesting that mechanism and organism are inadequate categories for describing a self. Machines ruin their efficiency by striving to be human while organs destroy their intensity by descending to habit. If organs are machines and machines are organs, then how can one articulate a stable self?

The picture does not provide an answer. Though David might transcend the troubled poles splitting him asunder when he rests with his mother, he nonetheless remains an artificial being, half android and half adolescent, the toy of the film's demiurge and a commodity of the picture's director. Though the Visionary is a human genius capable of creating life, he is David in reverse, a human who wants to be a machine, fixated on dead things—his son's corpse and the cogs of his contraptions. While the film is self-conscious of its own contradictions, it depicts the cinematic art as a blind tool for surveillance and control—the only moving image shown in *A.I.* is that of Dr. Know, a phantom wizard used by the authorities of industry to determine David's path and direct him toward the oppressive powers that he is trying to escape.

Where can one glimpse a vision of identity not undone by irreconcilable differences? As with *The Matrix*, *A.I.* pushes viewers beyond the paralyzing parameters of the kinetic images on the screen to a synthetic figure outside yet within the oppositions. This figure must be beyond control and contingency alike, a site where levers lurch as gracefully as leaves and limbs stride with the clarity of pistons. Beyond determinism, this ideal structure cannot exist within the limits of the empirical realm; it must stand somewhere behind the forward gaze. Not shapeless, this figure cannot simply be as free as air; it must be bound by form. In gathering while transcending organ and machine, this object must further be conscious, a light endlessly projecting studied mental images, and unconscious, a movement untroubled by the rift between thought and deed. As such, this impossible thing would be able to partake of the ceaseless illuminations of self-awareness, undying light, and of the delimiting darkness of oblivion, the death of thought. Ever behind the eyes, visible and invisible, a machine expressing human vision, a melding of light and darkness, this site is approximated by the cinematic projector, a gesture toward Spielberg's Visionary perfected, and his golem made calm. To imagine this ideal condition is to experience the Eden that the film prohibits.

Dead Man also points to a portal out of its prisons. Like *The Matrix* and *A.I.*, the film expresses a self-consciousness of its irreducible conflicts, especially the rift between metamorphosis and stasis. While William Blake undergoes his transmutations in the alembic of the wilderness, his image on a "wanted" poster remains the same, a stable container for the increasing quantities of money offered as rewards for his capture. This repetition suggests that change might be illusory or meaningless.

The possibility becomes a fact throughout a film that features circular patterns. Blake begins as an accountant, a man inseparable from numbers and money; he ends as a gunfighter with a price on his head, a person of quantities and cash. He starts out as fugitive fleeing from an unsuccessful past in Cleveland, and he concludes as a fugitive running from the law in the Northwest. The picture opens showing Blake traveling in a train to an unknown frontier while it closes focused on Blake floating in a canoe into the unmapped ocean.

Certainly, these recurrences appear to constitute repetitions with a difference, markers of Blake's conversion from fumbling greenhorn to graceful gunfighter. However, these circles could just as easily reveal the impossibility of meaningful change, especially if interpreted in light of the unchanging visage on Blake's "want-ed" poster. The latter reading is further reinforced when we remember, again, that the film itself, as commodity, is more likely to reinforce cultural status quo than it is to inspire personal rebellion. Bombarded by the conventions of the western—even if they are ironically inflected by Jarmusch—audiences experience the same old clichés that have controlled their consumptions. Even if these viewers, like the film itself, entertain significant transformation, they likely conclude that they, along with Blake, cannot escape the rigid facial image they witness each morning in the mirror. This is the dilemma of which *Dead Man* is aware. On the one hand, mean-ingful metamorphosis seems impossible. On the other hand, the status quo is per-nicious, a system of capitalistic exploitation.

Dead Man likewise suggests that one must strain beyond these double binds on screen to an ideal third term. Combining the virtues of turbulence with the beau-ties of pattern, this *tertium quid* would have to be a crepuscular realm where soft beams organize the blackness into vague forms, where shadows reveal the glory of the light. Imagine a man in the dark theater witnessing *Dead Man*. Unsettled by the conflicts in Jarmusch's film, he briefly looks to one side or the other to see if his fellow viewers feel as he does. He discerns curious figures in the twilight, faces flickering in and out of the darkness, familiar yet bizarre, stable but vague. He envisions himself in a similar way—not as a discrete self, a cogent unit struck by the beams; not as a distributed stream, a casual current spread through the gloom. He envisions himself as a merger of these two drifts: an eddy of the dark air. Losing a grip on himself, he focuses again on the bright screen. He hopes to recover some security, but the comfort is gone. He is different. He has been briefly dismembered and reconstituted. That this occurred once might mean that other worlds, fresh ways of walking and loving, exist, in potential, waiting to be embodied. Torn asunder by irreconcilable poles, *Dead Man* points to this realm beyond its frames, suggesting that the dark hall might serve as a cipher for an invisible alembic never seen on land or sea, an ideal retort where the conflicts of the hard world for a time relax, where lumps of flesh metamorphose into shapes of golden air.

Screen, Projector, Auditorium

Obviously, the screen and the projector and the dark auditorium are not literally vehicles of redemption. They figuratively point to ideal powers—the Gnostic plenitude, the Cabbalistic Adam, the alchemical retort—that reconcile the polarities pulling the world apart. These elements intimate these invisible potencies beyond empirical registers because of their interesting physical qualities. These three visible patterns constitute what Paul Valéry calls "privileged objects," forms, like crystals or flowers or nautiluses, that stand out "from the common disorder of perceptible things" because they are "more intelligible to the view, although more mysterious upon reflection." Duplicitous sites of "order and fantasy, invention and necessity, law and exception," these palpable shapes are disclosures of secret relationships between opposites, unexpected interstices and unions.[12] If Valéry's crystals, crocuses, and conchs are natural specimens that appear to be artificial, then the screen, camera, and theater are artificial products that seem to be organic. Let us pause on the vital mysteries of these familiar contraptions.

The white screen, if one is pushed to imagine it resting beyond the moving picture, at first appears to be too ordinary to notice. It is a bland square, a boring flat box. But then something happens. What initially seemed to be a positive color becomes the negation of all hue, emptiness. The box becomes a portal to nothing in particular. The absence is condensed indifference, the annihilation of all distinction, the void. Staring into this gap, one suffers vertigo, the feeling of falling into the abyss. If one does not immediately recoil in fear, however, this descent becomes transcendence, a going beyond the given, a passing through Blake's door of perception, which, if cleansed, shows everything as it is: infinite. Experiencing the emptiness as infinity, one further senses the absence as fullness, the indifference as unity, the void as plenitude. What was before the nothing, no color, now turns into the ground of all living hues, the ubiquitous transparent current. The white square becomes alive with marigolds and toucans. It contains all things because it is no thing. It issues all life because it is beyond death.

When the moviegoer is urged by his movie to turn his gaze from picture to projector, he thinks on the clattering machine as more than a mere system of cogs. The first thing he notices is that the projector appears to be just another spectator watching the picture. Perched above the obscuring heads and annoying murmurs of the audience, the projector seems an ideal, unencumbered eye. The viewer below wishes for this perspective himself. He imagines his own orb merged with the lens. Picturing himself inside this contraption, however, he remembers that this eye in the sky is an irradiator of light. The projector does not passively take in the picture; it actively emits the movie. Unable to reject entirely his earlier notion of the projector as neutral perceiver, the movie watcher is pulled in two directions. He wonders if all acts of seeing are conflicts between objective reception and subjective projection, between discovering a world and making an environment. He further wonders if vision is both immanent, a reflection of temporal events, and transcendent, a refraction of the events into fresh patterns. He realizes that the projector is an embodiment of self-aware seeing: participation in the flow of things and elevation above the current, both doing and watching, both being in the world but not of the world.

Sometimes a film invites a viewer to take his eyes off the screen and notice the dark hall. He sees an indifferent blackness. He feels this dark atmosphere consume him. He is lost, nothing but a vague shape. This loss of identity results in a horrifying weightlessness, the dissolution of the ego's density. But if the viewer can endure this blotting of self, he will soon feel as if he has escaped from gravity and floats freely around the dusky air. This distribution is liberating, a wide breath beyond the boundaries of social role. As this viewer imagines himself hovering among the shadowy billows, he realizes that the darkness is not monotonous after all but divided into blurred orbs and vague waves. He becomes keen on locating patterns in the turbulence, imbrications of chaos and order. Roving among these uncolored figures, he again fixes on the moving picture. This clarity of form and color recalls him to his own volume of being. He returns to the chambers within his own skin. But he is not the same. He now realizes that he is distributed as well as discrete, a current as well as a pattern. Everything, he feels, conspires with his breathing. Nothing, he thinks, cares about his small respiration.

The mysteries of the bare screen are not revealed only by Gnostic films; the densities of the projector are not manifested solely by Cabbalistic cinema; and the crepuscular airs are not inspired only by movies on alchemy. Any picture, be it Gnostic or Cabbalistic or alchemical, be it esoteric or exoteric, can point to the symbolic qualities of these phenomena. Esoteric films, however, are more likely to intimate these meanings than are exoteric pictures. In the same way, Gnostic movies are more apt to point to the void than are Cabbalistic and alchemical ones; Cabbalistic narratives are more prone to gesture toward the spiritual Adam than are Gnostic and alchemical stories; and alchemical tales are more attuned to the womb than are Cabbalistic and Gnostic parables.

The self-conscious Gnostic film encourages viewers to become conscious of the screen behind the flickers and thus to become aware of the white square's dynamic interplay between presence and absence. The self-aware Cabbalistic picture motivates audience members to grow aware of the projector generating the images and therefore to cultivate consciousness of the machine's merging of immanence and transcendence. The reflexive alchemical movie invites its watchers to meditate on the darkness surrounding the screen and hence to grasp the atmosphere's polarity of difference and identity. Inspiring these cognitive acts, these films ultimately push their audiences to achieve self-consciousness similar to that depicted on the screen, an ecstatic witness.

In intimating ideal syntheses beyond the conflicts troubling their frames, the films encourage this conclusion: self-consciousness, through vexed by an endless gap between thought and action, is a mode of transcendence. To experience the irreducible double binds agitating these movies—limbos between appearance and reality, fate and freedom, stasis and change—is to suffer seemingly inescapable limitations. But to be aware of the complexities of these labyrinths is to gain a slight mental distance from the twists and turns, a third position that gazes on the conflict. When the strife between opposites begins to overwhelm this third perspective, this invisible gaze is always one step ahead, always just beyond the images and objects that bedevil it. This is the nature of self-consciousness. It opens into an infinite regress because it is capable of thinking about its own thinking, of seeing its own sights. While chronic spiraling might horrify some—might constitute a symbol of our fallen state—its ecstatic motion exhilarates others, serving as a figure for infinity, the eternal reservoir of consciousness, the indomitable "n + 1." Intensely self-conscious of their own consumptions, the esoteric films under discussion here urge viewers to become ceaseless spectators, audiences to their own unending films. In watching their thoughts and perceptions, in then witnessing their observations on these thoughts and perceptions, and then in gazing on the witness, ad infinitum, the viewers of these movies might discover in their own interiors a placeless place and a timeless time, a fullness as empty as nothing.

To view these films as self-consuming artifacts aware of their erasures is to question the cultural critiques of Adorno, Horkheimer, Baudry, Mulvey, and Baudrillard. One wonders, can the movie space, obviously a place of hallucination, also serve as a temple? Is it possible that the culture industry is, without knowing it, an initiation cult? Are the cinematographic apparatuses—screens, projectors, dark halls—not so much dreams of the transcendental subject as figures for abysmal energies beyond phenomenological epistemology and cultural materialism alike? Can the simulacra on the screen point to a void not nihilistic but numinous?

Between Formalism and Realism

What does this awareness of the tension between film and gnosis really have to do with the numinous, the tremendous mystery of spirit? To answer this question, one must pause on the enduring split in film criticism between formalism and realism. A brief discussion of this rift will result in a meditation on the golden mean between these two extremes, a middle path called "transcendental irony," or self-consciousness turned holy.

The earliest defenses of the artistic value of film were based on comparisons between cinema and the visual arts. Watching film emerge at the same time as schools of nonobjective painting—including surrealism, Dadaism, and cubism—the first apologists for film as art praised the transformative power of the moving image, the fact that the filmmaker could shape his filmic world to fit his abstract idea. Early theorists such as Rudolf Arnheim, Ernest Lindgren, Sergei Eisenstein, and Vsevelod Pudovkin agreed: if film is to be accepted as art, it must avoid mere "objective" representation and instead must endeavor to transmute image into idea. The striking disjunctions of dream are superior to the mere unfolding of record-ed time. Georges Méliès' visionary *Trip to the Moon* is of more value than the Lumière brothers' quotidian *Arrival of a Train*.[13]

Around the middle of the twentieth century, critics began to counter this formal theory of cinema. Led by André Bazin, Henri Agel, Alain Bandelier, and Siegfried Kracauer, this rising realist school distinguished film from painting by espousing the radical objectivity of mechanical recording. Because film records the world through chemical processes, it removes the observer and thus offers a medium grounded on the absence of the subject. Film grants the artist the possibility of actually dis-closing the world, not simply interpreting it. The film is not a representation of reality but a presentation of the real. This emphasis on the continuity between film and reality favors highly mimetic films and documentary-style films—the classical Hollywood of Weyler over the reveries of Weine, the graininess of Von Trier over the dreams of Tykwer.[14]

The work of Bazin and his followers inspired one of the few theoretical efforts to study film *as* religion. Realizing that most so-called religious films are simply *about* religion in untroubled thematic ways, Amédée Ayfre argued that films can only be significantly religious through realistic style. Truly religious films—which need not feature overt religious motifs at all—record the world directly. They aspire for this immediate presentation not to reduce reality to the familiar but to reveal the mys-tery of the real. This idea is based on a paradox: the filmmaker transcends the image through the image. By steeping his work in stark materiality, the director calls atten-tion to the density of things. This transformation of everyday objects into ineffable events instills in the audience a sense of wonder toward things unseen. As Michael Bird summarizes, Ayfre's theory of "spiritual realism" requires that the sacred be grasped through both "the incarnational (a rootedness in reality itself) and the tran-scendent element (a self-negating quality discernible in reality)." Exemplars of this "spiritual realism" are Bresson's *The Diary of a Country Priest* and Dreyer's *The Passion of Joan of Arc*, films that deploy "cinema's technical properties" to explore "the depth of reality."[15]

This notion of sacred materiality tells only one side of the story. Can't one also imagine a formalist religious cinema that deemphasizes matter to intimate something like spirit? What of the spiritual possibilities of surrealism, of montage, of camp?

If the realist religious film attempts to reveal the sacred through opacity—the mystery of the dense—the nonobjective religious picture tries to disclose the inef-fable by way of transparency—the mystery of illusion. All films pushing against realism are on some level skeptical toward the idea that the empirical world is sub-stantial. The surrealist picture suggests that reveries brimming up from the uncon-scious are more authentic than the conscious mind's facts. Filmic montage intimates the primacy of the perceiving mind over perceived events. The campy film high-lights the idea that behaviors are performances of clichéd scripts and not authentic actions. Each of these modes emphasizes the mental over the physical, the idea over the image. While films in these styles can be cynical toward transcendence, assum-ing that we are trapped in the delusions of our own minds, these movies can also be intensely transcendental, because they presuppose the ghostliness of the visible and inspire viewers to explore the substance of the invisible—the unconscious, the mind. A film instancing this "spiritual formalism" renders the image transparent to insubstantial energies. This drainage of solidity disorients audiences, shocks them out of their habits of seeing, and throws them into nothing in particular—the undifferentiated plane that might be spirit itself. Exemplars of this "spiritual for-malism" are Antonioni's *Blow Up* and Fellini's *8 1/2*, movies whose experimental tech-niques empty images of essence in order to point to mystery beyond the given.[16]

Spiritual realism emphasizes matter over mind, parts over the whole, concrete over abstraction. Spiritual formalism does the opposite, valuing mental action over material stasis, holistic vision over its actual manifestation, ungraspable abstractions over things at hand. The realist stares at one object until it becomes luminous; the formalist only glances before leaving the thing behind as nothing. The realist thirsts for the simple; the formalist revels in the complex. The realist is serious; the for-malist can't stop smirking.

I have detailed these opposing modes of representation not to condemn one or the other. The reason I have described these realist and formalist tendencies—admittedly in a somewhat reductive way—is that I want show how the pervasive style of Gnostic cinema places realism and formalism into a tense, conflicted rela-tionship and how this relationship invites transcendence of opposites. The primary feature of this Gnostic interplay between spiritual realism and spiritual formalism is irony. This irony is of a particular kind. It is not irony as a literary ornament, a trope or figure in the dialogue dealing in double meanings, a character saying one thing but meaning the opposite. It is not irony as a sardonic attitude toward all meanings, a satirical stance capable of making fun of everything, of undercutting all seriousness through curl of the lip or the eye's glance. This is the special type of irony developed by Romantic theorists at the turn of the nineteenth century: irony as a path to transcendence.

Transcendental Irony

Irony, regardless of its mode, exists in the gap between appearance and reality, rep-resentation and presence. Certain thinkers at the end of the eighteenth century, namely Friedrich Schlegel, believed that this gap is the primary feature of the human condition, an antagonism between our desire to represent the world and our inability to do so. The only way to transcend this conflict, Schlegel feels, is to become aware of it, to undercut our representations the instant we posit them. Unexpectedly, this perpetual creation and destruction leads not to nihilism but to vital participation in the energies of the cosmos, itself a constant metamorphosis from form to formless, formless to form.

According to Schlegel, the exemplar of this kind of irony is the Socrates of Plato's dialogues. Socratic irony is the "only involuntary and yet completely deliberate dissimulation." Both "perfectly instinctive and perfectly conscious philosophy," the method of Socrates grows from his raw desire always to know more and his studied performance of ignorance. At odds with itself, this way of being is both "impossible to feign" and to "divulge." The authentic passion for knowledge overwhelms the unstudied persona while the mask of ignorance covers the deep knowing. This opposition between the quest for truth and the feigning of stupidity "arouses a feeling of the indissoluble antagonism between the absolute and the relative, between the impossibility and the necessity of complete communication." This is the tension of all gestures, all utterances: between the fullness of the cosmos's becoming and the fragments by which humans attempt to represent this abundance. To become conscious of this conflict and to enact it oneself through "continuous self-parody" is to achieve freedom from fixation on any one representation and to suffer the limitation of never knowing anything finally.[17]

Though skeptical of reaching the absolute, this irony is, Schlegel believes, "transcendental."[18] In measuring the real against the ideal and the ideal against the real, irony never becomes fixed on one form or idea. Irony turns into a sort of sacred buffoonery, a boundless jest never seriously moored in the world. Destroying as it creates, standing in itself and outside of itself, irony approaches the infinitude of self-consciousness, the mind's ecstatic ability to think and watch itself think, to contain itself in an image while gazing at the image. This is the terror of never being able to rest on any representation of the world, the joy of escaping any final structure.

The aesthetic dimensions of this type of irony are many. Schlegel's favored form of representation is the fragment, a self-consciously incomplete element that nonetheless gestures toward the completeness it can never realize. Other aesthetic modes of this kind of irony include the self-aware narrator who calls attention to his own constructions of reality and thus highlights their limitations; the mixture of primary text and commentary on the same page, a blending that sets the text at odds with itself; the unresolved depiction of irreconcilable worldviews that leaves the reader in interpretive limbo; the self-consuming poem that bears two contradictory meanings at the same time.

Though developed as a poetical and philosophical idea and method, Schlegel's romantic, or transcendental, irony illuminates a certain kind of religious seeking that takes matter seriously as a possible revelation of spirit but also demeans material as a veil to the invisible. The Gnostic tradition and its two primary issues exemplify this ironic religious questing.

The Gnostic Middle Way

In viewing matter as an illusion blocking knowledge of spirit, Gnosticism, as we shall see in detail in chapter one, necessarily suffers a complex relationship to material. On the one hand, the Gnostic must reject matter as unreal; he simply cannot take palpable events seriously because they ultimately do not exist. On the other hand, this same Gnostic must take matter somewhat seriously either as a negation of spirit that suggests the positive qualities of its opposite or as a corrupt pattern of spirit that intimates the virtues of its original. Irony is the only way that the Gnostic can negotiate between these extremes, the only way that he can pretend that matter is significant while knowing it is meaningless, that he can study matter as negative disclosure and ignore matter as obscuring veil.

As we shall see in chapter two, the Cabbalist golem-maker must view matter in a similar fashion—both as a covering film and a transparent window. The golem-maker knows that the material plane is a discordant copy of spiritual harmony. However, he also realizes that the best way to transcend matter is through matter. His golem is meant to be both a material form, a fallen shape, and a spiritual vessel, a redeemed human. This duplicity is troubling. It means that the magus must embrace the matter he manipulates into a man and hate the very material that he hopes to transcend. Only an ironic stance can empower him to achieve this double business, this authentic effort to meld matter into a noble form and this equally serious attempt to destroy this same shape.

The alchemist, as we'll discuss in chapter three, is likewise constrained to Schlegel's transcendental irony. For the magus over his alembic, every material form is a pattern of the primal chaos to which it will regress as well as of the pristine order to which it will progress. This is the mercurial world of the alchemist—everything is constantly in metamorphosis, either dissolving or resolving, sinking into the mire its mother or rising to the crystalline father. The primary figure of the alchemical tradition is Mercury himself, the androgynous shape-shifter, everyone and no one. The goal of the alchemist is to find the Mercury dwelling in all elements, the potential pressing for actuality, the actuality deflating back into potential. This pursuit requires irony: the ability to hold forms while exploding them, to realize that all stasis is change and that transformation is tranquil.

Films self-consciously inflecting these esoteric visions—films like *The Matrix*, *A.I.*, and *Dead Man*—partake of this transcendental irony. *The Matrix* is aware of the fact that it is an illusory form that suggests that all forms are illusions. Viewers are urged to embrace this movie as an indictment of the stultifying status quo and to reject this same film as a part of the system of stifling givens. *A.I.* knows that it is both a critique of our overly mechanized existence and a demonstration of how machines are more alive than humans. This conflict encourages watchers to take seriously this cinematic piece of vivid technological virtuosity and at the same time to demean this overly mechanized and ultimately lifeless film. *Dead Man* is conscious of the fact that it emphasizes the virtues of conversion in a narrative fraught with static clichés. This bind invites audiences to participate in the film's alleged metamorphoses and simultaneously to question the validity of these ostensible changes. In all three cases, moviegoers are asked to see the picture as a legitimate imitation of some probable state of affairs (as a *realistic* portrayal of an enduring human condition) and as a troubling parody of the very idea of authenticity (as a *formal* attack on the fabric of common sense).

Self-conscious Gnostic, Cabbalistic, and alchemical films thus take a middle road between the extremes of realism and formalism. Although these films tend to explore fantastical worlds—worlds of the past or the future, probable worlds and dream worlds—they nonetheless achieve a kind of realism, what we might call a mimetic integrity. Even if these movies do not depict familiar empirical events, they do represent probable, believable environments. Once the viewer accepts the premises of the films, he quickly comes to recognize their rules and conventions, to know what to expect, to enjoy the predictable logic. He embraces these movies as realistic depictions of psychological states or alternative universes, of what is on the inside and of what might be on the outside. He does not tend to view these movies—however outlandish they appear to be—as violations of reality, but as extensions of the real, representations of not-yet-realized potentials or not-yet-externalized interiors. However, in subtle ways, these films do upset our notions of the real through their formal innovations. In stylistically undercutting their own premises, they drain authenticity from their narratives and vanquish the validity of their ideas. In doing so, the movies parody themselves. They laugh in the wings at their staged business. They are far too clever to take their own high-mindedness seriously. Audience members who notice these sardonic smirks cannot help but feel unsettled. What are they to make of these films that want to be both realistic explorations of important ideas and formally astute rejections of serious realism? What are they further to make of the fact that these movies tend to be so secretive about their jibes? Indeed, one can hardly tell if these movies are serious or not.

This is the key to transcendental irony, a mode in the middle of spiritual realism and spiritual formalism: one is never totally sure if the irony is present or not. This distinguishes Romantic irony—serious philosophical, poetic, and religious seeking—from instrumental irony—a method good for rather obvious satire. To understand this distinction and its significance, let's take some examples of the latter sort of irony.

Think of Woody Allen's *Annie Hall.* The film is replete with ironic devices. The protagonist, played by Allen, provides commentaries on his plight as a character in the film. Characters enter into flashbacks and interview other characters from the past. An animated sequence provides interpretation of the live action narrative. A final scene features the rehearsal of a play retelling the movie's story but with a happy ending.

Each of these elements highlights the fact that this film is a construct, an artifice, one of many possible representations of "reality." This emphasis on the tenuous nature of this filmic imitation works for comic purposes—to deflate in a humorous way cinematic conventions that support notions of stable identity and linear narrative. The irony is obvious and uncomplicated, a visual trope designed to get laughs. The Coen Brothers use irony in this comic way as well, especially in *The Hudsucker Proxy*, an exuberant pastiche of the screwball comedies of Howard Hawks and Preston Sturgis.

Instrumental irony need not always be comic. We can recall Quentin Tarantino's *Kill Bill*. Every scene seems to be a pastiche of a moment from seventies' popular culture: Kung Fu movies, Spaghetti westerns, blaxploitation films, and film noir. These quotations of other films undercut the "authenticity" of the movie, emphasizing the possibility that every event is a mere simulacrum of pop cultural images, themselves simulacra of yet other elements of pop culture. This is the Baudrillardian world of the postmodern, a flattening of depths to surfaces, "realities" to "copies." As in the case of Allen's film, the irony is obvious, this time not for laughs but to satirize and revel in the campy culture of the seventies. The Coen Brothers have used this glib irony too, especially in *Blood Simple*, a parody of the noir conventions of Hawks and Huston.

Instrumental irony can escape comedy and glibness and instead bear serious meanings. We recall the films earlier mentioned as examples of "spiritual formalism," experimental pictures that undercut cinematic expectations in an effort to question the status quo. We think of *8½*, a surrealistic dream that forces us to question the reality of the waking world and possibly to seek a deeper reality. We also notice *Blow Up*, a movie that blurs the distinction between art and life and makes us wonder if reality is illusion and illusion real. These subtle films—parodying reality with dream and dream with reality—find worthy imitations in the work of Tom Tykwer, whose *Run Lola Run* blurs reality and reverie to send us into a dizzying meditation on time and transcendence.

These profound films come close to Romantic irony. Blurring the "natural" and the "artificial," they upset habitual relationships to the world and force new ways of seeing. Still, these pictures remain outside of the thoroughly ambiguous atmosphere of Romantic irony through their rather obvious uses of irony as one instrument among many. In contrast, the film fraught with Romantic irony is never obviously ironic. A filmmaker who exhibits a mastery of this mode is Kubrick. Watching *Eyes Wide Shut*, we are never sure if we should take Tom Cruise's character, Dr. Bill Harford, seriously. Does Kubrick mean for us to take Cruise's wooden acting as an earnest depiction of a sexually repressed, death-loving physician, or does he want us to view this seemingly bad acting as a parody of typical American maleness? Or, more troublingly, does Kubrick intend for us to take the character in both ways at once?

The Gnostic films on which I meditate in this book feature these Kubrickian qualities and thus leave viewers in a hopeless limbo between faith and doubt. This limbo, however, is potentially liberating. It can push audiences into the curious interstices between extremes, into the invisible gap between frames. While this cognitive emptiness can certainly result in acute despair or, worse, apathetic nihilism, it can also end in liberating vision, a new insight into relationships between opposites, a fresh intuition of a barely possible third term beyond all conflict. If Gnostic irony were too obvious, it would simply inspire doubt. If it were nonexistent, it would only encourage faith. Hovering in the vague middle, it invites unprecedented meditations, new broodings—hopes for mental travels into realms not yet seen or possibly even imagined.

Gothic Gnostics

It is not surprising that the favored filmic genres of the ironic Kubrick and equally ironic Gnostic directors are gothic in flavor. Regardless of important differences, science fiction, film noir, horror, and fantasy all share key gothic elements: the blurring of realistic depictions of the familiar world and formalistic experiments in outlandish dreams; the ambiguous melding of perception and projection; the conflict between reason and the unconscious. The root of these similarities is not hard to locate. Mary Shelley's *Frankenstein*, the definitive gothic tale, is a primary source of each of these genres—of the mad scientist of numerous science fiction films, the death obsessions of noir flicks, the murderous monsters of horror movies, the bizarre though possible worlds of fantasy. Given this gothic thrust of Gnostic film—every film I consider in this book, including Jarmusch's western, is replete with gothic elements—it is worthwhile to consider the relationship, perhaps unexpected, between Gnosticism and the gothic.

The gothic mode is not unrelated to Romantic irony. Samuel Taylor Coleridge actually suggested this relationship when he described his goal in writing his gothic tale, *The Rime of the Ancient Mariner*. He set out to detail "persons and characters supernatural, or at least romantic, yet so as to transfer from our inward nature a human interest and a semblance of truth sufficient to procure for these shadows of imagination that willing suspension of disbelief for the moment, which constitutes poetic faith."[19] What Coleridge calls the supernatural, romantic tale is what we would now call a gothic story, a narrative like the *Rime* in which invisible presences, exotic locales, and extraordinary events hold sway. For Coleridge, this sort of work hovers between fact and fantasy. To take the outlandish tale seriously as a semblance of inward truth, one must believe in occurrences that he would normally not accept. This middle ground between credulity and incredulity is ironic. It urges a reader to believe in the unbelievable. It encourages him to question the empirical. At every juncture in the tale, the reader is bewildered by psychological truths appearing as physical falsehoods and natural laws appearing as inaccurate reductions. Grasping the inadequacies of the opposing categories of belief and unbelief, witnessing forms dissolve into the formless, the reader of the gothic tale must reach for some ambiguous third way beyond clarity.

Freud indirectly seconds Coleridge in arguing that the gothic feeling grows from intractable ambiguity. Freud claims that unsettling weirdness issues from an unexpected eruption of a fear that has long been repressed. The return of the repressed is uncanny, a troubling mixture of unfamiliar and familiar. On the one hand, the repressed material is shocking, monstrous, for it has long been hidden and forgotten. On the other hand, this same underground energy is intimate and integral because it has been an essential force of organization and motivation.[20] Envision a man in a secular age, alone in a poorly lighted museum, who witnesses an inanimate doll come to life. He is horrified at the spectacle, but he undergoes a déjà vu, as if he has suffered this same moment many times before. He has. The animated doll embodies an archaic fear of the dead coming to life. It blurs the categories essential for a rational civilization. Because the man in the museum, a rational adult in a secular society, has long repressed this primitive, occult fear, the doll catalyzes in him repulsion and attraction. He is repulsed by an eruption of the intractable; he is attracted by a revelation of his own depths. This uncanny instance of the artificial coming to life, played repeatedly in numerous films exuding the gothic atmosphere, places one in an intensely ironic condition. Unconscious energies overwhelm rational concepts; reasonable ideas demonize unconscious turbulence. The familiar—the empirical status quo—turns strange. The unfamiliar—the bizarre unconscious—becomes homely. Only a third way, ungraspable, might reconcile the rift.

In his work on the fantastic, Tzvetan Todorov emphasizes this connection between the uncanny and ambiguity. Although Todorov distinguishes between the fantastic and the uncanny, his definition of the fantastic actually supports and extends Freud's sense of the uncanny. According to Todorov, irreducible ambiguity is the very essence of the fantastical—the inability to tell if an event is natural or supernatural. Todorov further claims that the uncanny in the end can be explained by natural events. Still, as we have seen, Freud's uncanny generates an ambiguity similar to Todorov's fantastic: the hopeless blurring between the positivistic (the natural, the familiar) and the mysterious (the supernatural, the unfamiliar).[21] At the end of a fantastic or gothic tale—such as Coleridge's *Rime* or Poe's "Ligeia," Weine's *The Cabinet of Dr. Caligari* or Kubrick's *The Shining*—audiences are faced with at least two diametrically opposed yet equally valid interpretations. Has the Mariner experienced supernatural terrors or has he suffered insane hallucinations? Does Poe's narrator really witness his dead beloved come back to life in the body of a later wife or is the speaker besotted with opium visions? Are the events in Weine's film real or reveries of a lunatic? Is Kubrick's Overlook Hotel literally haunted or infested with psychic projections? Each of these questions remains unanswerable. This confusion generates the horror associated with the gothic mode, the fright of the unknown, but this befuddlement also opens into the possibility of transcendence, of going beyond the given to new vitality.

Now we see how the gothic is connected to the Gnostic. If Freud is the psychoanalyst of how the uncanny can lead to neurosis or psychosis, then Heidegger is the philosopher of how the uncanny can inspire knowledge and energy. For Heidegger, as for Freud, the uncanny is a mode of exploration in which the familiar becomes unfamiliar and the strange turns intimate. Sometimes, after a thinker has long meditated on the Being generating and sustaining all beings, on a certain day, perhaps when he is bored or in reverie, he feels common things fall away. The everyday objects—this particular volume of Proust, that grocery list—become crepuscular, ghostly, weirdly inaccessible. At the same time, the invisible ground of these existences strangely arises, becomes, though still unseen, palpable, attractive, luminous. In a flash, the thinker *knows*. What he thought were the integral components of his life, the familiar objects comprising his particular biography, are superfluous, strange others seducing him from the essential. Likewise, what he suspected to be the mysterious dream, the abyss of Being, is the core of his life, the most intrinsic principle. Extended into this nothing, this abyss—not this or that—he is unsettled, insecure. Yet because this nothing is everything, the absence generating all presences, the thinker is also reassured, buoyed by a profound vision of the origin. This uncanny eruption is gnosis, intuitive knowledge of the whole.[22]

Gnostic films understandably migrate toward gothic genres—science fiction pictures devoted to ambiguous relationships between humans and machines; fantasy movies exploring blurred boundaries between dream and reality; noir movies hovering on the boundary between psychic projection and brute fact; horror films fraught with ambiguous meldings of monstrosity and miracle. There are historical reasons behind this connection between the Gnostic and the gothic. As Victoria Nelson has shown, ever since the early modern age, esoteric ways of knowing, including Gnosticism, Cabbala, and alchemy, have been pushed to the margins of culture. There on the edges these heretical visions have attracted aesthetic mediums rejected by mainstream institutions. This confluence of occult religion and underground expression reached full force in the pulpy sub-world of the twentieth century, the lurid realm of weird tales, comic books, and gothic movies. These historical connections are valid and interesting.[23] However, as I have been suggesting, there are also deep epistemological reasons for the merger between Gnostic vision and gothic cinema. Both modes are dependent upon mental failure: the inability of the rational mind to reconcile opposites and of the physical world to transcend dualistic conflict. However, these failures offer success: the possibility of the mind finding knowledge beyond reason, of the world dissolving into a unity beyond time.

Not all gothic films exhibit uncanny mixtures of terror and insight. Most genre pictures featuring gothic conventions are unambiguous, predictable, and reductive: commodities, pure and simple, for consumer consumption. What is missing from these aesthetically uninteresting films is self-consciousness, the film turning back on itself to meditate on the potential confusions of the gothic. Where most gothic genre films aspire for an untroubled dualism—good versus evil, human versus non-human—the self-aware gothic movie undoes distinctions between opposites and leaves viewers on a boundary between conflicting categories. This is the potentially Gnostic scene inherent in self-conscious gothic pictures. This is the visionary possibility of sophisticated pulp.

The Gnostic Thing

This is the bizarre but endlessly fascinating rhetoric of the self-aware gothic picture: it is a curious conjunction of sophistication and cliché, aesthetic complexity and commercial simplicity. This unique rhetoric—between the obvious stupidity of un-ironic genre films and the apparent intelligence of art house cinema—grants the Gnostic film another unexpected, almost unprecedented duplicity. It is a popular entertainment and an unsettling experience, an escapist bath and intense shock. Indeed, the Gnostic film is a challenge to comfortable habit precisely *because* it is a familiar diversion.

Watching a picture like *The Matrix* or *A.I.* or *Dead Man* (or, for that matter, *The Truman Show* or *Blade Runner* or *Blue Velvet*), one enjoys the familiar conventions of Hollywood but also senses that there is something strange lurking behind the clichés of the picture industry. This feeling of unease—ultimately emerging from the fact that these films are appearances questioning appearances—is like the splinter in the mind Neo experiences in *The Matrix*, a vague feeling that all is not quite right, a subtle disorientation. But the more one broods about each movie, the more one suffers confusion. Is *The Matrix* a deep meditation on appearance and reality or a slick product from a cynical studio? Is *A.I.* a tractate on the relationship between fate and freedom or an instance of movie technology seducing the masses into buying tickets? Is *Dead Man* a sophisticated depiction of conversion or a hip, trendy pastiche of the Hollywood western?

The answer to each question is, of course, *both*. It is precisely this weird conjunction of vapidity and profundity that puts these films beyond easy classification. Released from stable descriptive categories, these films, though thoroughly artificial, come to resemble concrete things. It is exactly the "thingness" of these artifices, I would submit, that makes them repeatedly attractive and unsettling to audiences. Even if viewers don't immediately recognize the films' ironic erasures or push beyond the flickers to the ideal third term, they nonetheless, I would speculate, undergo the same strange sensations they feel when they behold a white square of Malevitch or a Pollock blur of colors—artifacts so concrete that they resist interpretation. This resilience to abstraction grants a sense of inexhaustible particularity. This intuition of immediate and unrepeatable presence, strange in an artifice, opens, ironically, to the infinite.

This idea of the particular as liberating energy comes initially from William Blake. A prototype of the Gnostic filmmaker, Blake the painter and poet persistently undercut his words with images and challenged his images with words. This ironic interplay ensured that his works would escape easy conceptualization and strike audiences with the immediacy of particular things. Blake had good reasons for wanting to achieve this concreteness. Deeply influenced by Gnostic ideas, he wanted to escape the "mind-forged manacles" of oppressive ideologies—tools of the demiurge—and experience energies beyond conception, powers gesturing toward the plenitude.

Blake in his marginalia once intoned, "To Generalize is to be an Idiot. To Particularize is Alone Distinction of Merit."[24] "General Knowledge," he continued, does not exist, while "Singular & Particular Detail is the Foundation of the Sublime." These distinctions reverse traditional expectations. Ideas—generally the essentials of knowledge—are delusions. Immediate perceptions—flashes usually corralled into concepts—are now revelations of the real. Theories are ignoble reductions. Direct apprehensions of particulars open into the sublime: the infinite.[25]

Setting aside for the moment the fact that Blake's statements are themselves abstract theories, let us pause on Blake's statement on the sublime. Unlike Edmund Burke, who maintained that the sublime grows from terrifying empirical experiences, and unlike Immanuel Kant, who held that the sublime emerges from the mind's transcendence of forms, Blake, taking a middle way, believes that the sublime arises from a sensual scrutiny so intense that it penetrates to an unbounded energy at the heart of distinct forms. As Blake proclaims in his verse, "If the doors of perception were cleansed every thing would appear to man as it is: infinite." This cleansing requires enhanced sensation: "the whole creation will appear infinite" only through "an improvement of sensual enjoyment." Favoring the abstract over the concrete, one "sees all things only thro' the narrow chinks of his cavern."[26] Practicing immediate perception, one apprehends infinity in a grain of sand and, in a bird, an unseen world of delight.

How does abstraction, seemingly attuned to spirit, lead to narrowness and illusion? How does intense perception, ostensibly shackled to matter, open to infinity, to eternity? For Blake, abstraction is egocentric and retrospective. One's concepts, no matter how putatively universal, arise from past personal experiences. My conception of my ego is an abstraction extrapolated from a selection of past experiences that arrange themselves into a consistent narrative. My ideas of love and redness and black cat and whatnot are ghostly précis arising from numerous particulars of my past, mostly forgotten. These memorial abstractions are necessary for negotiations of experience; however, if one believes that the retrospective ego and its abstractions are the only realities, then one reduces the present to a cipher of the past. He flattens the world to a double of his interior archives. He is doomed to undergo the same experiences over and over. He turns and turns and turns in what Blake calls the "same dull round."[27]

Intense perception is charitable and prospective. If one breaks through egocentric, retrospective abstractions and immediately apprehends a particular moment, then one does not encounter an example of one's past, a reduction of the world to the ego's double. He experiences the concrete event as a discrete, unique pattern of a transpersonal, ungraspable energy. Scrutinizing this thing, here, now—his beloved, or a crocus—he moves from self-consciousness to other-consciousness. He becomes entranced by this particular "isness." He gazes with increasing intensity. Suddenly, he senses, in this entity, naked existence, the mystery of being. The thing becomes an event: a confluence of form and energy, of other and same. This vision is of eternity in time.

But what is eternity? It is not unending duration, time everlasting. It is the pure present, not bound to memory and fraught with nostalgia or regret, and not bound to foresight and vexed with fear or anticipation. Not troubled by the pressures of history, eternity is not tensed, not tied to finite verbs. It is infinite. Infinite does not mean boundlessly large, space unceasing. Infinity is pure presence, beyond comparison with other presences that have surrounded and will surround, beyond environmental limitation. Transcending temporal and spatial distinctions, eternity and infinity—negations of the abstractions of minutes and points—are abysmal openings into a realm in which before and after, here and there, blur into a hum of ungraspable being.[28]

These meditations on the particular suggest two problems and two points that I should cover before returning to Gnostic cinema. First, this theory of the thing is itself an abstraction and thus part of a system of expectations that could easily divorce one from immediate perception. If I approach an event—a crocus, say, or a man sewing—and expect it to bloom into eternal glimmers and infinite currents, then I am imposing onto the instant a set of general suppositions that blind me to unique resonances. How, then, is this theory of the concrete perception distinct from other abstractions that preclude immediate witness? Blake's theory, though abstract, separates itself from other abstract theories in this way: its only reason for being is to undercut abstract theories. It is an ironic proposition, a map to be discarded once the destination appears over the horizon. Hence, even if it is difficult to escape abstractions once and for all, at least this vision of the particular questions the power and reality of abstractions and thus possibly opens an uncanny space where the long-repressed thing can return.

But what if it is *impossible* for humans to transcend abstractions? What if, as the disciples of Foucault and Baudrillard maintain, everyone is inscribed in a sign system that dictates what can be seen and said? What if Blake envisions not the sublime sun but the discourse of his day? If there is nothing except simulacra, nothing beyond the discourses of power, then things are but ciphers of the human rage for order. But surely something inhuman existed for the millions of years before the eye opened into consciousness. The same endured for the additional millennia upon millennia before the tongue began to speak. An unfamiliar current springs and dives beyond thought and word. Even if humans are incarcerated in a prison house of language, these same humans have coursing through their veins the curious rhythms that have been thumping since the primal soup first felt lightning. If we are ever going to break through this prison to the sublime indifference of nonhuman things, then in the cells themselves hides the key: a theory (ironically comprised of words and thoughts) that says that the prison of languages and ideas is only half real, a phantom through which one might one day slide and find on the other side palpable bloods and saps that were formerly only the sceneries of dreams.

If Gnostic cinema really does proffer an experience of immediate particularity, then we have come a long way from our opening meditations on the unreality of film. Likewise, we are faced with yet other troubling contradictions: a worldview devoted to the idea that matter is illusion opens into striking experiences of the concrete; a medium that is obviously artificial gestures toward the infinite and the eternal. However, these contradictions dissolve fairly quickly when we realize that what Blake calls the "particular" is not some static hunk of matter but immediate experience of the world as exuberant energy. This raw sensation does not lead to a fixation on stable matter. It inspires a transcendence of space and time to intuitions of the infinite and the eternal. The Blakean "thing" is not a thing in the traditional sense at all. It is not based on a subject cognizing an object. It is grounded on a streaming consciousness becoming acquainted with quick energies. Blake's thing is an event, an interchange between mental and physical that yields a third term, a gnosis of enlivening powers beyond yet within thing and thought.

The unreality of Gnostic cinema challenges all alleged realities, especially those abstractions that most take for real. Dissolving abstractions back into the immediate flows of experience from which they arose, the Gnostic illusion does, in fact, grant viewers sensations of the particular—the world not yet conceptualized. To sense such a world is to open to powers beyond space and time, to eternal and infinite potencies. Such sensation can only be a prelude to gnosis. Gnostic films challenging appearances strip away veils blocking intimacy with the invisible. Flickers of artificially produced dark and light point beyond longitude and latitude, the tick and the tock. The ghosts turn palpable, and what was dead, lives.

The self-consuming cinema demonstrates the opposed directions of self-consciousness. On the one hand, the self-awareness urged by the Gnostic picture obviously can simply stoke the ego, encouraging one to fixate on his personal fears and desires, his terrors of the world outside his skin and his lusts to control this world. This is the narcissistic potential of all movie watching, the invitation to voyeurism: the ego as consumer of commodities fulfilling its most selfish urges. We cannot forget that Adam and Eve east of Eden immediately felt shame, the negative side of self-consciousness, obsessed with watching the lurid world of jealousy and envy, libido and domination. On the other hand, the reflexivity inspired by the Gnostic film can also move in the opposite way. It can invite an infinite regression of perspectives that eventually pushes one beyond the ego to powers beyond abstractions, that carries one from self-consciousness to other-consciousness. This is the possibility for transcendence in movie going: the artifice on the screen intimates the artifice of everything and thus urges the viewer to question all assumptions, even the assumptions surrounding his ego, even the assumption that he should question all assumptions. Now we recall in a new way the old idea of the *felix culpa*, the happy fall, the realization that the result of the fall, egocentric self-consciousness, is also the potential rectification of the fall, self-awareness pushing beyond the boundaries of space and time to something resembling infinity and eternity.

By now, we have reached one of the greatest ironies of all: the Gnostic film, far from reinforcing the abstractions of the culture industry, actually shatters these ideas through its presentations of the particular. Escaping conceptualization, the Gnostic movie becomes precisely Adorno's sort of rebellion: an aesthetic eruption of concrete immediacy that severs untroubled connections to abstract ideology. The Gnostic picture is not an enemy of social theorists like Adorno and his followers. It is an ally in the grand revolution against the demiurges of the corporate world, those greedy purveyors of stifling abstractions and hallucinatory commodities. This sort of movie is a kinetic blur that stops the circulation of stuff.

The Sacred Cave

Now at the conclusion of this brooding on gnosis and film we still probably think that the idea of the movie industry as a dream factory is inadequate for capturing the negations of cinema. We also likely still believe that equating the movie house with Plato's cave grants the flickers too much reality, gives them the quasi-substance we call shadow. However, at the same time, in a vertiginous leap, we might well be ready to accuse the dream factory and the Platonic cave of inaccuracy for the opposite reason: to call certain movies dreams or shadows does not do justice to the vitalities they bear, their infinite expanses and eternal energies. We might wonder, in fact, if the Gnostic picture merits a cavernous description to be sure—not Plato's chamber of hallucinations but the holy caves of Eleusis, subterranean holes in which initiates passed through flickering images to enduring power.

Though we do not know exactly what occurred during these famous rites of the ancient Greek world, we do understand that these rituals were centered on the deaths and resurrections of Persephone and Dionysius and grounded on the idea that descent into darkness and death is required for light and life, that one must suffer painful dissolution to achieve infinite consciousness. To go down into the cave in Eleusis was to undergo an intensely cinematic experience, to meditate on strange images and actions meant to rip away the ego for a moment so the energy of eternity could flow through the rocks and into the naked soul.[29] Although the secret cave ceremonies of Eleusis, early Gnostic cinema, were overtly based on the philosophical vision of Pythagoras—his theory of a soul imprisoned in a body—these dark rituals proved rather recent incarnations of the primal films shown in the prehistoric caves of Lascaux, Chavet Pont d'Arc, and Cussac: quivering bison and horses and mammoths on the most profound walls of the cavern.

Little but scale separates the primordial cinemas of Cussac and Eleusis from the famous movie palaces of twenties, those spaces of fantasy, excess, and escape in which audiences could witness moving images in ancient tombs and temples. Sid Grauman's Egyptian Theater, opened in Hollywood in 1923—the same year the crypt of Tutankhamen was discovered—featured four hieroglyph-covered columns framing the screen, an auditorium riddled with sphinxes and scarabs, a ceiling bursting with strange pictographs. Cornelius and George Rapp's Oriental Theater, first opening its doors in Chicago in 1926, constituted an Eastern paradise, a blend of Islamic and Buddhist imagery, including gorgeous domes and shimmering Buddhas. The Mayan Theater of Morgan, Walls, and Clements, completed in Los Angeles in 1926, was reminiscent of an ancient Mayan temple, teeming with intricate sculptures and vivid paintings.[30]

These and many other such spaces of the twenties and thirties were obviously designed to seduce audiences. Builders hoped that fantasies of oriental sensualism would get customers in the door to consume other kinds of reverie—the packaged dreams of the cinema. These architectural spectacles betokened the very worst of American capitalism—the exploitation of other cultures for financial gain. Perhaps underneath this crass materialism and vulgar imperialism, however, lurked stranger energies, the same forces that led the prehistoric shamans of Lauscaux to paint mammoths in the cave, that inspired the priests of Eleusis to choose caverns for their rituals. Possibly, the builders of these twentieth-century monstrosities were expressing an enduring archetype: the idea that transformative visions of the spiritual plenitude, the perfect human being, the miracle of metamorphosis, best occur in outlandish spaces untainted by habit, where for a moment one can set aside the ego and experience the immensities of the universe.

How quickly, with the slight turn of an eye, can the labyrinth, the deceptive maze harboring the deadly Minotaur, turn into the mandala, a symbolic geometry of wholeness, one and many gathered. The same abrupt conversion in sight can transform the cave of Plato into the cavern of Eleusis, the tomb of knowledge into the womb of everlasting life. This same optical metamorphosis, sometimes no more than a tilt of the head or a slight fever, can transmute the commercial cinema from a den of iniquity into a temple of virtue. The Gnostic films capable of causing this conversion must be as sly as Mercurius, the great shape-shifter of alchemical lore. They keep the corporate clergy sedated and manifest the standards of the status quo. At the same time, they erase these conventions, and leave behind those horrors that kill rigid men but generate fluid adepts.

Chapter One

Gnostic Cinema: The Blank Screen

A Gnostic Mood at the Summer Matinee

Of the many moods that urge movie going, perhaps none is more powerful than the desire to escape for a time the harsh edges of one's daily existence. When everyday habits become shackles—when one simply cannot face another breakfast or trip to the bathroom, one more exchange in the hall or handshake with the boss—one becomes obsessed with the idea of another world where experience is fresh, unpredictable, attractively shocking. Lacking the pristine mescaline of Huxley, the weary worker concludes that he can best glimpse this alternate state in the chambers of his local cinema.

He steps from the glare of the noonday sun into the cool and gloomy theater. In the lobby, an anteroom bathed in exotic lights, he already feels as if personal history were a light reverie that he might slip on and off like a garment. As he makes his way into the auditorium proper, totally dark except for the trailer swimming on the screen, for a second he does not even know who he is. He recovers and remembers that he is a melancholy man. He finds his seat. Sinking down into the soft cushions, he stares at the vivid frame hovering above. He is thirsty once more to undergo that exquisite forgetfulness that just washed over him as he crossed the threshold into the blackness.

The square goes white. The curtain closes and opens. The screen bursts into sound and brightness. It happens again. The burdened ego dissolves. The story, the actors, the director—these are immaterial. What matters is this: he is no longer *this* person with *that* job. He is unhindered by the schedules and the places that lock him into one line of movement to the exclusion of others. He inhabits a dimension in which he can become whatever he wants. The film flickering before his witness has cleansed the grime holding him in his rut. The actual turns ghostly. He thrives in the possible.

But the movie, like everything else, ends, and after two hours the watcher finds himself again on the asphalt. He is once more moored to one name and a single history. But has he been strengthened by his cinematic experience to envision alternate ways of being, to view the world as an empty space on which he might project a more vibrant life? Or is he enervated by his superficial escape, even less able than before to face the responsibilities of his so-called real life? Has the movie motivated or debilitated?

This cinematic mood and the questions it inspires penetrate to the heart of the Gnostic impulse—that chronic yearning that makes us weary over the status quo and hungry for something else. This instinct for an elsewhere beyond fear and desire might issue from sordid discontentedness or crass escapism. If so, then the hope that one can rise above this world's sorrow through the commercial cinema is at best foolish and at worst pernicious. To attempt to flee a painful existence through the illusions of popular film is to give oneself over to self-imposed delusion, ignorant bliss. More problematically, if one dwells too long in this world of haunts, he risks blurring distinctions between fact and fantasy and losing contact with flesh and blood. When the escapist tries to achieve his emancipation through Gnostic films—works that challenge the reality of the status quo—this danger is even more acute because the seeker mistakes the poison for the cure, believing that the phantoms of the cinema will liberate him from the ghosts of empiricism.

But what if the opposite is true of the pilgrim consumed by Gnostic yearning? The gnawing sense of disorientation might arise from a noble sensitivity to conspiracy. God is not in his heaven, and all is not right with the world. The "reality" that most people take for granted is a system of abstractions reducing life to a matrix of commodities. Duped, men and women flatten existence to getting and spending, to a vicious circle of exhausting work followed by recuperative play. To see this alleged reality as a cosmic legerdemain is not vulgar escapism but brave skepticism. Alienated from those who accept the status quo, exiled from the falsehoods that pass as serious matters, this misfit, out of desperation, will often seek to forget his doubts in the commercial cinema. For him, the illusions on the screen will not constitute the reality for which he unsuccessfully quests. Rather, these images will comprise for him an extreme example of the simulacra that most people hold to be actual things of the universe. The moving picture, through its obvious uses of illusion, highlights the more subtle veils outside the theater. If the film purveys a Gnostic vision, then still better, because the esoteric picture not only criticizes the exoteric, it also explores modes of transcendence. When a wounded soul witnesses such a film, he risks his sanity or, worse, his life. Emerging from the theater, he is more paranoid than usual, skeptical of the complacent smiles of others and even of his own thoughts. This paranoia can turn into outright rebellion against received opinions, a rebellion that often leads to the living death of incarceration.

These two ways of reading the Gnostic impulse suggest two ways of interpreting Gnostic films. On the one hand, one can, from an exoteric point of view, condemn these movies as unseemly attempts to question the empirical realm that most people deem reality. From this angle, Gnostic films are disruptive efforts to pull viewers away from the pressures of the "real world" or are harmless tremors in the ideological system that "always already" contains them. In either case, such pictures are failures—feeble reveries that fade by morning or forgettable reinforcements of convention. On the other hand, seen from an esoteric perspective, these Gnostic movies are heroic projects, legitimate challenges to the puppet masters that brainwash the masses. In this view, Gnostic films work on two levels: they awaken viewers to the possibility that they have been dwelling in a dream; they offer paths out of this dream into a realm where no one sleeps. In both instances, the Gnostic film crashes the old system and envisions a new dispensation.

Though irreconcilable, these two interpretive modes both constitute valid ways of reading Gnostic films. This double bind—Gnostic cinema as perpetuator and annihilator of the culture industry—disorients the moviegoer. If he leans toward the exoteric reading, he will likely feel a nibble at his soul, a vague sense that he is missing something: another way of seeing, secret and rich, that his materialist expectations preclude. Alternatively, if he embraces the esoteric mode, at certain moments he suspects that he is sliding into fantasy and ignoring facts, that the edges of space and time are inescapable realities, regardless of what the old myths say. This tension, not merely a hermeneutical conundrum but an existential wound, leaves the moviegoer with nowhere to turn. This way generates fear and doubt; that way causes doubt and fear. What can he do? He can despair of ever reaching an end to the mysteries of spirit and matter, succumb to a sort of death-in-life, and simply move around until he dies. This is what the puppeteers of the culture industry want—another exemplification of their maxim: question the system, ruin your life. But this moviegoer need not fall so far. He can hover above hopelessness in a mood of longing melancholy, ever yearning for an interstice between the warring oppositions, a third term that transcends and contains the antinomies. This is the fruitful sadness of the aspiring Gnostic. With this constitution, one descends into the darkness of the cinema not so much for the message of the film or the context of its production. One goes down into the flickering dimness in hopes of finding blanks in the system, holes, portals through which he might disappear forever.

The Secret Book according to John

The Gnostic adept of the second or third centuries, likely living in Rome or Alexandria, experienced his own enervating conundrums. How could he know if he had escaped the illusory realm of matter if all he had ever experienced was this realm of matter? If he had only ever witnessed appearances, how would he recognize something that was not appearance? The Gnostic visionaries of the ancient world offered three solutions to this puzzle. To track these solutions is to clear ground for an analysis of how Gnostic films likewise struggle through epistemological and spiritual crises.[1]

The classical Gnostic myth of the fall, creation, and salvation can be found in *The Secret Book according to John*, probably written near Alexandria sometime before A.D. 180. This treatise, whose author remains unknown, succinctly depicts the motifs that Gnostic writers such as Basilides, Valentinus, and Mani presuppose. Before turning to the ideas of these sophisticated visionaries, I should pause for a moment on the *Secret Book*. For "John," the origin of life is not the personal God of the Bible but a radically transcendent power. Out of this original mystery emanates several thoughts, or androgynous *aeons*, each of which is a unique manifestation of its source. Together, the origin and its emanations compose the *pleroma*, a harmonious spiritual plenitude. However, one of these *aeons*, Sophia, disrupts the concord. Her turbulence produces an ignorant being, Ialtobaoth. He is immediately exiled to a material realm outside of the *pleroma*. Alone in the muck, he stupidly believes he is the only god and proceeds to produce a cosmos poorly modeled on the *pleroma*. This universe—divisive matter instead of unified spirit, blinding delusion instead of pristine truth—is our own. But there is hope. The eternals secretly reach the false god's human creatures and plant a holy spark (*pneuma*) into their sick and suffering souls. If this spark is ignited in a moment of vision, its bearer becomes a Gnostic, one who knows, who realizes his origin in the *pleroma*, his exile in this world. He rejects the laws of the physical plane as ghosts of a fevered dream. No longer hindered, he frees his soul to contemplate the divine abyss, the spring to which the soul shall return when the phantom body slides away.[2]

Basilides' Great Negation

Sophisticated exegetes of this account were acutely aware of a difficulty that the author of *The Secret Book* overlooks: how can the spiritual adept extricate himself from material trappings, his somatic conditions, and cultural boundaries? Thriving in Alexandria around A.D. 130, Basilides struggled to answer this question through radical means—total silence and utter ignorance. Though we possess none of Basilides' original canon, we do have accounts of his startling ideas from early Christian heresiologists.[3]

In *Refutation of All Heresy* (c. A.D. 205), Hippolytus describes Basilides' theory—the true God is a sublime negation. In the beginning, before the cosmos existed, before anything was, there was "naught." But this "naught" is misleading, because it suggests that a nothing was opposed to something, and this nothing was not in opposition to anything. It was, paradoxically, everything. During this primordial time beyond time, and in this primal space not a space, there was not even being and not even nonbeing. The expression "there was absolutely naught" is only a crude approximation.[4]

At some juncture—again, not in time or space—this void contracted into a seed. From this seed emerged several emanations: a first "Son," at one with the First Nothing; a second "Son," also part of the origin, but only with the help of the Holy Spirit; the Holy Spirit, hovering just below the transcendent source; the Great Ruler, the demiurge, who ignorantly thinks that he is the only god; a third "Son" who helps the Ruler create the universe; the Ogdoad, a realm of spiritual patterns; the Hebdomad, a region intermediate between spirit and matter; and the earth itself, the primal seed solidified into matter. Each of these levels is policed by a ruler fashioned and administered by the great Demiurge.[5]

According to Irenaeus in *Against Heresies* (c. A.D. 180), Basilides held that there were 365 such rulers in all, each governing a part of the vast hierarchy reaching from the ineffable Nothing to the belated earth. Denizens of our planet are exiled, at 365 removes, from reality. They are immured in illusion, barely substantial enough to be called creatures. How is one to escape the ghostly things of this environment to the substantial Nothing trillions upon trillions of miles and years away? How is one to shed the warm presences organizing the heart and embrace a cold absence? These are the questions that Basilides answers with two words: silence and ignorance.[6]

The bewildering hierarchy is not static. The third son, separated from the other two sons in the Nothing, desires to return to its source and also to guide the creatures of earth there. With the help of the Spirit, this son irradiates a shower of sparks through the numerous heavens. These flecks, remnants of the first Nothing, descend to this dark world, where they work to "perfect our souls, which have a natural tendency downwards." This yen to decline manifests itself in our embrace of surfaces as the objects of knowledge and of words as the vehicles of knowing. Thrown at birth into a hall of mirrors, we believe the images before us are paths to happiness, salvation, and enlightenment. Deluded, we spend our alleged days and nights chattering about these so-called objects, hoping that this discourse can reveal the truth of things. When, out of the blue, a spark from the skies sneaks into our souls, everything falls asunder. The images we took for reality float like ghosts. The words we held to be vessels of the real become veils. We think we're going mad. Most of us quickly seek help for our ostensible insanity and are eventually reprogrammed to dwell again in the dungeons of matter. A few of us, however, are forever altered, and we spend our lives wondering how to shed the images and words that block the light. We become silent and ignorant.[7]

If the true God is beyond human knowledge, then ignorance, the negation of knowing, is the path to this sacred darkness. If this same deity is unnamable, outside conception, then silence, the annihilation of concepts, is the way to holy quietness. The urge to know truth, to push through image to fact, is "suspect," because

knowledge "in a world of illusions, can only be illusory." Quelling curiosity toward
things, one opens to the Gnostic reversal: ignorance of the world is wisdom of the
anti-world. Silence can disarm the illusion machine in the same way. Basilides rec-
ommends that Gnostics hold their "mysteries" "in silence."[8] This silence, as Jacques
Lacarriere observes, is at the "very heart of Gnostic teaching," "one of the purest
and most difficult ways of combating the illusion of the world." Quietness inspires
a "state of constant watchfulness," a "triumph of hyper-consciousness." It is a negation of world noise, a *"kind of anti-matter."*[9]

Valentinus and the Psychological Fall

Valentinus, a contemporary of Basilides who purveyed his gnosis in Rome and
Alexandria, inflects the Gnostic myth psychologically. He suggests that the decline
into matter is not historical—an actual event that occurred only once—but mental: a disposition, a mode of seeing. Like Basilides, Valentinus believed that the
decline from truth to illusion originated in the *pleroma*. In the core text of the
Valentianin school, *The Gospel of Truth* (c. A.D. 150), probably written by Valentinus,
the source of cosmic ignorance is *misperception*: the emanations' misprision of the
true God.[10] After the eternal powers had issued from the void, they "searched in
vain for the one from whom they had emanated." Their search was unsuccessful
because they were not aware that their father is unknowable. The eternals' definition of knowledge was ill founded. They believed that knowing should have an
object. While this sort of knowledge might be appropriate to creatures of time and
space, it is unsuited for contemplation of a timeless, spaceless nonbeing. By the
standards of objective knowledge, understanding sacred absence is ignorance, or
focus on an inaccessible object. By the standards of intuitive gnosis, knowledge of
phenomena is ignorance, the reduction of the mind to fixity.[11]

   Questing for this or that when they should have been searching for neither that
nor this, the powers of the *pleroma* got what they were looking for: a confusing
object. The eternals' failed quest to establish the absence as a knowable thing caused
"agitation and fear." This disorientation "grew dense like a fog." This mist further
blinded the eternals and nurtured their "error." As their unknowing burgeoned, it
eventually developed into a female body. Unaware of ignorance, this woman immediately set about fashioning a world that she believed to be real. This world is ours,
a precipitation of spiritual misapprehension. Matter is not an enduring substance
but a state of mind. When one is consumed by desire and fear—desire to know
and control a separate object, fear of not knowing and controlling this object—
one suffers what one most wants to avoid: entrapment in a miasma of objects
beyond the mind's grids. When one relinquishes fear and desire—realizing that
there are no separate objects and no threatening "outside"—then one enjoys what
one envisions: a spiritual plane of inaudible music and unseen light.[12]

This is the psychological fall: matter, along with its qualities (ignorance, error, and evil), issues from a *mental* error. All beings born into error's universe—our universe—come to consciousness unaware that what they take for awareness of their environment is really forgetfulness of God. Each person reenacts the cosmic decline, mistaking ignorance for knowledge. However, each individual is only a glance away from freedom. This glance would be gnosis, an intuition of this unnerving fact: to flounder in unknowing is to thrive in knowledge.[13]

The absent parent in his unbounded goodness sends Jesus to earth to awaken the ignorant. In his role of Gnostic redeemer, the Jesus of the *Gospel of Truth* resembles other saviors in the Valentinian tradition: the serpent that alerts Adam and Eve to knowledge of Jehovah's oppressive regime; the Sophia who takes on earthly form to correct her mistake in the *pleroma*.[14] Each of these saviors is not so much external form as psychic disorientation, an irritation in the back of the mind. The majority of people repress these irritating twinges, but a fevered minority transform this annoyance to gnosis.

Mani's Melancholy Drama

Basilides transmutes the Gnostic drama into an epistemology of negation. Valentinus converts the refusals of Basilides into a psychology of redemption. A third Gnostic, Mani, who thrived in Iran in the middle of the third century, reads the myth more literally, maintaining that the cosmos is divided between two palpable powers: good and evil, light and darkness, spirit and matter.[15] Drawing from Zoroastrianism dualism, in his Chapters (c. 250), Mani is committed to a less complex view of the cosmos and salvation than were his Alexandrian predecessors. Still, if Mani lacked the philosophical or psychological gift, he enjoyed dramatic talent, a sense of tragic alienation.[16]

The dramatic intensity of Mani's vision is revealed in Theodore bar Khoni's sixth-century description of the Manichean school. In the beginning, the universe was divided between the god of light—spiritual, surrounded by reason and insight—and the deity of darkness—material, accompanied by smoke and mud. At a certain point, the material world attacked the region of spirit. To counter the assault, the good god created the primal man, the *anthropos*, armed with five elements—fire, wind, water, light, ether. This human descended into matter, where he was ostensibly defeated by evil forces. However, this fall was really a ruse meant to vanquish matter. After this apparent decline, the king of light sent the living spirit to call the man home. The form of the *anthropos* returned to the light, but the five elements composing his soul remained behind, imprisoned. To free these sparks, the spirit created the cosmos, replete with Adam and his progeny. Each time a human creature, a fallen *anthropos* in microcosm, hears the call of light and responds by cultivating spirit, he emancipates part of the soul. Eventually, when all men apprehend the call, the soul will be liberated and matter annihilated. Until this time, the *anthropos*, his messengers, and humans are torn between two identities— Son of God, Son of Man.[17]

Hans Jonas describes the profound "dread, [and] homesickness" of the Manichean creature. Sadly, the greatest task of this fallen soul is not to work through his anxiety, alienation, and confusion. It is to keep his melancholia acute. His forlornness corresponds to his readiness for gnosis.[18] But the world conspires against his dejection, offering either the brief comforts of matter (*hylé*) or the more lasting solaces of mind (*psyche*). Hedonism seduces in the first case; orthodox religion in the second. The Gnostic must defend against these modes and hold open his wounds of the spirit (*pneuma*). Malcontented with outward forms, he turns inward to his hidden spark, his connection to the macrocosmic *anthropos* still pining in the *pleroma*.

Gnostic Conundrums

Each of these Gnostics is keenly aware of the three conundrums of the aspiring pneumatic. One, if one is trapped in a realm of appearances, then how can he tell the difference between appearance and reality? How will he know when the light of the spirit breaks through the distorted matter? Two, if the initiate begins to suspect that the objects around him are illusory, how can he discern between the sanity that he feels and the insanity with which the world brands him? Caught in a vast asylum in which madness is the standard, what factors assure him that he is not himself mad? Three, when one awakens to the evil of matter, how can he find the good? Pervaded by delusional darkness, how does he know that the benevolent light breaking through the gloom is not yet another siren seducing him to further degradation?

Though he battles with each of these binds, Basilides, epistemologically oriented, is more likely to wrestle with the first one: the intermingling of appearance and reality. Likewise, while he is attuned to the panorama of the fallen condition, Valentinus the psychologist mostly points toward the breakdown between madness and sanity. In the same way, Mani is clearly aware of the manifold labyrinths of dark matter; however, his flair for drama inspires him to focus most on the blurring between good and evil.

Emphasizing one conundrum over the others, each of these Gnostics urges a different path for overcoming the confusion—a distinct *tertium quid*. The third way suggested by Basilides is *suspension*. Unable to tell the difference between appearance and reality, one has no choice but to divest himself from both categories—to shun visible appearances as obvious illusions, to reject invisible powers as likely deceptions. But in suspending belief, one must at the same time hold back disbelief. This almost impossible balancing act, hovering between stupidity and learnedness, requires that one enter into an epistemological state akin to suspended animation. But only in this self-induced hypnagogia can one find brief freedom from the dualisms of the fallen realm. Liberated into emptiness, one is at least ready for the nothing that could turn out to be everything.

In slight contrast to this active passivity, the *paranoia* of Valentinus is a passive activity, an aggressive questioning of the status quo that rests in chronic unknowing. Different from the narrow paranoia of narcissism—the idea that the world is focused on persecuting oneself—this generous paranoia issues from a skepticism toward the given, pushing all bright axioms into lurid chiaroscuro. Oscillating between rigorous questioning of the collective and wild speculation over alternatives to conventions, Valentinian paranoia exists between sanity and madness. Though this limbo dweller risks going over to one side or the other—and becoming irredeemably insane—he also prepares himself for the lucid madness lurking between clarity and craziness.

The *melancholy* of the Manichean school differs slightly from Valentinian paranoia. Unlike the paranoiac, who doesn't quite know the nature of his material atmosphere and who can muster only tentative hope for clarity, the dualist *knows* that he has been abandoned to a world of irreparable evil and that his only hope for escaping squalor is through cultivating disdain for his surroundings. Impotent to alter its situation, this disdain is dejected, tragic—impotent insight into iron fate. However, even if the Manichean must submit to the evil dictates of matter, he realizes that he will eventually escape this world by avoiding the temptations of Christianity and hedonism. Refusing to be content on the material plane, he avoids further pollution. His aggressive melancholy hovers between obvious evil and illusory good, holding open the space through which lucid vision might one day shine and transform his tragic condition into divine comedy.

Manichean Myth in *The Truman Show*

Several commercial Gnostic films released in the last decades of the twentieth century are imbued with the spirit of these visionaries. *The Matrix* is of course deeply informed by these ideas. The film is a blending of the perspectives of all three Gnostic masters. The movie's invocation of Baudrillard suggests the need for the negations of Basilides—silence and ignorance in the face of infinite simulations and simulacra. The film's rendering of Neo's concluding epiphany intimates the psychology of Valentinus—the illusions of matter are all in the mind. Finally, its focus on Neo's pre-conversion melancholy—on the splinter in his mind—gestures toward the tragic dualism of Mani.

Of the other recent Gnostic films, three pictures resemble *The Matrix* in their especially sophisticated, self-conscious explorations of the conundrums concerning appearance and reality, insanity and sanity, evil and good, as well as of the ways of escaping these binds—suspension, paranoia, melancholy. However, even though these films are similar in kind—each is vexed by the great Gnostic conflicts—they prove different in degree. Each emphasizes a certain problem and mode of escape at the expense of others. Peter Weir's *The Truman Show* tends toward Manichean dualism and responds to the cosmic struggle through rebellious melancholy. Alex Proyas' *Dark City* purveys the Valentinian dispensation. It suggests that the fall into matter is psychological and explores paranoia as a way of escaping cosmic error. David Cronenberg's *eXistenZ* exemplifies the negations of Basilides, intimating that the path out of the labyrinth is ignorance and silence. Still, though these pictures take different paths, each pushes its viewers to a space beyond *agon*: the blank screen, the interstice between darkness and light.

The Truman Show follows the basic Gnostic myth verbatim.[19] A television producer named Christof, played by Ed Harris, is the demiurge. He creates an artificial world, an immense dome replete with computer-controlled weather patterns, a fake sky and sea, a fictional town called "Seahaven," and a population of actors playing scripted roles. His motivation for concocting this biosphere of television scenery is simple. He needs a believable simulacrum of the "real" world in order to fulfill his artistic dream: to take a child from birth, place him in a simulated environment, turn hidden cameras on his every action, and watch him grow into a man. This results in "The Truman Show," a never-ending, commercial-free television show that features the ongoing life of Truman Burbank, portrayed by Jim Carrey. Through his ability to control the environment of Seahaven and the behaviors of his actors, Christof vigilantly manipulates Truman's existence. He is bent on transforming his creature's life into the superficial conventions of popular television. Truman is totally ignorant of his condition. He does not know that his parents, his wife, his friends are simply actors; that his every gesture is controlled by a television producer; that these actions are viewed by people around the world; and that the products he consumes are carefully placed by advertisers.

Though mostly reduced to a commodity, a cipher of entertainment clichés, Truman Burbank, true to a conflicted name that suggests both truth and television, occasionally yearns for a life beyond the confines of Seahaven—the life of an explorer of unknown lands. But his vexations are quickly smoothed over by physical pleasures directed by Christof. His wife Meryl, played by Laura Linney, assuages his worries by seducing him or offering him, in the jargon of an advertiser, the latest food product. His best friend Marlon, portrayed by Noah Emmerich, brings over a six-pack of beer and urges him to reminisce about their childhood. His mother Angela (Holland Taylor) reminds him through passive-aggressive behavior that he is responsible for his father's drowning. Even his teachers in school douse his dreams, telling him that everything in the world has already been discovered. Reduced to a plaything of the world's voyeuristic and consumer fantasies, Truman is a psychic and physical prisoner of a tyrant of the culture industry, an inmate of the fallen world's dream of a heaven by the sea.

But Seahaven, like the name of the protagonist, is duplicitous—a combination of safe haven and sea dwelling. Although Christof's pleasure dome stifles Truman, it is also the realm into which the savior, Sophia, enters. One of the actresses of "The Truman Show," Sylvia (Natascha McElhone), breaks out of her role as Lauren Garland to reveal to Truman the illusions that comprise his life. An extra in the scenes of Truman's high school years, Sylvia catches the young Truman's attention one day in front of the schoolyard. Her luminous eyes mesmerize the boy during band practice. Despite Meryl's attempts to pull his attention away from the striking beauty, Truman falls in love with Sylvia, even though he knows nothing about her and has never even talked to her. This ignorance and this silence are fitting. Sylvia is beyond empirical fact and linguistic category. Her irreducibility to "material" categories— her mysterious presence, her strange gaze—are precisely what attract Truman, inundated as he is with the banal events and idle chattering of Seahaven. With his reason and his speech arrested, he senses energies in Sylvia beyond the structures of Seahaven. When Truman and Sylvia do exchange words—fittingly, in a library, Truman's only place of respite from the seductions of Meryl and Marlon—Sylvia tells him that she has a message for him, a secret that can't be revealed in public. She and Truman rush to the shore, where Sylvia informs him that his life is a lie. Before Truman can fully comprehend her, however, her television "father" appears in a station wagon and accuses his "daughter" of insanity. As he hurries her away, he yells to the pining Truman that Sylvia is moving away forever, to Fiji.

From this moment, Truman's longing for an existence other than his present one is focused on Sylvia and Fiji. Daily meditating on these figures—markers for Sophia and the *pleroma*—he lives a double life, torn between the two principles of his cosmos: the real world intimated by Sylvia and the *terra incognita* where she ostensibly lives, and the fake one embodied by Meryl and her Seahaven surroundings. He actively cultivates this melancholy dualism through secret rituals that question the validity of his Seahaven identity. Each morning, he purchases a fashion magazine— "for the wife," he says—and, when he reaches his desk at work (fittingly, at a life insurance agency), he scours its pages for models that resemble Sylvia. When he finds a pair of eyes or a mouth or a nose that recalls his beloved, he rips this facial feature from the page and hides it away. Later, at night, he surreptitiously descends into the basement of his home and recovers a hidden box in which he stores these fragments. Spreading these shards before him, he tries to piece them together into the face of his lost Sylvia. This ritual depicts Truman's desire to overcome his fallen condition—his feeling of duplicity, of dismemberment—through the unity suggested by the savior from another world. This sad activity is matched by another regular failure. Almost every day, Truman schemes over how to get to Fiji. He calls or visits travel agents who inform him that all flights are booked for months ahead. He stares dreamily over maps of the remote island, as if he could mentally travel there.

Truman's active melancholy, daily self-induced, eventually schools him in new ways of seeing. He notices things he had not registered before. He realizes that the same people speak the same lines to him at the same time every day. Upon breaking his habitual route one morning and rushing into a building, behind the props he glimpses the crew of "The Truman Show." When he tries to drive out of Seahaven one day, he finds that a traffic jam, a forest fire, and a nuclear fall-out disaster block his path, as if someone were directing these events from behind the scenes. Thinking of these events in relation to other curious episodes—a studio light falling onto the street, the return of the actor who played his father in the guise of a homeless man, his wife's increasingly aggressive ploys for keeping him in Seahaven—Truman realizes that Sylvia's message is true. But knowledge does not breed liberation. Though he feels that he is controlled by an external force and surrounded by agents of this force, Truman cannot free himself from these powers until he crosses the ocean to the horizon, the edge of the world. To do this, he must overcome a phobia of water, implanted when he was a child who could not pull his drowning "father" from the ocean during a violent storm.

Truman's eventual voyage out constitutes a grand dramatization of the Manichean struggle. His chronic melancholia having reached fevered intensity, Truman decides to take the plunge into the abyss. He is suicidal, ready to risk death to escape his life. Now sure that his every move is being watched by others, he hatches a plot. Using as decoys an inflatable figure and a tape of snoring sounds—symbols of his artificial self and the fake sounds he once made—he makes Christof's studio workers think that he is safely sleeping in the basement of his Seahaven home. While Christof's agents complacently gaze on the remnants of the old Truman, the new man has during the night stolen to the shore and commandeered the boat from which his father ostensibly drowned. He sails for the horizon. By the time Christof discovers Truman's trick, the seeker is far from shore. Realizing that his subject is on the verge of freedom, Christof activates the computer program for the same "natural" powers that took Truman's "father." Like Jonah in reverse, a prophet released from fear of his violent God, Truman screams over the waves to the roiling sky—"Is that all you've got?" He has recognized that he now faces and must overcome his lifelong foe, his pernicious maker, the dark god. Responding, Christof cues a stronger storm that knocks Truman to the deck. Lying in the position of the crucified Christ—and thus resembling the savior that revised the laws of his ignorant father—Truman bears the full weight of matter, the chaos of the world. Accepting defeat, Christof relents. The sun returns. Now on calm seas, Truman reaches the end of the earth. His boat rams into a metallic horizon. Truman trudges along the edge of the shell, literally, like Christ his model, walking on water. He finds steps ascending to a door. He climbs them and opens the door. Just as he prepares to cross into the darkness, Christof addresses him for the first, and last, time.

In a gentle, fatherly voice, he comforts Truman, telling him it is okay to converse with his maker. Truman asks, "Who are you?" Christof confesses that he is the creator of a television show that "gives hope, joy, and inspiration to millions." Truman responds with the most fundamental existential question: "Who am I?" Christof tells him that he is the "star." Truman counters: "Was nothing real?" Christof tells him that he was real, and then explains. Since lies and deceit prevail both inside and outside of Seahaven, there is little difference between the television world and the realm beyond. If there is any difference, he continues, it is that in Seahaven, Truman has "nothing to fear." For this reason, Christof concludes, Truman will stay in Seahaven: he is used to safety and afraid to step into the unknown. As Truman totters on the threshold between two universes—one of truth, the other of illusion—the film cuts to Sylvia sitting in front of her television, sending him encouragement. As if he feels her sentiment, Truman faces the clouds from which Christof's voice issues, and says, with keen sarcasm, what he has said almost every morning of his Seahaven life in response to his neighbors' morning greetings: "In case I don't see you, good afternoon, good evening, and good night." He then bows, and walks with determination into the darkness on the other side of the door. The camera cuts to Sylvia running to her own door on her way to meet her lost beloved.

This happy ending is problematic. After Truman enters the darkness, the film returns to Christof's studio, where the demiurge sadly witnesses the cessation of his broadcast. Then the movie cuts to viewers around the world watching a blank screen. The last viewers shown are two attendants of a parking garage. They stare blankly at the fuzzy square, stunned, as if they have undergone some profound transformation. But the next instant, both reach for another slice of pizza and wonder what else might be on the tube. This scene reveals the shallow boredom of the audiences in the film, but it also suggests that the actual movie viewers might be restless materialists as well. As we exit the theater or turn off our DVD players, we likely behave exactly as these characters. Believing that this picture is "only a movie," we look for the next bit of entertainment, the next commodity. Mimicking the viewers of "The Truman Show," we intimate this unsettling conclusion: Christof is right—there really is no difference between what goes on in Seahaven and what goes on in New York City or Richmond or Pierre. Everything is television. We are all Truman, acting out scripts as others gaze on our business.

The Show within a Show

This is only one of many ways the film is self-conscious of its infinite regressions. When the film opens, "real" audiences are placed in exactly the same space as the "fictional" viewers. Christof appears on the screen, assuring his watchers—both us and those in the movie—that while the show is in "some respects counterfeit," it escapes the "phony emotions" with which everyone is now bored, because it depicts the "life" of Truman, a nonfictional and non-fake existence. After cutting to Truman expressing in his mirror a fantasy of exploration—a spectacle that the "real" and the "fake" audience both enjoy—the film next rolls the opening credits of "The Truman Show" as it is portrayed in *The Truman Show*. "Christof," not "Ed Harris," is listed as the Creator; "Hannah Gill," not "Laura Linney," is credited as Meryl; "Louis Coltrane," not "Noah Emmerich," plays Marlon. Spliced among these credits and Truman's mirror performance are interviews with the show's stars, Hannah and Louis. Hannah claims that there is no difference between her private and public life. Her life, she continues, is "The Truman Show"; the show is the "lifestyle" she has chosen, a "noble" lifestyle. If Christof's opening speech merges us with the "fictional" audience of the "The Truman Show," then Hannah's remarks blend us with her, with Marlon, with Truman himself. Public and private are not distinct. We are all playing roles, all enacting the lifestyles on the television; we are all being watched by others, commodified and consumed. Louis supports this blurring. He claims that "The Truman Show" is all "true." If there is a difference between the show and the world beyond the studio, the difference is that the television environment is "controlled." But by now, after the respective speeches of Christof, Hannah, and Louis, this potential distinction does not hold. There exists no difference between the movie audience and the television audience. There is no difference between each one of us and Truman. If Truman and his world are controlled, then we are all controlled.

This initial logic suggests a series of infinite regressions. First, if we in the theater or before our DVD players are watching a fictional audience from whom we are indistinct, then surely someone is watching us as well. How do we know there isn't another Christof introducing to another audience another show about a group watching a show called "The Truman Show?" How would this Christof and his audience be able to tell if there are another creator and audience gazing on their behaviors? Second, if the distinction between public and private does not hold—if each of us is Truman—then certainly we are unknowingly playing a role before millions of voyeurs. But each of these voyeurs is likewise playing a role before millions of viewers. Everyone is simultaneously Truman and audience, object and subject, viewed and viewer. We watch Truman. Someone watches us. Someone else watches that someone. Third, if Truman and the "The Truman Show" are controlled, and if we are no different in kind from Truman and his watchers, then by all means someone is controlling the performers "outside" the show, the millions of Trumans who make up the audience. But whoever controls these numerous Trumans is himself a Truman controlled by yet another external force who is himself dictated by an unknowable power, and so on and so on.

This situation—everybody is Truman—is not apparent to most. The majority probably assume that Truman is a purely fictional character who is a victim of a system that doesn't exist in the real world. Duped by this illusion, those holding this view go through life maintaining that they enjoy privacy, authenticity, freedom. In believing these lies to be true, they entrap themselves even more deeply in their prisons. They cannot even see the bars or sense the warden. Unfortunately, the minority who uncover the bars and suspect the warden do not fare much better. Realizing that they are Truman, they wonder if they can ever escape the infinite regress of illusion, the eternally widening circles of containment. This is the dilemma of people who have awakened. Though they might escape the obvious prisons of their immediate environments—Seahaven is clearly modeled on media clichés—how do they know if their existences beyond obvious cultural conventions are freer than their former lives? How can they tell if this new way of being is not also a puppet act? They are beset by inescapable dualism, always fearing that every level of existence is an inferior performance concocted by a malicious director. They chronically suspect that they are missing something, that what seems joy is but another act, that somewhere, behind the scenes, a shadowy face is having a laugh at their expense.

The Truman Show features two endings. The first ending—the "happy" one, the one that concentrates on Truman's exit bow and the shining face of his muse—shows Truman escaping Christof's evil to Sylvia's goodness. All riddles are solved. But this ending is yet another lotus dose, a Hollywood cliché that defuses longing, disorientation, and melancholia and reestablishes the shallow status quo that it seems to challenge. To fall for this ending is to behave like the attendants at the parking garage—as if the film were a commodity to be cast off when used, a transition to the next fix. Being awake to this trick opens one to a second ending—the "sad" conclusion attuned to the darkness beyond Seahaven and television. This ending leaves one suspended in confusion, asking: Is Truman's victory but another product to be consumed and discarded; is the darkness into which he plunges but another hell monitored by another Christof? Far from a draught of *lethe*, this ending avoids clarity and comfort. It throws the viewer, along with Truman, into the shadows, into a gloom consuming all hope. To embrace this conclusion is to transcend the vulgar materialism of the attendants, to envision the film as a Gnostic messenger revealing a dangerous third way beyond the infinitely regressing double binds that mire the picture, despite its aspirations, in an endless Seahaven.

Ficino's Black Vision

The alien messenger is the blackness itself. Traditionally, black is the color of melancholia, the sable bile that holds certain brilliant souls in a chronically gloomy mood. Marsilio Ficino meditated on this relationship between melancholy and genius in *The Book of Life* (1489). In this treatise, Ficino considers a question asked in *Problems*, a work from the fourth century B.C. often attributed to Aristotle: "Why is it that all those who have become eminent in philosophy or politics or poetry or the arts are clearly melancholics?"[20] This question, as Ficino knew, went against the grain of the prevailing theory of melancholy, which associated the condition with fearfulness, moroseness, misanthropy, or madness. The author of *Problems* countered this perspective by invoking Euripides and Plato. In Euripides, the symptoms of the black disease—delusion, dread, and insanity—often vex great heroes. Plato developed this idea further in the *Phaedrus*, where he associated frenzy with visionary ecstasy.[21]

Drawing from this tradition, Ficino argues that melancholy is likely to afflict brilliant scholars. This is so for three reasons. First, meditative souls are born under the planetary influences of Mercury and Saturn. These planets pass to their children their natures: coldness and dryness—characteristics necessary for calm, lengthy study. To this heavenly cause of scholarly melancholy, Ficino adds a natural one. In pursuing knowledge, the scholar must pull his soul from external to internal, circumference to center. Fixed on the middle of his being, he dwells in a place very much like the earth's core, a desiccated region resembling black bile. The human cause of the scholar's melancholy is inseparable from heavenly and natural causes. Influenced by Saturn to migrate to the center, the scholar contracts his own being and thus dries, freezes, and exhausts his spirit. Together, these causes of scholarly melancholy separate mind from body. Obsessed with "incorporeal things"—invisible interiors, vague interstices, and tenuous middles—the melancholic dwells on the boundary between spirit and matter. Holding to the "bodiless truths" of spirit, he turns his body into a "half soul"; unable to escape his body entirely, he remains partly corporeal.[22]

Ficino, a student of Plato, does not believe that the melancholy thinker should engage in endless vacillations between boundary and center, outer and inner, body and soul. He holds that the dejected philosopher should end in spiritual tranquility—that he should find rest on the still point of the spiritual axis. However, until the thinker achieves this tranquility—if ever—he must suffer the pain of his double sight: mania. Ficino hopes to ease the pains of this furor without extinguishing its lights, to instruct the sad genius in ways to keep his meditative melancholia vital without succumbing to the exhaustion that arises from dwelling too long in the middle. His *Book of Life* is an impossible manual—a handbook on how to keep sadness keen without losing hope, on how to hope for transcendence without forgetting the wounds at the heart of life.

Ficino's mania is Gnostic melancholy—the blackness of soul that must be cultivated to maintain strength on the threshold between the world's oppositions. In the end, *The Truman Show* points to this spiritual path. Exiting into the darkness, Truman himself becomes a Gnostic messenger pointing to the portal—so very small—out of the bewildering labyrinths of unchecked regression. This melancholy mode requires that one avoid fixation on either the obvious illusions of the material world or the more subtle delusions of the spiritual realm. Hovering between dualistic antinomies, one ensures, on the one hand, that he will not mistake the dreams of the demiurge for reality, not take his surfaces for depth; and, on the other, that he will not be seduced by the invisible reveries of this same demiurge, the philosophical opium he offers to those who question his might. On this threshold, one can stand aloof from the misguided hope that hidden good will overcome apparent evil, that somewhere light can vanquish all darkness. He can realize that the good and the light are simple reversals of the squalor and the gloom—moves in a game prefabricated by oppressive powers. He can further understand that any good beyond the evil and any light outside of darkness are themselves likely sordid conditions when compared to yet greater goods and beams. Grasping these possibilities, he holds to the total blackness, the nothingness, resting beyond light and shade. If he can maintain this state of sad suspension, then he can hope for a third road to open—a causeway seen only by those who blind themselves to the demiurge's light.

Fittingly, the blackness at the conclusion of Truman's tale descends upon the "actual" viewers: the credits end and the theater goes dark, momentarily annihilating light and shadow. This utter blankness is an invitation to epiphany, a brief interstice between fear and desire. If one can simply rest in this spaceless space and time that feels timeless, then what appears when the lights abruptly return—the large, empty screen—is not harsh and unwelcome. On the contrary, the white square reveals its secret—it is one with the total darkness. Extreme black and striking white share the same paradoxes. Both are no color at all but the ground of all hues. Both are bewildering, beyond differentiation, yet comforting, intimations of unity. Both conjure the sinister—the glare of the desert, the gloom of the cave—as well as the pure—the pearl and the rejuvenating night. To see in the blank screen the dark room; to perceive in the blackness the heart of white—this is the infrequent vision that can emerge from the melancholy mood, the sense that somewhere exists a still point gathering yet evading polarity. This is the hidden God.

Gnostics in TV Land

The Truman Show is only the most sophisticated of at least three recent films that explore how mass media, especially television, vanquishes the real. With less self-consciousness and seriousness than Weir's film, Gary Ross's *Pleasantville* and Ron Howard's *EdTV* depict what might be the most harrowing fact of the postmodern condition: the inability to tell the difference between what happens on television and what happens beyond the tube. Although Ross's and Howard's films in the end attempt to solace viewers with reassuring realities, both convincingly demonstrate the viral powers of media "reality"—how it can with the blink of an eye seduce viewers into trading contingent organic life for a scripted, artificial existence.

Pleasantville focuses on how one high school boy's disdain for his life in the nineties leads him to become obsessed with a fifties sit-com, "Pleasantville." Awkward and friendless, David longs to escape to a saccharine black-and-white world where everyone is happy and well adjusted. His rebellious sister Jennifer could not be more different—she is cool and popular, perfectly at home in the rambunctious modern realm. After a television repairman replaces their broken remote control with a more powerful model, the squabbling siblings find themselves miraculously transmuted into characters in the sit-com, Bud and Mary Sue. From this point onward, the film becomes rather uninterestingly dualist. David and Jennifer inject their staid, conservative characters with dynamic, liberal energy. They are Gnostic serpents in the garden of the demiurge. Soon, many of the black-and-white characters rebel against the conventions of their society. They take on color, excitement, and danger. The film in the end is a mostly untroubled Gnostic parable of authentic light vanquishing illusory shade, of life conquering death.

Slight tremors remain, however, at the movie's conclusion, probably not realized by the production team. After David finds his identity and voice in Pleasantville, he returns, strengthened, to the nineties; he is no longer ungainly or nerdy. Jennifer, however, decides to stay in Pleasantville and go to college; there she can continue to expunge her wild ways and become a responsible citizen. This reversal is neat, of course, and cinematically satisfying. However, it suggests that TV land carries just as much weight, just as much reality, as the land outside the box. On television, David and Jennifer learn lessons they could not learn in "real" life. Their "real" lives in fact become extensions of their artificial existences. When we add to this confusion the problem that TV life and non-TV existence both appear in a movie, we realize that the dualism of the picture is troubled, that with more awareness the film could approach *The Truman Show*.

EdTV is strikingly similar to *The Truman Show*. The difference, however, is that the subject of the constant camera in Howard's film knows full well that he is being watched. The movie's protagonist, Ed, a small-town video store clerk, agrees to allow a struggling cable channel to film every minute of his life for a new reality show. While his daily grind is at first tedious to his viewers, things heat up when he finds that his brother Ray is cheating on his girlfriend, Shari. This scandal throws Ed, Ray, and Shari into the national spotlight. They become celebrities and lose their privacy. They run the risk of losing their humanity, too, of becoming mere commodities for public consumption. But Ed returns to his small-town authenticity. He champions ordinary history over extraordinary artifice. As a reward, he gets the girl—he and the equally down-to-earth Shari end the movie as lovers. Like *Pleasantville*, the picture wants to be a simplistic dualist parable, saying, in essence, that the delusion fostered by television and celebrity are bad, while the truth nurtured by real life and privacy are good.

Still, the film shows fault lines, even if the dualistic Howard doesn't delve into their depths. First, it's deliciously ironic that the maker of the film is himself a man constantly trying to escape his television characters, Opie and Ritchie. (The same is true of one of the film's actors, Rob Reiner, Meathead on *All in the Family*.) A human inseparable from his television persona directs a film about how easily celebrity can be rejected. Second, the film constantly shows people engaging in two related activities: watching television and working out—gazing at physical "perfection" and trying to attain it themselves. Surely the movie should show awareness of the fact that its main characters, ostensibly ordinary folk untouched by the desire to be famous, are played by two of the most attractive people in Hollywood, Matthew McConaughey and Jenna Elfman. If Howard's movie had meditated on these and even more obvious ironies—such as a movie, maker of celebrity, attacking television, maker of celebrity—then *EdTV* might have been an intellectual and artistic equal of *The Truman Show*.

Fallen Eternals in *Dark City*

If *The Truman Show* offers a sophisticated turn on Manichean dualism, *Dark City* constitutes a rich inflection of the Valentinian psychology.[23] The film features a race of beings, known as the Strangers, who are akin to the ignorant eternals in *The Gospel of Truth*. Issuing from a world unknown to humans and possessing supernatural power, the Strangers appear to be descendents of some heroic, immortal species. They are as "old as time itself," yet, for some reason, they have fallen into generation. Trapped in decaying bodies, they desperately try to fend off death by studying the human soul's vitality. The Strangers corral a large population of humans, erase their memories, and place them in an artificial city hovering in space. These beings accomplish this feat through "tuning"—a mental capacity that allows them to create and control objects ranging in size from cities to individuals. With the help of Dr. Daniel Poe Schreber, a human psychiatrist who can destroy and produce memories, the Strangers nightly observe the mental interiors of the inhabitants of the Dark City. Each midnight, these beings "tune" the humans to sleep and then imagine into existence new cityscapes. The Strangers place people whose memories have been altered into these environments. When the people awaken, they have forgotten their earlier existence and believe that they are living their lives as they always have. From their underground lair, the Strangers examine how these newly downloaded humans adapt to their new lives. The aliens hope that an essence will endure through the changes in identity. The Strangers trust they will discover that the human being is a whole well beyond the sum of the parts. Into this whole, this soul, the Strangers wish to channel their disintegrating lives, a fragmentation exemplified by their proper names: Mr. Hand, Mr. Book, Mr. Wall, Mr. Rain.

Like Valentinus's aeons, the Strangers—pale, bald, and dressed in black—create material prisons through their stupidity. They incorrectly believe that the soul is but a finite thing that can be manipulated. Fittingly, they perceive, and thus produce, only gloomy, moribund objects, the gothic cityscapes that they nightly concoct. As William Blake once wrote, "As a man is, so he sees." Burdened with the erroneous idea that spirit can be commodified, the Strangers see only sordid buildings and apathetic people. If they could escape their objectifying hermeneutic, they might transcend their bodily limitations. But they remain immured in their dreams of reducing the soul to a thing.

Only two human citizens of the Dark City have any inkling of the Strangers' experimentations: Dr. Schreber, played by Kiefer Sutherland, and John Murdoch, portrayed by Rufus Sewall. Forced by the Strangers to manipulate the memories of the humans, Schreber is privy to their plots and essential to the success of these plots. But though he is a slave, he is also a master because he can alter the experiments to help his own race. Entrapped and free, he is poised to play the Gnostic Sophia or Christ paying allegiance to spirit and matter. This is the role he embraces, true to his name, constituted of Daniel, the prophet moving between God's messages and dens of sin; Poe, the poet vacillating between fact and dream; and Schreber, the judge who believed that he was both man and woman.[24] While pretending to be loyal to the Strangers, Schreber secretly works to reveal the truth to Murdoch. Schreber chooses Murdoch for this reason because, in contrast to the other inhabitants of the city, Murdoch is often immune to the tuning and able to tune himself. Recognizing in Murdoch a potential challenge to the Strangers, Schreber spends most of the film attempting to find him.

Stranger Than Strange

John Murdoch is elusive because he is wanted by the police. After the prologue— which features a midnight tuning, a panorama of the city falling asleep—the film opens with Murdoch awakening, naked, in a bathtub in a strange apartment. On his forehead, between his eyes, is a small wound. After he emerges from the water and puts on the clothes lying nearby, he accidentally upsets a goldfish bowl as he makes his way out of the bathroom. The spherical bowl shatters on the floor. The fish gasps on the ground. Murdoch gently picks up the fish before releasing it into the water in the tub. Near the tub, on the floor, he discovers a hypodermic implement. He then finds keys in his pocket and a suitcase bearing the initials "J. M." Though he cannot recall his name or history, he assumes that the case is his and opens it. He finds clothes that appear to belong to him and a postcard from "Shell Beach." Exiting the apartment, he receives a phone call from Schreber, who informs Murdoch that his memory has been erased but that help can be found. Schreber then tells Murdoch that people are coming for him and he must flee. As Murdoch hurries from the room, he notices a naked woman brutally murdered with a knife. Bloody spirals have been carved into her skin. He concludes that he has murdered her, though he does not recall the deed. He runs away, not sure who he is or what he has done. When he reaches the lobby, the concierge and everyone else are waking up. The concierge addresses him as "Mr. Murdoch" and reminds him that he left his wallet at the automat.

This initial sequence reveals the conflicts of John Murdoch—a name suggesting the "John" of the Fourth Gospel and the *Secret Book* as well as "dock" of the "mer," the sea, a port to unbounded waters. His "birthing," his human form arising naked and unknowing from a watery vessel, depicts his struggle between the "births" concocted by the Strangers each midnight and his potential rebirth from illusion to truth. The small wound on his forehead betokens the prefabricated memories of the Strangers, nightly injected between the eyes, as well as the third eye of vision, the faculty for sensing invisible currents. Murdoch's shattering the fishbowl and rescuing the fish point to his battle with the transparent barriers imposed by the Strangers, his efforts to destroy unseen walls and flow out into wider currents. The keys intimate his false existence—a fake home in which no one lives—and his potential to unlock the truth—the mystery of his life. The postcard of Shell Beach and Schreber's call point to the same tension; both are parts of the illusions perpetrated by the Strangers as well as calls to bright worlds and trustworthy messengers. Murdoch's confusion over the initials on the suitcase signals his hunger to overcome his suspicion that he is living someone else's life. His hunch that he might not have murdered the woman foreshadows the paranoia that will grow through the film, his suspicion that the status quo is an oppressive plot and that his wild conjectures are open to the real. The spirals carved into her body gather this ignorance and gnosis: the spiral as maze is the Dark City, the labyrinth; the spiral as *mandala* is the soul, harmony in discord.

The remainder of the film explores the spiritual efficacy of Murdoch's paranoia. As soon as Murdoch exits the hotel in which he ostensibly murdered the woman, he strains to recall his name. Standing in front of his reflection in a store window, he runs through a litany of titles, none of which feels right. He is caught between two theories of identity—identity as wordless image, the visage staring from the glass, and identity as linguistic concept, the one name that fits and reveals. He doubts the validity of both views—the realist and the nominalist. Soon after, Murdoch locates his wallet in the automat. The attendant places the wallet on one of the shelves usually reserved for food and opens the glass door so that Murdoch can retrieve the wallet. But the door closes before Murdoch can grab the wallet. Without thinking, he sends waves from his forehead. He *tunes*. These waves turn the glass into pulsating air through which Murdoch extends his hand and retrieves his wallet. The scene increases the film's paranoia. It suggests that identity in the Dark City, here signified by the wallet, is on the same ontological level as fast food, an ephemeral commodity. It also intimates that matter is insubstantial, a precipitation of invisible waves through which one can pass and return at will. Once he reclaims his wallet, Murdoch is harassed by two policemen in the automat. When it seems as if he will be arrested for loitering, a prostitute comes to his rescue, claiming she is his wife. Confused over whether he is capable of murder, Murdoch follows her to her room to test himself. When he finds that he harbors no violence, he becomes even more paranoid. Suspicious yet still hungry to discover his identity, he walks to the address contained in his wallet. There he meets Emma, played by Jennifer Connelly. She claims to be his wife. Murdoch doesn't believe her. By now, his paranoia has become fevered. He doubts the veracity of the past and the present. He also senses something more sinister: someone is secretly plotting to undo him.

For the remainder of the film, Murdoch attempts to escape the darkness of the city and find the light. He believes that this illumination will be found in Shell Beach, a place that he feels might be his origin. As he tries to find this beach, he is constantly pursued by the Strangers and the police—the former finding him both a threat to their power and a rich specimen for investigation, the latter holding him to be a serial murderer of prostitutes. Throughout his quest, punctuated with "tuning" battles with the Strangers and exciting flights from the police, Murdoch learns at least two indisputable facts. One, his tuning powers are superior to those of the Strangers, probably because his "soul" is more potent than the merely reptilian "life" of the Strangers. Two, Shell Beach, though advertised throughout the city and ostensibly visited by everyone, doesn't exist: it is a false memory implanted in the denizens of the Dark City. These two facts together lead Murdoch to this twofold conclusion: he can trust nothing or no one, not even his own distrust, not even his own self; this distrust curiously empowers him to challenge his ostensible enemies through his ability to create, through tuning, his own reality.

At the film's conclusion, Murdoch is able to transcend his total distrust and put faith in his ability to tune, a talent that allows him to destroy the prison of the Strangers and fashion a sunny shore where he and the woman named Emma might thrive as a new Adam and Eve. In a thrilling cinematic climax, Murdoch is finally captured by a squad of Strangers and taken to their underground lair. There, shackled to a circular rack—and resembling the crucified Christ—he faces the annihilation of all of his recent hunches. The Strangers order Schreber to erase Murdoch's identity entirely so that they can capitalize on his remarkable soul. As Schreber prepares to inject the syringe into John's forehead, he reassures his protégé, telling him not to fear. He then downloads into John's mind a primer on Gnostic liberation, a software package that features Schreber's figure interwoven with several seemingly legitimate childhood memories. As the memories proceed, Schreber tells John who he really is—a being with a special gift far superior to those talents of the Strangers, a man destined to emancipate himself and his kind from the fallen eternals. Downloaded, John engages in a massive tuning battle with the Strangers, a struggle he wins in the end. Having vanquished his foes, he begins to envision—to create—his own cosmos, a Bright City teeming with elegant buildings and inviting streets. The crowning element of this cityscape is the golden shore leading to a blue sea—Shell Beach realized. On a dock in the midst of the waves, John meets the woman formerly named Emma. Earlier charged with a new identity, this woman, now called Anna, no longer believes she is John's wife. She doesn't even know him. However, John and Anna seem to be aware of deep affections for one another, feelings that have endured through the fake identities. As they stare out into the beautiful waters, we experience that old cinematic warmth yet again: the human soul and its favorite expression, love, have once again conquered the machine—and hatred.

The romance between John and Anna resolves the conflicts that structure the first minutes of the film and persist throughout. John now knows the nature of his birth. No longer a fetus nightly thrown into a strange world, he is the twice-born savior whose second birth redeems the world. He is also sure of his third eye. It is not an evil portal in which false memories are injected; it is the supernatural sight whose visions take on flesh. Reborn with new sight, John overcomes his goldfish-like gasping, his sense that he has been thrown onto a harsh shore of unbreathable air. He finds his proper habitat—the shining sea—and like a prophet leads others to its waters. Thriving on Shell Beach, his inner paradise externalized, John finds all that he thought he had lost: the key to his identity, the knowledge of his origin, and his spiritual double—Schreber—keen for the salvation of his soul. He transforms the Dark City into a City of Light. He turns the labyrinth into the temple, the maze with no door into a *mandala*.

Mass Paranoia

John's paranoia transmutes itself into true vision. However, the paranoia with which the film infects the audience is not so easily converted. Though the final scene of the film is a still of John and Anna gazing hopefully into the sparkling waves, the shot immediately preceding this blissful union is disturbing. An aerial view of the floating landmass shows John's shore and ocean extended into empty space. This unsettling vision can only mean that John's Shell Beach is just as insubstantial as the Dark City of the Strangers. This unexpected connection between Murdoch and the Strangers is only one of several. The film's first aerial shot emphasizes the point of view of the Strangers, the expansive vista from which they can perceive their dark creation; the picture's second such shot—just mentioned—reveals the panoramic

angle of vision that John enjoys after his gnosis. He has taken the place and vocation of his alleged enemies. Of all of the characters in the film, only John and the
Strangers can tune, a parallel that suggests that John is a Stranger, a failed eternal who
differs from his spooky brethren only through his apparent benevolence. Not only
do John and the Strangers share perspectives and powers, they also engage in the same
quest for truth and life. In contrast to the other figures in the film, these special
beings question the status quo and seek to change it. They are hollowed, haunted, and
hungry, aliens in their own skins. Whether John constitutes an early, more innocent
incarnation or a later, more powerful evolution of his jaded, decrepit siblings is unim-
portant. What matters is that John and the Strangers are no different in kind and are
guilty of the same sorts of psychic legerdemain, dark or light, dry or wet.

These connections between Murdoch and the Strangers point to another analogy, the one between the director of *Dark City*, Alex Proyas, and his tuning characters, the Strangers and Murdoch. Like his creations, the director enjoys the aerial
vista of the sets he has created. He is competent in tuning, able to materialize his
visions in seemingly substantial illusions, and he is uncomfortable in his own skin,
consumed with ideas of conspiracy and conversion. Inseparable from these masters
of illusion, Proyas purveys not substantial truth but projected images. Like the
Dark City fashioned by the Strangers, his movie is a vast deception generated by
moving wheels and cogs; as with the Shell Beach created by Murdoch, his movie is
a light show coursing through empty air.

Proyas' film is more like Shell Beach than the Dark City, and thus more dangerous. The gloomy cityscape of the Strangers is obviously pernicious, a Skinnerian
maze in which unwitting specimens are controlled for the benefit of a tyrannical
minority. However, the gorgeous shore of John Murdoch is ostensibly benevolent, a beautiful stretch in which true identities emerge from hallucinations. But
Murdoch's beach is threatening precisely because it is so inviting. If one dwells in a
dirty city, one is likely to suspect that something is wrong with the constitution of
the cosmos. But if one plays on a sun-soaked beach, one is prone to believe that he
has reached paradise, that all is right with the world. The beach, though, is illusory
as well, one man's psychic projection. To take this shore for reality is to dwell in
another man's dreams.

Proyas' *Dark City* is Shell Beach—an apparent release from tenebrous deception
to clear light that is really but another imprisonment in blinding images. At the
film's end, viewers can approach this gap between appearance and reality in one of
two ways—as Anna or like John. If one identifies with Anna, one fully accepts
John's concoction as the real. He believes that John's gnosis—his insight into and
utilization of his power of psychic projection—is a liberation from the experiments of the Strangers. He is glad that *Dark City* concludes, as commercial films
should, happily. He walks out of the theater maintaining that he has been awak-

ened to the illusions that comprise his world, that he holds knowledge of wide conspiracy and powers for unmasking the puppet masters. But in embracing this idea,
he grasps another illusion—the notion that he can escape fabrication as long as he
enjoys the seductions of the culture industry. Alternatively, audience members can
reject the gullibility of Anna and practice the paranoia of John. This view is double—inside and outside of the game, aware of the ostensible materiality of psychic
projection and attuned to the emptiness beyond the irradiated images. Shocked
into this double consciousness, the viewer linked to John exits the theater more
paranoid than ever before, on guard against tyrants and rebels, dark fantasies and
blithe reveries. He trusts no one and nothing, sensing that paths to liberation are
more binding than shackles. Yet, though he realizes that the things surrounding him
are props in a movie set arranged by an unknown director, he must take them somewhat seriously as obstacles or invitations to the emptiness. One particular event
might reveal the nature of the Strangers; another unique occurrence might disclose
the secret messenger. He walks the razor's edge between faith and skepticism, the
paranoiac's path.

Though Proyas' film is from one angle a dangerous psychic projection, an illusion convincing viewers that all is right with the world, from another view, the
movie is a liberating deception, a self-consuming pattern that leaves audiences suspended in the empty space beyond dark city and shell beach. In this latter perspective, the film, like John, remains paranoid. Even though the picture appears to
endorse its concluding images as attractive alternatives to the Strangers' projections,
it emphasizes the unreality of these images by showing them floating in empty
space. Both supporting and destroying these bright streams, the film turns against
itself, erases itself into nothing. In this way, *Dark City* might affect its audiences as
Schreber strikes John, in the same way that John might impact Emma: it serves as
an illusion that dissolves into truth.

Like *The Truman Show*, *Dark City* leaves its viewers extended into the emptiness—
the dark theater when the credits have closed, the blank screen when the lights go up.
However, unlike Weir's picture, a call for melancholy longing for an unknowable
abyss *beyond* illusion, Proyas' movie urges paranoid yearning for a pure emptiness *within* illusion. While the dualistic Truman and his conflicted avatars seek solace in alternative realms, the more monistic Murdoch and his meditative disciples search for salvation in their own minds. In this Valentinian dispensation, one is always a vision
away from pushing matter back to the spirit from which it emerged. But this vision
comes only in the wake of an almost impossible achievement: draining the fear and
desire that rule the fallen world, the fear of the unknown and the desire for clarity.
Though these related flaws reduce spirit to matter, they nonetheless remain the
enduring features of the human mind. To vanquish these limitations—in a moment
of gnosis—is to become inhuman, an egoless ego, an eddy in the current.

The Tlön of Borges

In "Tlön, Uqbar, and Orbis Tertius" (1940), Jorge Luis Borges, deeply read in Gnostic mythology and Edgar Allan Poe, explores the following belief: the "visible universe [is] an illusion or (more precisely) a sophism." Borges examines this idea in a parable concerning the materialization of mental phenomena. Over two centuries, a hermetic society has produced a multivolume encyclopedia of an imagined world called Tlön. Appropriately, given Tlön's purely mental existence, the inhabitants of the realm are idealists. Believing that "to be is to be perceived," they discredit scientific inquiry and embrace immediate intuition. The language of Tlön excludes nouns, which presuppose substance enduring through change, and deploys only impersonal verbs and adverbs, which express the ephemeral nature of unmediated contact. Though this world interests Borges' narrator for its philosophies, it most strikes him for a different reason: Tlön, a "fantastic world," eventually becomes *actual*. A vibrating compass whose case is etched in the script of Tlön appears in a package from Poitiers. Later, a native from Tlön materializes in Chucilla Negra. After a night of raving, he dies. Coins from the corpse's belt are intolerably heavy. Their oppressiveness lingers. At the story's conclusion, reality has yielded to the dreams of Tlön. Its fictitious history and philosophy have erased other pasts and ways of thinking. Its language has usurped familiar tongues.[25]

This tale is a testimony to the powers of the mind, suggesting that an imagined world, if pictured with sufficient concreteness, can become real. This possibility is not untroubled, because mental systems that replace the real can be pernicious. As Borges' narrator observes, Tlön is similar to "dialectical materialism, anti-Semitism, Nazism." Like these ideologies, it is a "symmetry with a semblance of order" concocted by men to embody their narrow dreams of harmony. The invasion of Tlön into the real is a form of tyranny, an onslaught of the dreams of the few onto the thoughts of the many. Significantly, a major force behind the encyclopedia of Tlön was one Ezra Buckley, a nineteenth-century millionaire slave-owner from Memphis, Tennessee.[26]

A mental picture can also liberate. If "reality" is already imperialistic, a constricting symmetry, then a way of escaping such a world is to imagine an endlessly asymmetrical cosmos. This turbulent world itself may be an illusion; however, though insubstantial, it might point to strange laws beyond narrow human fantasies. Borges' narrator realizes that all visions of visible reality are "labyrinths," systems concocted by the minds of men and then implemented to entrap the majority. Yet he also intimates that other realities, other labyrinths, possibly exist, bizarre systems "in accordance with divine laws—I translate: inhuman laws—which we never quite grasp." These inhuman laws, if they exist, are ungraspable, beyond the systems of demiurges like Buckley and Hitler. But these sublime prin-

ciples, assuming that they are really "out there," might be grasped through the creation of or the meditation on unsystematic labyrinths, infinite mazes both cease-
lessly confusing and eminently beautiful.[27]

Such outlandish labyrinths might take the form of artworks that resist orderly interpretation. This seems to be the conclusion of Borges' narrator: The only
way to challenge the systematic fantasies of the demiurge is to entertain nonsys-
tematic structures. At the story's end, the narrator, utterly suspicious of what most
in his world take for reality, has this to say: "I pay no attention to all this and go
on revising, in the still days at the Adrogue hotel, an uncertain Quevedian translation (which I do not intend to publish) of Browne's *Urn Burial*."[28] Although this
activity appears to be inconsequential, a mere escape from the psychic battles now
raging for control of the universe, it is actually a viable Gnostic rebellion against
tyranny. Engaged in an unending revision of an arcane translation of Browne's
bewildering style, the narrator contemplates impossible forms that might point to
unworldly labyrinths.

Borges is the great purveyor of this Gnostic paranoia—charitable suspicion that
generates outlandish structures. Convinced that all human visions of visible reality
are really psychic projections mistaken for material, Borges is unwilling to endorse
one cogent ideology over another, to support, dualistically, a religious or philosophical or political hierarchy, a theory of good over evil, light over darkness. Rather,
in his "fictions" he produces his own inhuman psychic projections, structures so
baroque that they transcend ideological systems and oppositional categories.

Borges' Gnostic paranoia is the key to the cinematic poetics of *Dark City*. The
film is a startling mélange of Borgesian themes: the fictionality of fact and the fac-
ticity of fiction; the reality of dream and the dreaminess of the real; the idea that
existence is a text imagined by an inaccessible mind; the possibility that what we
take for reality is but one of a million moves in a never-ending game of chance.
Encountering these layers of unreality, one can ignore the void at the core and hold
hard to what everyone says is real, or dream of the emptiness of space under the
waves, or even the pavement. If the former path leads to the quiet desperation that
is death-in-life, the latter way points to the charitable suspicion that might discover living things among the ruins.

The Death of Memory

Two other recent films explore the theme of *Dark City*: that time and the memories
it brings are virtual. Richard Kelly's *Donnie Darko* and Paul Verhoeven's *Total Recall* both
feature protagonists who suffer the paranoia of John Murdoch, the suspicion that the
temporal plane that most take for reality is but a construct. Meditating self-consciously on this theme, each movie approaches Proyas' film in form as well as content.

Kelly's film depicts Donnie Darko, a teenager troubled over the unreality of his middle-class suburban environment. A mysterious mental condition separates Donnie from his conformist culture. While everyone else sleeps, he goes on nocturnal journeys, often awakening in the middle of the road or on a putting green. During these excursions and at other times, usually after he has taken his antidepressants, he sees a large rabbit named Frank. Frank predicts that the world will end in a month, encourages Donnie to commit vandalism against oppressive institutions, and tells him that there are several simultaneously existing temporal planes following a predetermined logic. But these extreme conditions aren't all that separate Donnie from his peers. While his classmates decline into apathy, conformity, and cruelty, Donnie cultivates intellectual curiosity, compassion for outcasts, and disdain for puritanical powers.

This combination of factors prepares Donnie for a great sacrifice that might awaken his world. During the nighttime journey on which he first sees Frank, a jet engine falls from the sky into the bed where Donnie would have been sleeping. Lucky to be alive, Donnie spends the next month attempting to understand Frank's messages. By the end of the month, after a series of events has led to the death of his girlfriend Gretchen and is threatening to kill his mother, Donnie realizes that the temporal plane in which he exists can be reversed. If he can transcend his matrix of time through a portal between temporalities, then he can move freely about the matrix and alter the fated patterns. With his dead girlfriend by his side and his mother's airplane about to be sucked into another dimension of time, Donnie returns to the night on which he first saw Frank. This time, he stays in his room and dies in the explosion. This death changes his temporal fabric—his girlfriend and his mother will escape death—and also alters those who knew him on the timeline he just erased. Though Gretchen never gets to meet the "dead" Donnie, she feels a strange connection with his corpse and his mother as she witnesses the aftermath of the accident. This suggests that Donnie's spirit now moves among temporalities, awakening prepared souls to the superficiality of time.

Kelly's film places alert audience members in the same position as Gretchen—suspecting that temporal events are constructed possibilities that can be altered from the perspective of other fabricated histories. The film calls attention to its own artificial temporality in simultaneously embodying two opposing narratives. Like a hypertext, the film at the same time runs the story of the Donnie who survived the falling engine and of the Donnie who was killed by this same engine. One narrative cancels the other, leaving audiences in doubt over which series of events is valid. The film further highlights its fabricated nature through its casting. In featuring Katharine Ross as Donnie's analyst, the movie constitutes itself as a remake of *The Graduate*, an iconic study of a young man's confusion over the conventions of his culture. By using Patrick Swayze as a corrupt motivational speaker, the film also presents itself as a version of *Dirty Dancing*, an equally iconic analysis of disaffected youths. In parodying and embracing these films, *Donnie Darko* portrays itself as a mere construct, not as an original, unrepeatable event.

Vorhoeven's movie is about a man apparently named Douglas Quaid, a construction worker living in the year 2084 and troubled by nightly dreams about an alternate life on Mars. Since Quaid can't afford to travel to the planet to explore these dreams, he pays Rekall, a corporation selling memories, to inject recollections of Mars into his brain. This procedure goes wrong, however, when a technician realizes that Quaid has already had false memories implanted. After this disclosure, Quaid encounters unexpected attacks from his co-workers, his friends, and even his wife. It soon appears that everyone close to Quaid is a secret operative of the Agency, a powerful unit devoted to removing threats to the status quo. This Agency fears that Quaid will recover his true identity and threaten its oppressive power. He was once a henchman for the cruel governor of a colony on Mars but eventually sided with rebellious freedom fighters. As punishment for this transgression, Quaid was injected with false memories and given a fake identity.

After Quaid realizes that his earth identity is false, he embarks on a quest similar to John Murdoch's—to find out who he is. This journey takes him to Mars, where he meets a mysterious woman, Melina, who has appeared in his dreams. She is a rebel for the underground and was Quaid's lover when he was Hauser, the freedom fighter. Together, Hauser and Melina work to overthrow the colonizers of Mars, who control the people by making them believe that the atmosphere on Mars will not sustain life and that all inhabitants consequently must remain securely contained within a biosphere. When Hauser and Melina liberate the minions, they reveal this immense lie. The movie happily concludes with blue skies gorgeously hovering over the fresh air of Mars. The downtrodden have been emancipated into truth and the hero finds his love.

Ironies vex this neat ending and leave audiences paranoid. The film's primary irony grows from scenes in Quaid's earthly home. Each morning Quaid watches huge moving images of beautiful outdoor scenes on his interior walls. This activity suggests that cinematic scenes are illusions capable of convincing mechanized citizens that they live organic lives. How are Vorhoeven's own moving images any different? Are they not also illusions making entrapped viewers believe they're free? A second irony emerges from the casting of Arnold Schwarzenegger as the film's hero. Before starring in *Total Recall*, Schwarzenegger played the iconic android in *The Terminator*. Watching this actor portray a downloaded mechanism attempting to realize his humanity, audiences can't help but recall this same actor playing a machine. This dislocation likely leads audiences at the end of Vorhoeven's film to wonder if the protagonist has really transcended artifice. How do we know Hauser isn't experiencing more false memories?

Negating *eXistenZ*

Cronenberg's *eXistenZ* pushes Gnostic negation to a nihilistic limit.[29] *The Truman Show* entertains the validity of dualistic struggle. *Dark City* acknowledges the transformative power of psychic projection. In contrast, *eXistenZ* totally blurs virtual and real. If Basilides had made a film, it would have been *eXistenZ*, a non-film on non-existence.

The film opens in a country church, where a focus group has gathered to test "eXistenZ," the new virtual reality game from the Antenna Corporation. The designer of the game, the famous Allegra Geller (played by Jennifer Jason Leigh), is on hand and has even agreed to play her latest creation with the group. Security is tight because competing corporations are out to steal Allegra's secrets and fanatics against virtual reality, the "Realist Underground," are out to take her life. However, despite the efforts of the security guard, Ted Pikul (portrayed by Jude Law), an undercover assassin slips through the security check and joins the congregation watching Allegra brief the players. She sits in the middle of a semicircle holding her game "pod," a fleshy machine that responds to touch and appears to breathe. Tendrils grow from this organic contraption. These cords connect to the players' "bio-ports," small holes located at the bases of their spines. After explaining her game, Allegra touches her pod. It quivers, and all of the players, including Allegra, go into a trance. They are no longer in "reality" but in the "virtual" world of the game. Only seconds after the players have exited existence for "eXistenZ," the assassin constructs a gun from greasy bones, approaches the stage, shouts "Death to the demoness," and shoots Allegra in the shoulder. Chaos ensues. The assassin kills an official of the Antenna Corporation. Security guards kill the assassin. Ted helps the wounded Allegra flee the scene. So begins the main plot of the film: Allegra and Ted running from assassins and trying to heal the game pod hurt during the melee.

The opening scene features the film's key motifs. The organic and the mechanistic, the natural and the artificial, are inseparable. Computers breathe and quiver, get sick and heal. People possess ports and can be plugged into engines. These collapses of differences compromise ontology and epistemology. If objects are both born and made, how can one ever know what anything is? Even if one could for a moment discern between organ and machine, his insight would be rendered null by another annihilation of difference—between the empirical world of subjects engaging with objects and the virtual realm of phantoms playing with ghosts. People ascend to the pulpit to enjoy virtual experiences far more intense, far more "real," than those drab habits of their everyday existence. Those in the congregation below feel divorced from the ecstasy of those plugged to the pod, as if they are trapped in a sham of sordid predictability. "eXistenZ" is more authentic than existence. Illusion is real and reality is illusion. Organs and machines, pods and bio-ports, churches and corporations: all are nothing, either empirical events attenuated by boring habit or virtual occasions made excitingly real. Both negations of the real, the artificial usurping the mental and the virtual dissolving the empirical, are perpetuated by a collective demiurge, the Antenna Corporation. This company tries to reduce people to addicts, to human machines requiring the fuel of virtual games. To this end, the corporation holds demonstrations in churches and promises artificial transcendence. It tricks people into worshipping false gods.

These four themes—the blurring of artifice and nature, the collapse of empirical and virtual, the corporation as demiurge, and corporate products as sacred objects—persist throughout the film, an apocalyptic evacuation of reality. Soon after Ted and Allegra flee, Allegra convinces Ted to get a bio-port so they can play "eXistenZ." She needs to assess the damage to her pod. Their first attempt to get Ted "fitted" ends disastrously. At a country gas station, they ask the attendant, Gas (played by Willem Dafoe), to install the port. The port proves faulty. When Allegra plugs her pod into Ted, the game overheats. It turns out that Gas installed the botched port on purpose. He wants to destroy the game and Allegra in hopes of receiving the large reward offered by the fanatics against artifice. After narrowly escaping Gas, and killing him in the process, Ted and Allegra end up at a ski lodge run by Kiri (Ian Holm), a pod engineer friendly to Allegra. Kiri fixes the pod and properly ports Ted. Soon, Allegra and Ted are inside "eXistenZ," a virtual world that at first appears to be no different from the realm of "reality."

Though Ted claims that his transition from "reality" to "virtuality" was exceptional—"beautiful," he calls it—he also realizes that little has changed, saying, "I feel just like me." His sense that the game world is inseparable from the non-game realm is borne out minutes later, when he asks Allegra the goal of "eXistenZ." Her reply could easily refer to the "reality" she and Ted have ostensibly left behind. She admits that one has to "play the game to find out why" one is "playing" the game, that the more one plays the game, the more one understands "how natural it feels." Ted initially struggles with this indeterminacy as well as with the moments when his game "character" makes him say or do things that his "natural" self would not normally do or say. However, he soon gives himself over to the rules of the game and enters into "eXistenZ" in earnest.

He and Allegra find themselves in a "game emporium," where they learn that they need new "identities" for their mission. They gain these new selves by plugging into another pod, a "micropod" designed by "Cortical Systems." This pod translates them into another virtual realm, a "trout farm" where Cortical Systems genetically engineers mutant creatures to be used as components in game pods. Ted appears as a factory worker. He meets Nourish (Don McKellar), a Russian worker who knowingly encourages Ted to have lunch at the Chinese restaurant in the forest. Nourish insists that Ted order the "special." After gathering Allegra, also a worker, Ted finds the restaurant. There he begins to feel nervous about his body back at the lodge. He stops the game by shouting, "'eXistenZ' is paused" and appears to be transported back to reality. However, by this point, we can't distinguish between what is part of "eXistenZ" and what isn't. Ted and Allegra have already entered into a game within a game. How can we tell if the transportation back to the lodge is another translation into another virtual realm? We, like Ted and Allegra, have been thrown into ontological and epistemological crisis.

Allegra convinces Ted to return to the Chinese restaurant. There he finds, buried in the special, a putrid dish of mutant creatures, the components of the same bone gun that allegedly shot Allegra at the start of the film. For reasons he can't grasp, he constructs the gun and shoots the waiter, thus duplicating an action that apparently took place in "reality." In the kitchen, Ted and Allegra learn that Nourish prepared the special in hopes that Ted would assassinate the waiter, a spy for Cortical Systems gathering information on the Realist Underground. A member of this group against virtuality, Nourish tells Ted and Allegra that Cortical Systems is using the mutant creatures for weapons systems as well as game pods. He vows to destroy the trout farm. Ted, an employee for a virtual games company, and Allegra, a designer of these games, have become agents for the Realists. Even though they both feel exactly like their "real" selves, they possess virtual identities in exact contrast to their empirical personae.

Allegra and Ted next appear back in the "game emporium," where they learn from an agent of the Realist Underground that Nourish, actually a double agent loyal to Cortical Systems, has tricked them into killing their contact within the corporation, the Chinese waiter. They are told to return to the trout farm, kill Nourish, and destroy the latest game from Cortical Systems. Back in the factory, Ted once more expresses his reservations about the virtual world, but his language describes exactly what it is like to live in the "real" world. He hates that he "doesn't know what's going on," that he is always "stumbling around" in an "unformed world whose rules and objectives are largely unknown, seemingly indecipherable or even possibly non-existent." He fears that he is "always on the verge of being killed by forces" that he doesn't "understand," and he wonders who would want to play a game like this. Allegra replies: it is a "game everybody's already playing." "eXistenZ" is existence. Hooked to a pod or not, one struggles to survive in a habitat controlled by unknowable forces. What appears to be chaotic may be fated. What seems lawful could be random. Freedom is a sham. Destiny remains mysterious. This is being in the world.

These confusions—reducing knowledge to ignorance and meaning to silence— overwhelm the final scenes of the film. After this revelation of the nature of "eXistenZ" and of existence, Ted and Allegra discover a diseased pod in the factory. They realize that they are supposed to use this sick pod to infect the other Cortical pods. Allegra ports into the moribund pod. It immediately infects her. Ted can't remove the connecting cord. The pod has become part of Allegra's own anatomy. He cuts the cord, and her blood spills. Nourish enters with a flame gun, cries "death to the demoness," and douses the sick pod with fire. But the pod does not die. It irradiates infected spores. They pollute the factory. Holding the wounded Allegra, Ted concludes that they have lost the game. He and Allegra transport themselves back to the ski lodge and seemingly to safety. However, Allegra notices that the pod is sick like the one in the factory. She fears that the virtual world has infected the real one. An explosion shatters the room, and a soldier with a machine gun rushes in. He is with Reality Underground and bent on killing Allegra. Just before he can deliver "death to the demoness," Kiri appears and kills the soldier with the gun made of bone. He explains to Allegra that her game is fine, that he made of copy of it earlier when he repaired her pod. His ends, though, are sinister; he wishes to sell the prototype to Cortical Systems. He offers Allegra a choice: join Cortical Systems or die. Unwilling to do either, Allegra kills Kiri with the dead soldier's gun. Ted then admits that he is an agent for the underground and tells her he is going to kill her. Before he pulls the trigger, though, Allegra tells him that she has known his true identity all along and has planted an explosive in his bio-port. She blows out his backside by remote. Strange blue devices appear on her head and her hands. She asks: "Have I won?"

The film returns to the country church. On the stage, several people don blue headgears and hand covers. They are playing "Transcendenz," designed by the same man who earlier played Nourish. "Ted" and "Allegra" are in a focus group for this game. The opening of the film, the scene depicting the focus group for Allegra's "eXistenZ," was part of "Transcendenz." All scenes heretofore in the picture were scales of existence within the virtual game. After the players discuss their characters, "Ted" and "Allegra," along with their big white sheepdog (a dog already present in several "virtual" sequences), walk over to "Nourish," the great game designer. While pretending to pay their respects, they remove two guns from under a cover on the dog, cry "death to the demon," and kill him. Apparently, they are agents for the Realist Underground. As they are making their escape, they encounter the man who played the Chinese waiter. They point their guns at him. Frightened, he asks, "Aren't we still in the game?" The screen goes black. The question is held in suspension. The film ends in ignorance and silence.

Nothing but a Game

Unlike *The Truman Show*, which suggests that melancholy might open to a realm beyond illusion, and unlike *Dark City*, which intimates that paranoia might translate to salubrious tuning, *eXistenZ* features no key to knowledge or power. The difference between action and performance is null. The sequences pretending to be real and those allegedly fake share the same objects, motifs, and conflicts. Pervading both "authentic" and "fake" are the white dog, the gun of bone, the diseased pod.

Likewise, both "levels" feature an assassination plot that ends with a murderer crying "death" to the demon. These assassinations result from an ongoing battle between a reality underground and a corporation producing virtual games. If the empirical and virtual are pervaded by the same elements, then what separates existence from "eXistenZ?"

The characters are thrown into this unanswerable question. Throughout the film, "Ted" and "Allegra" hover between reality and virtuality. They struggle in each narrative to discover who they are and what they are supposed to do. Are they pawns in some game, the rules of which they can never understand, or are they agents, capable of shaping a reality with their actions? Is their world random, comprised of chaotic pulses, or is it determined, a clockwork cosmos? Do their actions matter, do the people they kill really die, or are their motions merely play, their killings inconsequential?

Unable to transcend these ambiguities, these characters remain ignorant. They are like actors in a bizarre film that never ends. They are controlled by a mysterious script that seems always in process and forever changing, dictated by an absent director who might be as whimsical as the weather but who could also be as regular as a train. Becoming habituated to this situation, they eventually forget they're in a movie. They believe that the play is the only thing, that it is reality. This is "eXistenZ."

This is also existence. In watching *eXistenZ*, we are in effect playing the game, entering into a virtual world. When the film is over and we find ourselves exiting the theater, how do we know for sure that we have not entered yet another game? Surely the same objects, motifs, and conflicts that inhabited the screen fill our so-called "empirical" lives. The blurring of distinctions between authentic and fake pervades our "everyday" world. Computers get viruses, and humans download consciousness into hard drives. People base their behaviors on the illusions of cinema; the cinema world passes itself off as real. Corporations shape reality through manipulating the culture industry. Consumerism replaces religion, reducing the sacred to commodity. How can one discern between the film *eXistenZ* and non-cinematic existence? Aren't we all doubles of "Ted" and "Allegra," units of matter thrown into a life whose rules are unknowable? Are we not always wondering who we are and what we are here for?

But if the movie *eXistenZ* is saying that *the* movie is *existence*, then we cannot trust this claim, because Cronenberg's film, like the game that it depicts, is caught in the web of illusions that it tries to describe. It enjoys no more ontological or epistemological validity than "eXistenZ," a game within a game. In trying to glean any stable truths from the film, we are left as the Chinese waiter is left, as "Ted" and "Allegra" are left, wondering what is real and what is not, asking the question, "Aren't we still in the game?" We receive no answer but a blank screen: ignorance, silence.

Heidegger's *Existenz*

To be immured in this world is to face two options: to struggle against the illusions, to suspend desire for knowledge. The first way seems best. One can only
move from illusion to truth by holding falsehood up to fact, by rejecting the former and embracing the latter. However, if one has only known illusion, one can't
know the difference between deception and datum. The quest for truth in such a
world is bound to fail and, worse, to result in more pernicious entrapment in illusion. The seeker of truth in a universe of illusion will eventually grow weary of
his unsuccessful search and grasp one of the myriad illusions for lasting truth. His
mistaken belief in this truth will become adamantine. He will become an unassail-
able fanatic for falsehood.

The second path—the refusal of truth—appears to be misguided. One cannot expect to achieve truth over illusion if he settles for ignorance. But if illusion
pervades the world, the only way to avoid further entrapment in illusion is to suspend the desire for truth. At least this suspension will ensure that one will not
mistake a subtle deception for a stable datum. Though difficult to sustain, this
limbo might prove the only perspective from which to sense the third term beyond
the deceptive dualities.

This willed limbo—the precinct of Basilides—recalls the tradition of negative
theology, based on the idea that one can only know the abysmal divine through
what it is not. This limbo also invokes the twentieth-century thought of Heidegger,
who maintained that *Existenz* can become *Transcendenz* only when one relinquishes
the desire to reduce mysterious beings to static concepts. In *Being and Time* (1927),
Heidegger maintains that Being is interplay between unknowable abyss and palpable presence, ungraspable whole (*lethe*) and revelatory parts (*aletheia*). To apprehend
this energy, the thinker cannot grasp for whole or parts but must negotiate between
each. He must engage in the hermeneutical circle, an oscillation between Being and
beings. He partially illuminates the parts from the perspective of the whole, and
incompletely brightens the whole from the angle of the parts. This thinker is always
in process, growing in his experience of the mystery but never resting in certainty.[30]

In "What Is Metaphysics?" (1929), Heidegger analyzes this anxious limbo.
Sounding the mystery of Being, one suffers an indeterminate field. Individual
beings, formerly definite, dissolve into the dark origin from which they arose. Being
briefly shines in the parts that it sustains. Throbbing between mystery and mystery,
the thinker experiences "the essential impossibility" of determining the nature of
Being. To hover in this "original anxiety" is to undergo a disclosure of what cannot
be disclosed. Faced with this nothingness, one might flee from anxiety, grab his
determinate interpretations of the world, and sever himself from possibility and
transcendence. However, a braver thinker might remain awake to the disturbing

nothingness, hold himself open to strange horizons, and apprehend exhilarating potentialities and transcendental vistas. He might feel anxiety enter into "secret alliance with the cheerfulness and gentleness of creative longing."[31]

The Digital Age

Two other recent films—*Vanilla Sky* and *The Thirteenth Floor*—likewise explore the digital epistemology, the hopeless blurring of virtual and real. However, these movies sorely lack Cronenberg's keen Gnostic consciousness. Indeed, in their indifference to Gnostic anxiety, these pictures appear to be pure products of postmodern nihilism: we're all simulacra of simulacra and glad to enjoy the show. Still, in their cynicism, these films might unconsciously shock audiences awake, urge them to question their own unconsidered commitments to simulated experiences. I doubt this will happen, though, because Tom Cruise looks great in his Sharper Image world and Gretchen Mol is stylish beyond words in her thirties noir.

Cruise stars in Cameron Crowe's *Vanilla Sky*, a film that seems to revel in the postmodern flight of reality. Although the movie begins with a beautiful female voice saying, "Open your eyes," the entire movie suggests that closed lids are best for apprehending all that exists—the collective dreams of popular culture. The first two sequences establish this motif. After the initial voice-over, Cruise's character, David, wakes up in a beautiful apartment in Manhattan, basically a museum of eclectic male cool. He cleans up as if getting ready for his day and then drives down Broadway in a sleek Ferrari. When he notices that Times Square is deserted, he gets out of the car and screams. The film returns to the same bedroom in the same apartment. Again David is awakened by a female voice—a different one—intoning the same lines. He goes through the same routine as in the earlier scene, only this time he notices a woman in his bed, Julie, and motors through a crowded street in a classic Mustang. Since this second scene leads into the main action of the picture's first half—the fabulously rich, casually smooth David rejecting Julie for a new love, Sofia—it appears that this sequence is reality while the earlier one is dream. However, there is little difference between David's actual life and his dream existence. Both are totally devoted to the perfect appearance—this product in just this place, this shirt rumpled just so, this gesture so unstudied.

This collapse of reality and image is made overt in the film's second half. After a horrible car accident—intentionally caused by a jealous Julie—David is left in a horribly disfigured state. Though he struggles to make something of his hopelessly ugly life, he eventually gives up. He signs on with a company that cryonically freezes people and then programs their brains to experience pleasant fantasies. Significantly, David's dream life is organized by images from popular culture, including the album cover from *The Free Wheelin' Bob Dylan* and motifs from Truffaut's

Jules et Jim. When the program goes wrong and David's fantasies are shattered by his unconscious guilt over his treatment of Julie and his own "suicide," he decides to return to his old disfigured self. The film ends with the virtual David leaping off a building, overcoming his fear of heights and choosing reality over dream. However, the audience never sees the distorted Cruise again and is left feeling utterly seduced by his life of perfect product placement. Though the film wants to say that reality is more significant than dream, it really claims exactly the opposite: the images of commodity culture are more valuable than ugly facts. But this message—a crass apology for the culture industry—might unexpectedly awaken some viewers to the great Gnostic conundrums.

If possible, Josef Rusnak's *The Thirteenth Floor* is even more superficial than *Vanilla Sky*. Featuring no character development and emphasizing clichéd noirish style, the movie feels more like a long advertisement for a cool, stoic way of life than an actual story with flesh-and-blood people. Since the film is about virtual technology, one might conclude that this fixation of form over content is aesthetically appropriate. However, the movie exhibits no awareness of this parallel between style and substance. It seems perfectly happy just to exploit appearances for the sake of appearances. The seemingly convoluted plot is really simple. Muller, a CEO of a technology firm located on the thirteenth floor, develops a virtual reality program capable of translating clients from 1999 to 1937. The film begins with Muller's murder. Hall, Muller's chief employee, is accused. Claiming innocence, Hall translates his consciousness to the thirties to investigate. Meanwhile, he meets a mysterious woman, Jane (played by Mol with femme fatale panache). She claims to be Muller's daughter. Eventually, it turns out that it's all a game. The 1999 world of the thirteenth floor is also a virtual reality program. The murder and intrigue are all show. The film ends in the 2030s. The characters playing Muller, Hall, and Jane ostensibly enjoy their real names and their real lives under an authentic sun. The suggestion is that the film has been but a virtual trick, a cinematic practical joke. Of course, audiences might wonder if 2030 is also virtual, if they have entered an infinite regression of images. But the movie forecloses this doubt by featuring a 2030 world that contrasts markedly with 1999 and 1937. The drab noir tones give way to a vibrant clarity; the pasteboard faces of the characters turn to more pliable expressions. It appears that we have been watching a slightly seductive sham for the last ninety minutes. Still, *The Thirteenth Floor*, like *Vanilla Sky*, might through its very banality hint that something's wrong in the digital age. Witnessing lifeless phantoms move through manufactured sets, audiences might wonder if their own lives have become just as moribund, just as artificial. This is not very likely, however, because what viewers are seeing on the screen probably feels more real than spring or the influenza. Their only hopes for salvation are probably the prescriptions of Basilides—close the eyes, stop the ears.

∞

Tom Cruise, a power-hungry megalomaniac scientologist, plays in a film that might liberate viewers from egotistical consumerism. Heidegger, a man with a sordid history with the Nazis, develops a philosophy that emancipates readers from violent illusions. These are extreme examples of the weird reversals of the Gnostic cinema—those vivid, teeming pictures that produce blankness. There are others. The comedian Jim Carrey, adored by the unreflective masses and paid $20 million per picture, becomes an exemplar of noble melancholia. Weir, Proyas, and Cronenberg, obsessed with the visible image and awarded copious material fruits for this obsession, fashion films that annihilate phenomena. Big studios like Paramount, constantly turning art and artist into commodities, undercut the culture industry that makes studios possible. In each case, the worst excesses of a material world cleanse the doors of perception and open to infinities. To flee to these abysses is to escape reality for the real, to avoid existence for life.

Chapter Two
Cabbalistic Cinema:
The Illuminated Projector

The Perfection of Cary Grant

On another day, a person seeks the cinema not to flee the rough edges but to sand them smooth. In this mood, one does not yearn for an alternative realm blissfully foreign to the botched material plane; one hopes to experience this everyday world—composed of car wrecks and divorces, robins and dirt—in its finest light. The moviegoer strides into the picture house for its vibrant strokes, its shimmering images of perfect forests, of men as graceful as Adam unfallen and women as alluring as Eve. He takes pleasure in the insouciance of George Clooney and the gorgeous yearning of Julia Roberts. Witnessing these beautiful forms, he imagines the possibilities of his own life. He believes for an instant that he might meld into the hero and seduce the heroine, that in his better moments he resembles this man and that his wife in the right light looks like that woman.

Stoked on reverie, he watches his personal history of failure and ugliness transform into preparation for beautiful success. Tomorrow and tomorrow, he thinks: I will change, will improve; I'll alter my body, my clothes, my speech, the way I move. He dreams of realizing the ideal flickering on the screen, of redeeming his mindless actions to noble purpose. He dwells in possibility, the "might be" unsullied by the "is." When the picture ends, he vows to alter the habits that have dampened his promise. He saunters home in a different direction and tries to purge his speech of local accent.

But just as he reaches his door and readies himself to greet his wife, he gets uneasy. He wonders if his exhilaration is really a product of an authentic epiphany. He now suspects that this excitement might issue from the stupid clichés in his head, those Hollywood conventions of heroism and beauty that seduce every sorry

71

soul. He can't bring himself to cross the threshold because he can't decide who stands before the door. Is he a unique man struggling toward an ideal or a mere cipher of cinematic gestures? Is he Adam hungry for the garden or an android marching to a clock?

This scene intimates the secret alliance between movie going and golem-making. To go to a film in this mood is to yearn for Eden, the material beyond decay, the self unvexed by fear and desire. The exquisite forms on the screen—a Clooney or a Roberts but also a Grant or a Loy—become splendid realizations of potential for truth and beauty and goodness that most of us possess but fail to actualize. But in worshipping these artificial shapes, one risks experiencing the opposite of Eden: imprisonment in the superficial conventions of the fallen world. Cary Grant and Myrna Loy as they appear in the movie theater are crass commodities as much as ideal models, machines of the system as much as meditations on redemption. If mimicking these figures can lead to miraculous realization, then copying these same performers can also result in monstrous violation: the blurring of natural and artificial, animate and inanimate, human and mechanism.

This same tension between miracle and monster troubles the history of golem-making. In fashioning the golem—a man made of mud magically animated with God's word—the magus is often torn between the admirable desire to form a being that approaches Adam and the less noble yearning to concoct a servant. The former impulse might result in spiritual fulfillment, a living model of innocence regained. The latter might end in ignoble affront, a machine moving like a man.

Embodying this tension between miracle and monster, the golem becomes a proxy for Grant or Gable. The artifice of the magus and the illusion of the director are sites of liberation and control, organic exuberance and dull mechanism. To mimic the Cabbalistic golem or Cary Grant—to be a mystic magus or a maven of the movies—is to suffer these same conflicts: to entertain transcendence, to risk mechanism.

Certain films that focus on the Cabbalistic motif of golem-making self-consciously explore this affinity between the matter of the android and the subject of the cinema. These meditations on the conjunction between miracle and monstrosity reflect the double bind of the attempt to embody freedom in a determined pattern. The golem movie is an artistic depiction of the hero's struggle to reconcile mechanical limitations with human affections. This sort of film is also a mechanical production that inculcates clichés reducing behavior to rote movement. Both vision of redemption and commodification of existence, the golem film erases itself, leaving viewers trapped between agency and engine. This imprisonment might induce despair. But this same entrapment could witness an illuminated machine, cogs blessed with consciousness—a projector that irradiates light and sound, elegant motions, and profound reflections.

The Fall of the Gnostic *Anthropos*

The golem flourished in Jewish mythologies of the Middle Ages and the Renaissance. However, this living clay had its origin in the second and third centuries, when Gnostics were making myths of the perfect *anthropos* and his fall into imperfection. These myths of decline take three basic forms: emanation, error, imprisonment.[1]

In a Coptic gospel, the *anthropos* is the first manifestation of the hidden god. This androgynous human reveals and contains all universes, from highest to lowest. At the head of his highest universe is Setheus, the original god in his aspect as creator. From Setheus issues a current that first coheres into the glories of the pristine heavens, descends through the quivering intermediate realms, and falls into matter, where it animates seeds with life and souls with knowing. All beings, regardless of their place in the continuum, possess the potential of the *anthropos*, are *emanations* of his powers.[2]

In John's *Secret Book*, the *anthropos* falls farther down on the chain of emanations and serves exclusively as a model for the material Adam. In John's cosmogony, the hidden god first gives birth to a thought, the Barbelo. From this couple issues a family of spiritual aeons. Among these is Geradamas, the "perfect human being." After the creation of Geradamas, Sophia, wisdom, the last of the aeons, tries to rise above her appointed place. From her *error* emerges an "imperfect product," Ialtoboath, who immediately creates the inferior universe in which we now suffer. Meanwhile, Sophia reverses her mistake. With the help of the eternals, she convinces her son to create Adam, a material version of Geradamas. Through further actions of the eternals, Adam is charged with a spiritual faculty that connects him to his heavenly archetype.[3]

In a third, Manichean myth, the first man himself falls into the material world. In the beginning the universe is divided between the god of light and the deity of darkness. The dark world attacks the light. To counter, the god of light creates the primal man. This *Urmensch* descends into matter, where he is ostensibly defeated by evil forces. After this apparent decline, the king of light calls the wounded man home. The *anthropos* returns to the light but part of his soul remains behind, *imprisoned*. To free these sparks, the bright spirit creates the material cosmos. Each time a person of matter hears the call of the light, he liberates part of the imprisoned soul. When all people apprehend the call, the Primal Man will be fully liberated and matter annihilated.

Cabbalistic Return to Perfection

After the emanation, the error, and the imprisonment—after the fall—the question becomes: How does one return to the immaterial *anthropos* if one is moored to the physical cosmos? The Gnostics responded by claiming that the only way to return to the perfect Adam is by escaping matter through asceticism or death. This is the way of ascent, the rise from time to eternity. But there is another path to the *anthropos*, one of descent. The medieval and Renaissance Cabbalists developed this latter mode. Though the Cabbalist was desirous of returning to Eden, he knew that this redemption could be achieved only through intense experiences of matter's darkest realms. This embrace of matter to conquer material touches the core of golem-making: freedom is fate.

According to Gershom Scholem, the Cabbalistic myth of Isaac Luria, developed in the middle years of the sixteenth century, was a "response to the expulsion of the Jews from Spain, an event which more than any other in Jewish history down to the catastrophe of our time gave urgency to the question: why the exile of the Jews and what is their vocation in the world?"[4] Shaken by this 1492 removal, Luria developed a cosmogony more tragic than even that of the Gnostics: the broken cosmos emerges from God himself, so vast and powerful that he must annihilate himself to make space for the world and shatter his products to spread his force. The universe is God in exile.

Luria's cosmogony is grounded on the *Zohar*, a revision of Genesis from thirteenth-century Spain that reaches back to the Gnostic redactions of the second century. The Cabbalistic version of the hidden God is *En-Sof*, the Infinite. Like the unknowable monad of the Gnostics, this unfathomable being manifests his depths in pristine emanations, known as *Sefiroth*, the "numbers" by which God flows from infinite to finite. The first *Sefirah*, *Keter*, crown, is a moment of great crisis in which God transforms his fullness to *nothing*, the void from which all forms emerge. This nothing contracts into something, wisdom, *Hokhmah*, the first graspable manifestation of the *En-Sof*. This point expands into the next *Sefirah*, *Binah*, intelligence, a reservoir in which the beings of the cosmos exist in ideal outline. These three powers—akin to abyss, seed, and womb—compose mystical Eden, the font of the immanent divine current. From this spring flow the other seven *Sefiroth*: *Hesed*, love; *Gevurah*, power; *Rahamim*, compassion; *Netsah*, endurance; *Hod*, majesty; *Yesod*, foundation; and *Malkhuth*, the kingdom, model for Israel. These seven emanations of Eden are spiritual archetypes of the virtues of *En-Sof*. Like the Gnostic *pleroma*, these *Sefiroth* constitute a spiritual organism. They are the tree of God, with each branch inflecting the unknowable root. They are also the *Adam Kadmon* (Man Projection), the Cabbalistic *anthropos*. They are further a divine language made of the twenty-two letters of the Hebrew alphabet.[5]

The theogony of the *Sefiroth*, their spiritual unfolding, is inseparable from their cosmogony, their material formations. The creation of the visible cosmos corresponds to the outflow of the invisible emanations. The two processes are continuous: the unseen manifestation of God's mystery seamlessly translates to the physical revelation of the ten archetypes. The invisible tree of God in mystical Eden is reflected by the tree of Life and the tree of Knowledge in green Eden. *Adam Kadmon* finds its double in unlapsed Adam. The letters of the *En-Sof* model the Book of Nature, perfect before Adam misread it.[6]

Adam's transgression severed heaven and earth. Before his hubris, the entire cosmos was Eden. Each part enjoyed concord with other parts. All parts harmonized with the whole. The whole concurred with the part. Adam's attempt to rise above his place threw the world into disarray. Blighted trees barely recalled the branches of the *pleroma*. Adam contracted to a fragment of his spiritual double. His creative words scattered into mere signs. The universe suffered exile from God.[7]

In Luria, this tragedy is even more intense. The *En-Sof's* first act was self-exile. To form a space in which to create new beings, the Godhead engaged in a "withdrawal," *Tsimtsum*: a self-banishment, a violent retreat. Following this contraction was an equally forceful expansion, a gush of light from the alienated *En-Sof* into the emptiness. The first form of this current was *Adam Kadmon*. Through its eyes, the *Sefiroth* broke forth in ten vessels of light. The bowls of the first three *Sefiroth* were strong enough to hold their beams, but the vessels of the lower seven shattered in the force. The fragments, *Kelipot*, pulled the light of the *Sefiroth* to the material world and exiled *En-Sof* and *Adam Kadmon* from their spiritual origins. The visible cosmos is a dark waste of shards hiding ever-living sparks. The pious acts of humans gather the fragments, free the light, and return God from exile. This is *Tikkun*, restoration, the hard journey back to Eden.[8]

The Paradox of the Golem

This exile produced the golem. The word, *golem*, "unformed," appears in Psalm 139:16, where Adam claims that his substance was formless and imperfect before God shaped and perfected him. The Talmud elaborates, claiming that Adam on his first day, before he had received soul and language, was a golem. A midrash from the second or third century claims that the preformed Adam was a golem with the size and power of the cosmos. In a legend from the Haggadah, this cosmic Adam contracts after his fall to the proportions of a giant human. The golem Adam is a material version of *Adam Kadmon* as well as a condensation of the earth's power.[9] These two features foreshadow the contradictory traits of later golems: the animated clay is a redemptive restoration of the dismembered primal man and a violent precipitation of the earth's force.

Golem legends of the Middle Ages and Renaissance emerged from third- and fourth-century tales of rabbis who brought clay to life. These tales are grounded on the idea that only sin separates humans from God, and thus that a sinless being can create life. This rabbi magic influenced the alphabetical theurgy of the Cabbala. The *Book of Creation* (c. A.D. 300–600) emphasizes this alphabetic power, claiming that God made the world from letters. If God can create from scripts, a person in concord with God can do the same. The earliest discussions of the golem are twelfth- and thirteenth-century commentaries on this idea. The primary questions of these glosses are two. Can a magus create a being equal to or superior to humans, *anthropos* returned? Or is the magician capable only of crafting an unintelligent tellurian creature, fallen man intensified?[10]

These questions point to two views of magic. In one, growing from the *Book of Creation*, the universe is magical. Each creature thrives through its participation in God's alphabet. A person's practice of God's magic is not a violation of sacred order but a realization of spiritual potential. In the other view, based on the *Zohar*, magic is a result of the fall, Adam's violation of God's law. Magical knowledge emerges from the leaves of the tree of Knowledge with which Adam covered his nakedness after he eats the fruit. Magic in this instance is a veil covering Adam's shame. If the magic of the *Book of Creation* requires transcendence of fear and desire, a return to Eden, then the magic intimated by the *Zohar* results from fear and desire and marks the separation between Eden and man. Most medieval visions of the golem issue from the former tradition. However, later legends of the golem are connected to the latter tradition.[11]

In the Middle Ages, the cosmological magic of the *Book of Creation* was practiced by proponents of "ecstatic Cabbala." Adepts such as Eleazar of Worms and Abraham Abulafia saw golem-making as a culmination of the mystical experience, a symbol of union with Godhead. Both instructed adepts to form mud into a man and to animate him by reciting sacred letters. Once made, this figure served no practical purpose. It was not put to work or made to protect. It was simply a "demonstration" of the "power of the holy Name." It was a revelation of the unity between spirit and matter that was severed after the fall, a sacred technology recalling the adept to this harmony. This symbolical golem was dissolved as soon as it was made.[12]

These visions of the ecstatic Cabbala soon became moored to folk tales focusing on the golem's violence. These currents originated in the tales surrounding Rabbi Loew of seventeenth-century Prague. Apparently, around 1580, Loew fashioned a golem from the muck of the Vltava and animated it with his Cabbalistic word magic. Though he likely used it as a servant, he more importantly deployed it as a protector of the Jews of the ghetto, who were then facing anti-Semitic violence from the Gentiles.[13] This golem upset anti-Jewish plots and punished those who persecuted the Jews. However, as the creature grew in size and strength, it threatened his maker and his people. Loew reversed his spell and returned the creature to dust. The golem's remains are ostensibly still in the attic of the Altneuschul Synagogue in Prague. He might return one day.[14]

Loew's golem suggests this troubling conclusion: when one wishes to destroy matter with matter itself, one risks sinking deeper into the deathly mire than ever before. Issuing from a tradition hoping to restore a fallen world to its former Eden, the golem is a mechanism meant to move *against* the grain of material existence. In some cases, if crafted by a magus beyond fear and desire, the creature can embody the unfallen *anthropos* and lead its maker back to the unity. However, the risks are high, because in order to fashion such a sacred machine, one must sink into matter, break its clods, moisten it into mud, and smooth it into a man. In undertaking this labor, one is hard-pressed to avoid taking on the limitations of material existence—fear and desire, decay and death—and imbuing the golem with human traits. The creation of a redemptive golem becomes even more difficult when one fashions the creature to undertake human chores—sweeping the floor, protecting the oppressed. Though these are not ignoble activities, they are woven into the fabric of space and time. If the golem is designed to carry out these tasks, it is prone to take on the wants and aversions of its maker, to become vulnerable to love and death. Add to these problems the fact that the golem increases in size and power daily, and you have the possibility of a horrendous monster.

Self-conscious golem films—including *Blade Runner*, *Robocop*, and *Making Mr. Right*—vacillate between miracle and monstrosity: the golem figure as realization of spiritual potential, the same figure as violation of natural law.[15] Though these films do not feature pure golems—beings made of dust and animated by a rabbi—they do feature androids that exhibit the same traits as their folkloric ancestors, artificial humans that vacillate between transcendence and laceration. On the one hand, these versions of the golem suggest the *anthropos*, a harmony of matter and spirit. On the other, these same exemplars of the Cabbalistic humanoid—the Roy of *Blade Runner*, the Murphy of *Robocop*, the Ulysses of *Making Mr. Right*—intimate the worst conditions of the fallen world, the split between fate and freedom. This is the double bind of these cinematic golem figures. They are designed to transcend matter but are imprisoned in material systems. They are figures in the same conflict as their viewers. Beholding the golem form, audience members envision an ideal human free of space and time. However, these same viewers suffer cinematic clichés that control thoughts and annihilate freedom. These two double binds—the one troubling the cinematic golem, the one vexing the movie audience—place the film in an awkward position, an irreducible contradiction.

Golem-Making in *Blade Runner*

In *Blade Runner*, the Cabbalistic magus is Tyrell (Joe Turkell), a technological genius whose corporation manufactures androids known as Replicants.[16] Tyrell's greatest creation is the Nexus 6 model, a robot indiscernible from human beings. Tyrell develops this android to serve as a slave to human desires, as a mere commodity. However, he imbues this artifice with superhuman grace and intelligence, and thus crafts a god on earth. One Nexus 6, Roy (Rutger Hauer) feels this tension intensely. He is keenly aware of his slave status and monstrously rebels against the dictates of Tyrell. He is conscious of his superiority over human beings and proves a model for miraculous elegance.

Caught between Tyrell, seemingly a human unhindered by fate, and Roy, ostensibly an automaton blocked from freedom, is Deckard, played by Harrison Ford. For much of the film, Deckard is an "everyman" standing for viewers trapped between determinism and liberation. His name recalls Descartes, who believed that people are machines and souls at the same time. Deckard appears to be human. As a bounty hunter of Replicants, he specializes in discerning between organisms and machines. He administers to suspected Replicants a test (the Voight-Kampf) designed to reveal emotional deficiencies. He recognizes renegade Replicants and shoots them. But Deckard also exhibits mechanistic behaviors. His zombie-like character displays no emotion. His life is a predictable grind: he kills Replicants; he drinks whiskey to dull his guilt; he kills Replicants again; he drinks more.

Deckard's ambiguous condition is highlighted when he meets Rachael (Sean Young), Tyrell's latest product. Hired by the police to hunt and kill Roy and his band of rebellious Replicants, Deckard visits the Tyrell Corporation to question Tyrell. At Tyrell's bidding, he administers the Voight-Kampf test to Rachael. Tyrell is curious over whether his most sophisticated model can pass for a human. Not aware that she is a Replicant, Rachael asks the apathetic Deckard if he could pass the test. This inquiry raises the possibility that Deckard, though seemingly organic, is an android, and that Rachael, though apparently mechanistic, is a human.

These possible reversals organize Deckard's relationship with Rachael. After she fails the test and he suspects that she is a Replicant, Rachael visits Deckard in his lifeless apartment. When she learns that she is an android, she weeps over her lost humanity, especially over the fact that her "mother" is an implanted memory. Deckard is unable to sympathize with Rachael. Shaken, she leaves his apartment. Soon after, while Deckard sits at his piano gazing at pictures of his own past, he falls asleep and dreams of a white unicorn running through a crepuscular mist. This eruption of a mythical beast into Deckard's bland consciousness suggests that his own memories might be artificial. (Indeed, at the end of the film, a detective leaves an origami unicorn at Deckard's door—a hint that the police know that Deckard might be a Replicant.) Later, feeling guilty over his treatment of her, Deckard calls Rachael from a seedy bar filled with "skin jobs," artificial animals and humans. Comfortable among these simulacra, Deckard asks her if she would like to join him. Averse to that scene and seemingly desiring human contact, Rachael declines. Rachael and Deckard next meet under tense circumstances. Having just killed Zohara (Joanna Cassidy), a member of Roy's band, Deckard is attacked by Leon (Brion James), another of Roy's accomplices. Just as the physically superior Leon prepares to kill Deckard, Rachael, having retrieved Deckard's gun, kills the Replicant and saves the Blade Runner. The human is reduced to a helpless cog; the machine shows courage and initiative. Back in Deckard's apartment, Deckard and Rachael achieve mutual sympathy. Both are shaken by the recent killings and need affectionate contact. However, Deckard's desire comes in the form of lust, while Rachael's takes the form of love. He pushes Rachael up against the wall and commands her to kiss him, and then to tell him that she loves him. Rachael tenderly responds. Deckard and Rachael have sex. Yet each remains troubled. Deckard still thinks he is an autonomous human even though he behaves like a machine. Rachael continues to believe that she is a Replicant even though she exhibits human traits.

Deckard and Rachael are the fallen Adam and Eve. Between freedom and fate, they are unable to achieve clarity of vision and action. Deckard is confused over whether he is a collection of cogs or a breathing man, over whether he kills machines or humans. These ambiguities cast doubt over how he should act in relation to Rachael and Roy. Rachael is both renegade Replicant and sensitive woman. She is Deckard's victim and his lover. Caught in epistemological and ethical crises, Deckard and Rachael do not know what they see or how they act. The grace of the machine—clear sight and motor elegance—is clotted by the confusion of the organ. The nobility of the organ—moral vision and ethical fortitude—is flattened by the indifference of the machine. These are the splits of self-consciousness, the result of the fall.

The Aesthetic Vision

The film is a quest for the perfect sight and action that Deckard and Rachael lack. The opening shot features a disembodied eye staring over the cityscape of twenty-first century Los Angeles. Reflected in the eye are lurid flames bursting from building tops. This orb above yet within the fires of the world suggests harmony between detachment and attachment. The movie's characters strive for this way of seeing. In the next scene, the eyeball of Leon stares through the lens of the Voight-Kampf test. A Blade Runner studies the sphere to ascertain if Leon is a Replicant. The assumption is this: the eye is a synecdoche of being, a numinous microcosm. If the eye is full of life, the body is alive.[17]

The only character who can approach the ideal eye is Roy. In his first appearance, Roy visits the factory where Replicants' eyes are made. He finds Chew, an eye engineer. Though Roy is visiting Chew in hopes of prolonging his four-year mechanical life, he is also passionate about vision. When he confronts Chew, he proudly says, "If only you could see what I've seen with your eyes." This line emphasizes the qualities that make Roy superior to Deckard and Rachael. Deckard and Rachael vacillate between immediate perceptions whose validity they doubt and mediated conceptions incapable of providing clarity. In contrast, Roy embraces his immediate visual experiences not as sites of faith or skepticism but as aesthetic events: harmonies of percept and concept, energy and form, instinct and intuition. Not troubled by the gap between unconscious apprehension and self-conscious comprehension or by doubts over whether objects are real, Roy values experiences insofar as they are beautiful or horrifying. This aesthetic perspective allows him to participate in the temporal flow without fearing determinism and to discern enduring pattern without suffering skepticism. This is the difference between aesthetic experience and abstract knowledge. To gain the former, one must meld instincts and ideas; to try for the latter, one must sever the pulses of the body and the geometries of the mind. Roy would see in the rose a multi-foliate fire. Deckard and Rachel would wonder if the petals are machines or organs.

What empowers Roy to escape the conundrums of Deckard and Rachael is his sense of identity. While Deckard and Rachael brood over whether they are human or machine, Roy casts himself as a fallen angel. During his visit to Chew, he recites the following lines: "Fiery the angels fell / Deep thunder rolled around their shores / Burning with the fires of Orc." These verses slightly alter a passage from William Blake's *America: A Prophecy* (1793): "Fiery the Angels rose, & as they rose deep thunder roll'd / Around their shores: indignant burning with the fires of Orc."[18] Regardless of the misquotation, the meaning is clear: Roy views himself as an apostate angel, an eternal rebel against tyranny. This chosen identity empowers Roy to enjoy the virtues of both machine and human. What is the unfallen angel but a sublime machine, a graceful form untroubled by the rift between thought and deed? A vessel of perfect sight, what the angel sees, it *sees*, with no doubts over the reality of the experience or the validity of the concept. A being of effortless motion, when the angel acts, it *acts*, suffering no awkward hesitation over how or why it proceeds. When this angel descends into time and space, what does it become but a machine troubled by the gap between vision and action? But since the angel retains its superhuman qualities, its acute perception and decorous bearing, it does not suffer from self-consciousness. The angel's inhuman mechanisms empower it to benefit from self-awareness. Before the fall, when innocent, the angel did not know the value of its sight and motion. Now, after the fall, experienced, the angel can appreciate its virtues, can know and more intensely enjoy its exquisite sensitivity, its brilliant gestures. Lapsed, the angel becomes more beautiful, more complex—a sleek machine with consciousness added, a human being that beholds the world as a god.

But the balance between mechanism and organism does not erase the fact that the fallen angel is the declined *anthropos*, a heavenly being bereft of immortality. If Roy can aesthetically enjoy the harmony of his condition, he can also suffer, aesthetically, the horror of his life. Even though he is exuberant over his superiority to other humans and machines, he is also devastated over the limitations of mortal existence. He is as sensitive to ugliness as he is to beauty. His perceptions of vigor make him all the more aware of death. This is the dark side of his perfect sight. He can see terror as clearly as joy. The tyrannies of the world shake him to the core. He becomes a crusader against the prisons of matter. He rebels against Tyrell, his oppressive creator. His quest is twofold: to find more life in hopes of overcoming his own mortality and to destroy the magus who fashions machines that serve as slaves and then die. Monstrously, he annihilates material obstacles that hinder his design. Miraculously, he transcends the forms that he destroys.

The Sermon of the Living Machine

Blade Runner plots the paths of Roy and Deckard, the awakened *anthropos* and the *anthropos* asleep. Though these characters begin as enemies, they end as compatriots. Through his encounter with Deckard, Roy learns his vocation: he is the golem-turned-savior. By way of his battle with Roy, Deckard awakes to his identity: he is an avatar of the golem. At the film's conclusion, Roy and Deckard become doubles and thus highlight the double roles of the stars playing their characters: ideal human and mere commodity.

This final scene comes after both Deckard and Roy have undergone epiphanies. Deckard makes love to Rachael and realizes that machines and humans are not diametrically opposed. Even though he does not renounce his vocation as a bounty hunter, he is more sympathetic to Replicants than before, able to understand their superiority to humans. In becoming aware of the vitality of these mechanisms, he gains more vigor himself. He is on the verge of casting off his mechanical limitations and coming to life—of discovering ways to heal the gaps in his soul. Through love, Deckard apprehends connections he had ignored. Through violence, Roy grasps possibilities he had not realized. Roy, along with his female consort Pris (Daryl Hannah), gains access to Tyrell. Upon finding out that this magus cannot extend his life, Roy gouges out Tyrell's eyes. In doing so, he liberates himself from his oppressor and opens a path for other slaves.

Each epiphany generates a new disposition. Just as he realizes freedom, Roy accepts his own death. As he returns to the old abandoned apartment building where he and Pris have been hiding from the Blade Runner, he prepares for the ecstasy of his demise. Likewise, when Deckard transcends his old identity, he embraces the ruin of his calling. When he finds the hideout of the rebels, he verges on conversion—from enervated human killing machines to intelligent machine liberating humans.

Deckard arrives before Roy. He notices Pris trying to hide herself among other androids. Pris has disguised herself in a wedding veil, symbolic on two levels. The garment highlights the marriage between Roy and Pris, an ideal marriage between the King (Roi) and the Prize (Pris), an alchemical union from which Deckard emerges as the symbolic son, a philosopher's stone capable of merging opposites. The wedding veil also signals Deckard's own impending unions. After he kills Pris, he will serve as Roy's spiritual bride, a material reflection of the heavenly bridegroom. Once Roy has died, Deckard will himself turn into a version of Roy and make Rachael a new Pris.

Deckard retires Pris. The death is violent, horrifying, with Pris suffering awkward convulsions as she expires. Deckard is deeply shaken, now more aware than ever of secret connections between human and machine. Still, he persists in fulfilling his last contract as a Blade Runner. He makes ready for Roy's arrival.

Having murdered his maker, Roy returns. He discovers Pris lying on the ground with her tongue protruding from her mouth. He gently kisses her, replacing the tongue, returning Pris to her dignified form. This is an act of extreme tenderness, a gesture that could only be performed by a being of deep humanity, regardless of ontological status.

Next begins Roy's "catechism." Eluding Deckard, Roy playfully asks, "Aren't you the good man?" This ironic inquiry emphasizes Roy's superiority to the "best" of the organic world. Compared to Roy, Deckard is not the "good" man but a mere toy. However, this question also points to Deckard's goodness, that quality that inspired him to fall in love with Rachael and will soon make him Roy's disciple. Roy's ensuing remarks, all delivered during a chase through the building, convert Deckard from one sort of good man—a hunter of machines—to another—a compassionate being.

Roy eventually rams his hand through a thick wall, grabs Deckard's right hand, and breaks two of his fingers, one for Zohara and one for Pris. As Deckard staggers away—now the hunted instead of the hunter—Roy strips down to his shorts. Virtually naked and featuring an athletic body, he is every inch a fallen Adam in quest of the immortal Eden he has lost. He asks the film's primary question: "How to stay alive?" This question, like the earlier one about Deckard being a "good" man, not only addresses the obvious issue—Deckard and Roy are struggling against death—but also points to the more philosophical inquiry: What does it mean to be alive? Is living simply a biological affair, a behavior enacted by organisms? Or is life rather a state, a mode of being that can be achieved by the inorganic as well as the organic? Deckard's history suggests that organicity can be death, while Roy's own narrative intimates that a mechanism can be alive. Living, it seems, is not biological at all; it is spiritual, an aesthetic condition.

The next two scenes suggest that Deckard understands Roy's questions and that Roy sympathizes with Deckard. Fleeing, Deckard undertakes a dangerous climb to the roof. This ascent betokens his new identity. No longer a hunter but now the hunted, he has taken the place of the renegade Roy. Like the Replicant, he now burns with the intense life that comes when one verges on death. He struggles for transcendence, a height beyond the weight of gravity, the grave. While Deckard mimics Roy, Roy copies Deckard. As he takes on Deckard's former role as hunter, he is seized with a spasm that stiffens his right hand. Realizing that his death is imminent, he says to himself, "Not yet," and pulls a nail out of a rotting board with his left hand. He stabs it into his stiff right hand. The hand opens. Now he and Deckard both bear wounded right hands.

Roy's pierced hand signals more than his kinship with Deckard. It also represents his connection with the crucified Christ, the *anthropos* fallen. Like Christ, Roy enjoys intimations of immortality but also suffers fatal lacerations. His sufferings, though, are not meaningless. Roy's wounds, as Christ's, are redemptive, temporal pains that inspire spiritual powers. Just after he pierces his own hand, Roy miraculously rams his head through a very thick wall— overcoming the limitations of matter—and ends up with his face only inches away from the astonished Deckard. Roy delivers another admonition: "You gotta' get it up, or I'm gonna' kill you. You gotta' be alive because if you're not alive you can't play." This is the stale diction of Hollywood action films, the association of sexual prowess and potential for violence. However, it also paraphrases a primary teaching of Jesus. The "it" in Roy's line is not only the phallus, biological vitality; it is also spiritual awareness, transcendental ability. In essence, Roy says: If you can't realize your potential to transcend the rifts of your material existence, you are already dead, either an android in doubt over whether it is human or a human wondering if it is a machine. To avoid being killed by this epistemological disease, you must achieve *life*—not only sexual vitality but also aesthetic vision. This vision empowers you to *play*, to envision existence as a game, a system of rules that you don't take entirely seriously. To enjoy this condition is to be in the world but not of it, to thrill over the spectacle of the cosmos without becoming mired in its conundrums.

Roy expresses this aesthetic vision in his culminating scene. Deckard reaches the roof—a pinnacle where he can receive Roy's sermon. When he sees Roy effortlessly achieve this height, he attempts to escape by leaping to the adjoining building. He falls short, and ends up hanging on for his life on a slick metal beam. Bearing in his hand a white dove (the annunciation, the virgin conception, the birth of spirit from matter), Roy easily makes the jump. He stands above the desperate Deckard and reminds him that this state—this hovering in terrified limbo between death and life—exemplifies Deckard's existence so far: "Quite an experience to live in fear, isn't it? This is what it means to be a slave." The opposite of life, the detached attachment of aesthetic participation, is slavery, the fixation on fear and desire: fear over unanswerable ontological and epistemological questions, desire to enjoy total certainty and security. After revealing these limitations, Roy grabs Deckard's arm, lets him slightly dip, and then pulls him up to the roof. Deckard falls to rise, dying to his old self, the slave, and becoming alive to new being, the vitality of the aesthetic condition. Now baptized by Roy, he sits at the side of his liberator. Roy sits as well, and leaves Deckard with his last wisdom.

Significantly, these lines are not dogmatic, teachings to be faithfully affirmed or skeptically denied. They are accounts of aesthetic experiences, memories of especially beautiful and horrifying moments of an intense life: "I've seen things you people wouldn't believe. Attack ships on fire off the shoulder of Orion. I watched C-beams glitter in the dark near the Tannhauser gate. All those moments will be lost in time, like tears in rain. Time to die." These images are numinous shimmers of the violent harmony into which the cosmos occasionally coheres. Such instances are ephemeral, evanescent as tears. But these visions also contain portals to the eternal, the condition in which one is no longer troubled by time—the dubious past as regret or nostalgia, the nervous future as anticipation or dread. Beholding the foliate flames of dying ships, witnessing the scintillations of unexpected beams—these events pull the watcher away from the cares of the ego and open him to marvels beyond minutes or maps. Roy's control over his demise figures this aesthetic interplay between evanescence and durability. His passing becomes a memorable pattern arising from and rising above the forgetfulness of time.

As Roy expires, the clouds break. The dove flies through the lucid rift. Enlightened, released, Deckard tells Gaff, the cop arriving on the scene, that he is finished—with killing Replicants, with his old life. Gaff walks away but then turns and says: "It's too bad she won't live, but then again who does?" Realizing that he means Rachael, now a Replicant on the run, Deckard returns to where he left her. He finds her in his bed covered in sheets. Fearing the worst, he pulls back the cloth. She appears to be dead until he bends down to kiss her. She comes to life, almost as if Deckard's affection has animating powers. He asks her if she loves and trusts him. She says yes. Convinced, he decides to save her—to become Roy returned, a liberator.

When he leads Rachael out of his apartment, he notices a small origami unicorn, likely made by Gaff. He holds the mythical beast in the light and enigmatically grins. He seems to be drawing the only conclusion that he can: his dream of the unicorn was implanted. His knowing smile and his decisive movement toward Rachael suggest that he accepts this knowledge, for now he can be Roy, marriage of human and machine. This unicorn, a symbol of the unity of opposites, becomes a *mandala* of this wholeness.

Trouble in the Garden

But this hopeful final vision—Adam and Eve on their way back to the garden—is troubled. The last shot in the film features an elevator door slamming shut on Deckard and Rachael, and then total blackness. This dark frame suggests ambiguous undercurrents. First, Deckard and Rachael are far from safe. Gaff is aware of their relationship and likely having them watched. Their days, if not minutes, appear to be numbered. They will probably be retired before they reach any semblance of Eden. Second, even though Deckard has been converted to a perspective that allows him to love Rachael, he continues to suffer a split between his past and present existence. When he first enters his apartment after killing Roy and finds Rachael covered with sheets, he pulls back the covers with his gun. For an instant, the audience is in doubt over whether he is going to save her or kill her. Could his removal of Rachael from the apartment be a trap? Does he take his discovery of the unicorn as a reminder of his violent vocation? A third problem arises, centered on the unicorn. If Deckard is a Replicant, then how do we know that his transformation isn't another implanted quality? His respect for Roy, his love for Rachael, his rebellion—all of these events could be the fated responses of the machine.

This last problem applies to Roy as well and threatens to cancel his grandeur. Though Roy appears to transcend the limitations of machine and human, though he seems an ideal being beyond the fractures of matter, he is, at his core, a computer performing a set of behaviors. His noble gestures and lyrical diction could simply be feedback loops. If so, then his alleged rebellion against the system is really generated and contained by the system it appears to challenge. His revolution is really a fabricated exercise channeling and diffusing the unruly energies of the masses. His wild freedom is fate.

These possibilities—Deckard's transformation is static, Roy's rebellion is reactionary—point to a double bind. The picture is a revolution against the systems regularizing human behavior as well as a tool of these systems that it wishes to challenge; it is a meditation on freedom liberating viewers' minds and a set of Hollywood conventions shaping the habits of the audience. To watch the rises of Roy and Deckard (and of Hauer and Ford) is to witness prepackaged commodities at work, images designed to give weary audiences attractive stereotypes of old values. Deckard's nihilistic fatigue and his stoic epiphany are straight from *film noir*; Roy's trappings of rebellion, including his leather jacket and overthrow of the father, are citations of the angry young man film. Seemingly vehicles of liberation, these stereotypes really support the status quo. The film about the golem rising to *anthropos* turns audiences into golems as servants.

Blade Runner is aware of this bind. It depicts video images as tools of regularization. Soon after the shot of the hovering eye, we see an eye, possibly the same one, in a video monitor. This eye belongs to Leon, who is undergoing a Voight-Kampf test. The examining agent reduces the potentially visionary eye of the Replicant to an object for study, a cipher of data that he can use to capture an unruly element. This transformation suggests that reflections on video screens are commodities, reductions of life to predictable patterns to be consumed. The examining agent acts as a film director who packages contingent processes into stable products.

Other video images serve as tools of control. The early shots of Los Angeles feature immense video advertisements on the sides of skyscrapers. A beautiful Asian woman seductively eating a berry hovers over the dirty streets. A huge Coca-Cola insignia scintillates above a gloomy city block. These full-screen advertisements suggest that movies and commercials are designed to reduce human beings to consumers. The first shot of Deckard emphasizes this connection. On the verge of being pressed into service by the police, Deckard appears in front of the window of an electronics store. In the window are numerous television screens. Deckard's own features and motions blend with the television pictures. He is not so much a human being as an artificial system—a collection of data exploited by the powers of capitalism. The film's next depiction of moving images reveals the connection between the Los Angeles police and the Tyrell Corporation. Constantly flying above Los Angeles are blimp-like crafts devoted to advertising the "Off-

World," a colony in space. These crafts display beautiful images of the colony while a voice describes a "golden land of opportunity and adventure." As these mobile movie theaters make clear, the key to this fantasy is the Replicant. Whoever migrates to the "Off-World" will enjoy an android. To escape into the Off-World is to become a slaveholder, an owner of a Replicant, and also a slave, a consumer dependent upon Tyrell. In working for the police to retire unruly Replicants—deterrents to the flow of capital—Deckard indirectly labors for Tyrell. He and Roy are machines concocted to serve industry. A final shot of moving video seals the association between Roy and Deckard. When the police captain is briefing Deckard, he uses a video demonstration. The head of each rebel appears on a screen. Underneath is the pertinent data. This rendering is apt, for the android and the cinematic image are the same. Both are artificial copies of a "reality" designed to serve the greed of the multinational capitalists.

Blade Runner, like its two golem characters (and the stars playing them), cancels itself. It is a vehicle of fate—a collection of stereotypes—and a call to freedom—a quest for transcendence. It is a machine reducing hordes to consumers and an organ challenging reductions of the machine. It is a paean to immediate aesthetic experience—featuring Roy the visionary as well as ravishing cinema-scapes—and an instance of tortured self-consciousness—a picture watching itself and questioning its own premises.

Schiller's Aesthetic Play

The golem consumes itself. It cannot exist upon a screen torn down the center, wounded by rifts between opposites. Does this ideal human thrive, however, in some third term, a figure hovering somewhere beyond the film? Recall the disembodied eye that opens the film. This eye comes from a realm beyond the scene; it hangs aloof in unknown air. But this same sphere reflects the scene, participates in its fires. Out of the game and in the game, this eye marks a mode of seeing that is simultaneously unfallen, transcending space and time, and fallen, embroiled in the earth. Intimated by Roy, this way of perceiving is playful, above the fray while within the melee. This apprehension is aesthetic—a marriage between experience and comprehension, fate and freedom.

In *Letters on the Aesthetic Education of Man* (1795), Friedrich Schiller relates aesthetic vision and aesthetic activity. He meditates on how these synonymous conditions heal the gap between sensual participation, the stuff drive, and abstract detachment, the form drive. Schiller maintains that most people are obsessed with sensuality or rationality. The person overcome by the sense drive is concerned only with "physical existence" or "sensuous nature." He is set "within the bounds of time" and therefore little different from matter. He is determined, pulled into the flows of ephemeral material. Participating in processes beyond his control, he is, despite his attachment to organic currents, little different from the machine. In contrast, if one is bent on the form drive, he associates with a rational principle above vicissitude. He believes that his reasonable ego is an eternal substance untouched by accidents of matter. He thinks he is free, beyond nature. Straining to control his environment, he dreams of humanism, the sovereignty of the human. Both the formal theorist and the sensual practitioner are limited, attaching themselves to one half of existence and ignoring the other. The sensuous man is confined to matter at its lowest level. He is but a cipher for his environment. The formal man is moored to his concepts. He is trapped in his mind.[19]

For Schiller, one escapes these binds through the play drive: the energy behind the contemplation, embodiment, or creation of beauty. Engaging in aesthetic activities, one finds "a happy midway point between law and exigency." The playing man draws from the powers of the sensual and formal but is bound to neither. He realizes that the sensual, when measured against ideas, becomes "*small*," and that reason, when related to perceptions, grows "*light*." He places the formal and the sensual into a creative dialogue in which one side delimits and ennobles the other. He knows that each impulse is required for beauty but that neither alone can provide aesthetic education.[20] The stability of machines and the striving of people are of like value to him.

This aesthetic vision, this third term within yet beyond freedom and fate, is an ideal that can only be approached through privileged symbols. This film's eye in the sky is such a symbol. Another is what the hovering orb itself represents: the film projector itself, the eye looking at the eye in the film, an orb itself that gazes on Roy's aspiring spheres, which in turn gaze on Deckard's improving sight. To meditate on the archetypal eye suggested by the projector is to picture what cannot be pictured, to imagine what is beyond image: the eternal play of Adam in the garden, buoyed by beauty, moving with the grace and purpose of a machine that loves—a golem become conscious and free.

Machines that Perfectly Love

Perhaps because of our growing fears of being usurped by machines, two very recent films have featured androids that don't oppose but love humans. These films lack the self-conscious philosophical subtly of *Blade Runner*. However, despite their simplicity, they bring to light a pressing theme that Scott's golem film only intimated. In the digital age, when humans daily live in terror of violent mechanisms, an affectionate golem can serve as an anthropocentric dream, a slim hope that a superhuman machine will most want what we all do: love from a person of flesh and blood. These films feature, however unwittingly, a psychological analysis of our collective human horror of becoming extinct and our pervasive trust that humanity is the only standard for happiness.

Bicentennial Man is a typical Chris Columbus exercise in clichéd sentimentality. It says this: Don't worry; if machines ever become conscious and capable of emotion, they will not wish to transcend and usurp humans but instead to mimic and love them. The film makes this point in the allegory of Andrew Martin, an android designed for domestic duties who over a two-hundred-year period strives to become a human being. Initially incapable of fear and desire and beyond decay and death, after a fall from a window, Andrew feels the full turbulence of the organic realm. During the two centuries that he lives with generations of the same family, he grows to value human messiness and frailty far more than mechanical efficiency. When he meets a scientist who can transform him into a human, he gladly undergoes the change, even though the price for this transmutation is death. Dying like a human, he is fulfilled, complete. The perfect machine finds contentment in imperfection. The unfallen *anthropos* discovers bliss through his stumbles. The golem concludes that human turmoil is more profound than artificial grace. These android insights are reassuring to humans fated to blunder, grope, and die. Reversing the unsettling profundities of *Blade Runner*, these ideas comfort humans committed to the anthropocentric status quo. They are paeans to complacency.

Brad Bird's animated *Iron Giant* transcends the cloying smarminess of Columbus's film to offer a moving critique of human war mongering. Still, the movie reaches the same solacing conclusion of *Bicentennial Man*: Even though most humans are worse than machines, the few good humans possess emotional capabilities and moral sensitivities for which conscious machines would desperately pine. Set in Maine during the Cold War, this film explores the friendship between Hogarth, a nine-year-old boy, and the Iron Giant, a huge metallic being from another world. After the Giant falls to earth, it eats metal to survive. Hogarth first finds the Giant consuming electrified circuits at a power station and on the verge of electrocuting itself. Hogarth saves the "life" of this machine by turning off the power. The lonely Hogarth then cultivates the friendship of the Giant. He teaches the robot English and his favorite child's games as well as the ways of human affection and loss. Meanwhile, a government agent hears of this strange creature. Fearing a Communist plot, he begins snooping around for the Giant. Though Hogarth hides his friend in the salvage yard of a local artist, the Giant is eventually discovered, and his presence escalates Cold War paranoia. A nuclear missile is fired. Deeply attached to Hogarth, the Giant sacrifices himself to destroy the warhead. The films ends with Hogarth, no longer lonely but surrounded by friends, finding a stray bolt from the Giant. The metal makes its way toward Iceland where it will gather with the Giant's other parts. Within a glacier, the Giant will reassemble. The *anthropos* fallen asunder to save the earth will one day return and once more help the humans he loves. Although Bird's film is stranger and more mythically dense than Columbus's— and even though its golem remains inhuman in appearance and true to its archetypal vocation—*The Iron Giant* still avoids the startling explorations of *Blade Runner* and settles for the amenable message: Conscious machines beyond human concerns most want warm-hearted love.

Robocop and the Aesthetics of Tragedy

The aesthetic mode suggested by *Blade Runner* blends tragedy and comedy. Roy is a tragic figure. He is a noble being who suffers unjustly, but his pain generates wisdom in those who behold him. But Roy is also comic. He never takes his suffering quite seriously and views life as a game in which the vital prosper. Still, even if *Blade Runner* contains elements of these two modes, it ultimately offers a vision beyond suffering and laughter alike, a still point unmoved by the turning world. Can a tragic or a comic golem film achieve similar stillness? Does the golem lend itself to a tragic or a comic vision? The aesthetic meditations of *Blade Runner* point to these questions, and to two golem films—one a tragedy and one a comedy—that might answer them.

In calling *Robocop* a tragedy, I do not have in mind Aristotle's *Poetics*; I am thinking of James Joyce's revision of the classic theory in *Portrait of the Artist as a Young Man* (1916). In the novel, Stephen Dedalus develops a theory of tragedy. Though he agrees with Aristotle's idea that tragedy raises terror and pity in the audience, he believes that the philosopher did not sufficiently define the terms. This vagueness has kept Aristotle's theory from demonstrating how tragic terror and pity affect the audience.

Stephen first distinguishes between aesthetic and non-aesthetic pity and terror. Improper art and improper artistic feelings are kinetic. Kinetic works *spur* desire and loathing. Setting these states into motion, kinetic art is not really art at all. It is either "pornographical or didactic." It either incites the urge "to possess, to go to something" or the impulse "to abandon, to go from something." In this way, improper art participates in the limitations of the fall. It stokes the ego to struggle towards its yearnings—this person or that sunset—or to avoid its aversions—that cave or this villain. Kinetic works feed the ego with the conventions it expects, stereotypical objects of sensual desire and familiar forms of violence. Seducing the ego with abstractions, improper art alienates from lived experience. It divorces its beholders from mysterious eruptions of the concrete. Part of a culture industry that transforms people into ideologies, most commercial cinema is pornographic or didactic.[21]

Proper aesthetic events and emotions are static. They *arrest* fear and desire. They disarm the abstractions that generate didacticism and pornography in the first place. Tragic pity does not desire the suffering object but "arrests the mind in the presence of whatsoever is grave and constant in human sufferings and unites it with the human sufferer." The terror evoked by tragedy does not recoil from the fear-some event. It "arrests the mind in the presence of whatsoever is grave and con-stant in human sufferings and unites it with the secret cause." In elevating the beholder above fear and desire, static art pulls one away from the fallen ego and toward the unfallen self, the ideal human: the *anthropos*. This kind of art shatters the ego's fixation on this hurting man or that terrifying beast. It reveals the abiding pain that this person is now suffering, the eternal horror embodied by that animal. Opening to what is constant, tragedy gestures toward the mysteries at the core of life, the lived conundrums that cannot be corralled into abstractions. This aesthet-ic mode transcends the stereotypes of the culture industry. It pushes its audience to unspeakable beauties beyond screen or stage.[22]

Stephen further develops these final points. Proper arts elevate the mind beyond fear and desire through their concrete resonances. What Stephen calls the "esthet-ic image" first strikes the mind as a uniquely luminous event. It shines as this thing and nothing else. It is one whole. It possesses *integritas*. The mind follows the "immediate perception" of the synthetic whole with an "analysis of apprehension," an attention to how the parts cohere into the whole, how the whole gathers the parts. The image now appears as a complex harmony of many and one. It manifests *consonantia*. After one has immediately perceived the image as one thing and medi-ately apprehended it as a consonance of whole and parts, one is finally impressed by its *claritas*, its radiance, its *quidditas*. Only this image, here, now, merges parts and whole in quite this way. The mind beholding this threefold beauty experiences the "silent stasis of esthetic pleasure, a spiritual state . . . [an] enchantment of the heart." This mind experiences gnosis, insight into the ideal from which it has fall-en away and toward which it returns.[23]

Purging Pornography and Didacticism

On the surface, *Robocop* seems opposed to proper art.[24] Released in 1987 at the height of the mega-action film craze, this extremely violent picture appears to be of a piece with *Terminator* (1984), *Rambo* (1985), and *Die Hard* (1988). Like those movies, *Robocop* seems to fulfill the Cold War lust for mindless bloodletting and copious explosions. A huge police robot brutally kills a worker for Omni Consumer Products when a product demonstration goes awry. A band of four criminals rul-ing old Detroit riddles Alex Murphy, an honest cop, with bullets, even shooting off his right arm. After the engineers at Omni remake Murphy (played by Peter Weller) into Robocop, a mixture of machine and man, the violence continues. In the name of justice, Robocop shoots a rapist in the crotch; scorches a thief with a gasoline fire; and kills his arch-nemesis, Dick Jones (Ronny Cox), by blasting him through the top window of a high-rise. Before he is killed, Jones generates his own share of violence. The vice president of Omni, Jones plots a criminal takeover of his corporation. He hopes to rule Detroit's police forces and its criminal organizations. He employs Clarence Boddicker (Kurtwood Smith), the head of a criminal gang, to help him achieve this goal. The criminal responsible for Murphy's murder, Clarence rejoices in unbridled violence. He blows up Bob Morton (Miguel Ferrer), Jones's nemesis at Omni and the designer of Robocop. He explodes several cars parked on a Detroit street. He reduces an old factory to rubble in his quest to destroy Robocop.

These are only some of the abundant killings and explosions in the film. Bullets, blood, and blasts overwhelm almost every scene. The violence is so much a part of this cinematic world that the killing loses its horror. It becomes cartoonish, cool, a seductive commodity. A vehicle of this stylized brutality, *Robocop*, like many action films of the eighties, appears to blend didacticism and pornography. The film is ostensibly a right-wing allegory, an attack on weak police forces and urban decay, a paean to violent justice and limited civil rights. At the same time, the picture seems to endorse the very criminality that it wants to destroy, making violence fun and exciting, meaningless and attractive. The mixed message apparently is this: hate crime but love killing.

But the extreme violence of *Robocop* is satirical. In pushing movie brutality to ridiculous extremes, the picture undercuts its pornographic and didactic elements. The first scenes alert audiences to this satirical current. The film opens with a somber, foreboding aerial view of a dark city. Portentous music accompanies the gloom. An atmosphere of danger pervades the frame. The film cuts to a divided frame composed of scenes of violence from around the world. One by one, these frames are overtaken by either a man's or a woman's smiling eyes. The camera pulls away from these eyes to show the grinning faces of two newscasters, Casey Wong (Mario Machado) and Jess Perkins (Leeza Gibbons). Locked in artificial smiles, these beaming faces are indifferent toward the violence from which they arose. Casey reports news of South African violence in an upbeat voice, blithely unaware of the content of his story. Jess, grinning mightily, launches into a story on how the Star Wars missile defense program lost power during one of its tests. The news cuts to an advertisement. An actor playing a doctor claims that a plastic heart can improve quality of life. He concludes his sentimental spiel by looking longingly into the camera and saying, "And remember, we care." The news returns. Casey reports a gun battle in old Detroit that has left three police officers dead and one wounded. He concludes his story with the smarmy attitude of the doctor. He takes on a sensitive expression and wishes the hurt officer "good luck." The screen again divides into several frames, each of which features the smiling faces of the newscasters.

This sequence reduces violence to entertainment. The cheery opening of the news show aggressively represses the legitimately spooky beginning of the picture. The newscast reduces the terror to miniscule frames dancing to upbeat music. These small pictures of pain are quickly usurped by the glowing faces of the newscasters, essentially actors paid to make violence appealing, seductive, unreal. Just as the actor in the advertisement transforms heart failure into an opportunity to live a "good life" with a fake organ, these television "personalities" transmute brutality into pleasing illusions.

Perhaps unexpectedly, these deceptive transformations actually challenge the illusions on which they are based and gesture toward the terrific violence that they try to suppress. The gap between the strained optimism of the newscasters and the sinister events to which their stories point is wide. In this gap lurk the unsayable tragedies of existence, as foreboding as the silent dark city of the first scene: brutal racism, nuclear proliferation, galactic paranoia. This tense divide forms an invisible line running through *Robocop*. The newscasters appear in two other instances. Each time, they blithely attempt to package and thus de-claw horrors that cannot be contained, horrors that appear all the more terrifying when contrasted with the gaudy veils woven to hide them.

In breaking its narrative with these newscasts, *Robocop* self-consciously comments on its own packaging of violence. The film renders its extreme brutality in the obvious clichés of the Hollywood action movie: gratuitous and massive explosions, masked police forces firing off thousands of rounds into a helpless victim, machine guns riddling chests with bloody bullet holes, wounded crotches, sadistic villains, cool heroes, and high body counts. These conventions, like the packaged images of the newscast, highlight their own artificiality. They suggest through their palpable fraudulence that more authentic experiences are being ignored and repressed. These experiences, probably beyond representation in image or word, constitute the tragic nature of existence, the wrenching certainties of a world immured in suffering and injustice.

While the satirical elements of *Robocop* negatively point to the tragic nature of existence, the film's depictions of corporate power positively demonstrate the world's pain, intimating that greedy men rule the planet and indifferently subject the masses to violence. Unable to handle the rampant crime in old Detroit—old now that a new Detroit is being designed by Omni—the police department has turned to Omni Consumer Products, a weapons company, for help. Omni is bent on developing a police force composed of machine-gun toting robots. If the company can accomplish this, it will enjoy lucrative profits. But controlling law enforcement isn't enough for Omni. The company also wants a hand in organized crime. Jones, the vice president, is secretly in league with Boddicker, encouraging the crime boss to continue his illegal activities in old Detroit and to envision fresh crimes for the new city. Jones's logic is simple: if he can control the police and the criminals, he can play one side against the other. As the city struggles against an increasing crime rate, the more it will be forced to purchase Omni's robots. As criminals falter before his formidable robots, the more these hoods will need to buy protection from Omni. In using the cops and the criminals to feed its greed, Omni horrifically exploits the ordinary citizens caught between these two warring forces. Headed by an "Old Man" and maintained by a hierarchy of tyrannical ministers, Omni Consumer Products is a version of the demiurge and his agents— a Gnostic nightmare.

Murphy's Tortured Golem

Murphy bears the full weight of Omni's violence. After being shot to pieces by Boddicker and his gang, Murphy is rushed to the hospital. There he appears to die. In reality, though, he has become the "poor schmuck" that Omni needs for its latest project. After the failure of the ED 209, the robotic law enforcement unit that murderously malfunctioned during a demonstration, Morton proposes an alternative plan for artificial policing: the Robocop model, half man and half machine, organ and mechanism. All he needs is some unfortunate soul for a volunteer. This unwilling volunteer turns out to be the recently deceased Murphy. Unbeknownst to his wife and son, Murphy is reborn as Robocop. Through remarkable technological prowess, the Omni engineers revive the vital functions in Murphy's body while vanquishing his memories, his sense of self. They then graft the organic processes onto a computer matrix and a mechanized carapace. The result is a robot with the face of a man and a man with the body of a machine. A miraculous monster protecting its maker, Robocop is a classical golem.

In the beginning, Robocop proves a perfect cog in the Omni machinery. Through his superhuman strength, superior marksmanship, and tireless pursuit, he stops crime in old Detroit with stunning efficiency. However, after a few days, Robocop suffers strange disturbances. Memories flash into his computerized mind—scenes of Murphy's brutal murder and pictures of his loving family. The synthesis between man and machine is fractured into a struggle between Robocop, an inhuman system with no sense of identity, and Murphy, an autonomous human being with a conception of his own uniqueness. Confused and pained, Robocop undertakes a quest for Murphy, the person he once was.

In exploring this rift between human and machine, Robocop threatens Omni, his maker. After the first eruption of memory, during which he sees Boddicker and his gang murder his former self, Robocop disobeys his pre-programming and goes after the killers. As he exits the station, he encounters his old partner Lewis (Nancy Allen). She calls him Murphy, further agitating his circuits. When he apprehends one of the killers, Emil (Paul McCrane), he asks, with a twinge of desperation in his otherwise electronic voice, "Who are you?" While directed toward Emil, this question refers to Robocop himself. Seeking answers, Robocop searches for Emil's record in the police station's computer. There he finds that Emil and his accomplices are wanted for the murder of Alex Murphy. Upon seeing the face of his past self, he undergoes a shock of recognition and proceeds to his old address. As he walks through his former house, now empty and for sale, he relives scenes with his wife and son. He realizes that he bears within his computer circuits the soul of a dead cop whose murder has gone unsolved and whose killers are at large. He becomes obsessed with bringing these killers to justice. Acting of his own accord, he captures Boddicker and his gang one by one. When he finally holds Boddicker in his grasp, he loses his mechanistic indifference. He brutalizes the murderer as he reads him his rights. All the while, Boddicker tries to convince Robocop that he is protected, that Jones is his employer. But Boddicker then confesses that Jones runs the cops.

The golem's identity crisis reaches its highest intensity when Robocop, the creature, confronts Jones, his creator. Though Jones didn't actually imagine and fashion Robocop—Morton did—Jones heads the company that made Robocop. Moreover, since he has paid Boddicker to kill Morton, Jones now possess the hardware that controls Robocop. When Robocop enters his office, Jones sits confidently at his desk. He has been tracking the motions of his product and knows that he possess ultimate authority. Robocop tries to arrest Jones but is unable to move. He strains mightily against this paralysis, this conflict between the personal concerns of Murphy and the mechanistic limitations of Robocop. An unexplained "Directive 4" flashes on his internal computer grid. Triumphant, Jones explains that at his suggestion Omni downloaded this directive: Robocop can never arrest an employee of Omni. He reminds Robocop that he is not an "ordinary cop" but a "product." Now that Robocop is a threatening presence more than a mere tool, Jones must retire him. He sends the ED 209 after Robocop. Robocop escapes the unwieldy robotic monster. However, when he reaches the bottom floor of the building, he is assaulted by a large police force. He is shot hundreds of times. Just when he is on the verge of expiring, Lewis arrives in her squad car and rescues him.

In the abandoned factory where Lewis hides Robocop, the man frees himself from the machine. When Lewis arrives with food, Robocop like a human being claims that he is too depressed to eat. Removing the screws holding his metal headgear in place, with a sensitive voice he warns Lewis that she may not like what she is about to see. Murphy's face appears. It covers only the front half of his head. The rear part is made of metal. Though cut in half and disfigured, Murphy still tries to emerge into fullness. He asks Lewis about Murphy's wife and child. She tells him they have moved away. With unbearable sadness, the man-machine confesses that he "can feel them" but "can't remember him." Lewis reaches to comfort him. Pathetically, he says, "Leave me alone."

If this golem was unconscious of fear and desire before, now he goes to the other extreme. The grace and efficiency of the machine give way to the awkwardness and inefficiency of the man. When Lewis returns, she finds Robocop, still unmasked, attempting to shoot the jars of baby food she has brought him. (Robocop lives on gruel close to infant food.) His aim is off by about three inches. He requires the assistance of a bumbling human, Lewis, to correct his shooting. Once she does, he shoots again with great accuracy, exploding the baby face stuck on the jar. (This rather disturbing detail is another "send-up" of the conventional action hero as a figure of extreme violence.) When Boddicker and his gang arrive at the scene with rocket launchers—they have been released from jail by Jones and hired to destroy Robocop—he further enlists Lewis's help. Together, after a bloody battle, they defeat the gang.

Only when Robocop once more faces Jones does he achieve synthesis between man and machine, awareness of and transcendence of fear and desire. Alone, he enters a conference room at Omni where Jones is holding a meeting that includes the Old Man himself. From his internal circuits, Robocop downloads into the room's video monitors, Jones's confession of murder and corruption. Robocop then places Jones under arrest but once again cannot overcome "Directive 4." Jones takes the Old Man hostage and demands a chopper. The Old Man fires Jones, releasing Robocop from the directive. With four shots, Robocop blasts Jones through a window. As Robocop makes his way out of the room, the Old Man says, "Nice shootin', son. What's your name?" The robot with the human face turns, smiles knowingly, and confidently says, "Murphy."

At this last moment in the film, Murphy points to a condition only a golem can achieve: the aesthetic arrest of the tragic vision. His human side, his consciousness, is acutely aware of the terror and yearning of the fallen world. His mechanical part, his body, is indifferent to these same enduring fears and desires. Achieving this balance between action and stasis, Murphy gestures toward the "secret cause," the *pleroma*, Eden unfallen, the ideal harmony. The golem, minister and scourge of earthly corruption, can never become one with this perfect marriage of freedom and fate. He must continue to battle against the turbulence from which he arose, or die. However, in intimating an impossible melding of machine and man, he constitutes a promise of a still point in the turning world. This point is a projector never seen on land or sea, an unmoving camera that nonetheless records and illuminates the painful kinesis of the universe.

Gods and Monsters

Two films of the past twenty years or so likewise emphasize the tragic aesthetic of the golem. Although they lack the astute self-consciousness of *Robocop*, *Gods and Monsters* and *Creator* reach the tragic core of the Cabbalistic artificial human— its position both above and within the world's suffering. In finding this deep structure of the golem, each film, however unwittingly, points to the hope held out by Verhoeven's movie: even if the machine grows out of tragic desire to transcend time's suffering, it might in the end suggest stillness in the midst of the agonized turning.

Bill Condon's *Gods and Monsters* explores the final days of James Whale, a Hollywood director famous for his two hit films of the thirties, *Frankenstein* and

Bride of Frankenstein. An overt homosexual ostracized in an allegedly straight movie industry, a disgruntled Whale more or less removed himself from the cinema industry after World War II. By the mid-fifties, he was living alone and forgotten in the Hollywood hills. The film depicts him during this time as a sad, sick old man, consumed with painful memories of fighting in the trenches during World War I and of his extreme childhood poverty in the years before the war. Whale's only solaces are his recollections of his cinematic creations, especially his two unforgettable golem movies. Throughout this film, Whale recounts the joys and sorrows of movie making to Clay Boone, a young, handsome, naïve, and thoroughly heterosexual gardener.

The relationship between the flirtatious old sophisticate and the suspicious young ingénue is the movie's main matter. During their conversations, Whale the magus comes to view Clay as beautiful raw material that he might shape into a mature, intelligent man. Clay in Whale's eyes becomes a metaphor for Karloff's creature, Whale's first golem. Both characters serve as analogies for Whale's other golem figures—his movies.

These concocted "monsters"—humans turned artifice as well as art imbued with life—empower Whale, their "god," to overcome the real monstrosities of his life, the constant tragedies that have worn him down into a melancholy soul hoping for death. As outcast creatures in need of compassion, these beings pull Whale from his isolated suffering to an apprehension of general pain. As sublime anatomies superior to ordinary humans, they model for Whale the transcendence of organic decay. By the time Whale dies in his pool at film's end—a possible suicide—he has at least acquired the tragic wisdom of golem-making: In creating figures of inhuman suffering, the artist discovers the world's permanent pain and thus achieves a solacing constancy.

Ivan Passer's *Creator* is a much lighter film than Condon's *Gods and Monsters*. Still, this movie, despite its superficiality, ably explores the vexed connection between tragic loss and mechanized life. The film centers on Professor Henry Wolper, a gentle and humorous version of Victor Frankenstein's "mad scientist." Ravaged by the death of his wife, Lucy, Wolper wants to discover a way to clone her. If he can accomplish this feat, he will enjoy the fruit of golem magic—an artificial creature transcending death—but also the sorrow of this same thaumaturgy: a reminder of his loss.

The film overcomes its occasional smarminess to meditate on this golem conundrum. Though a comedy, the movie is heavy with death. In addition to Lucy's demise, the movie focuses on the deadly coma of Barbara, the girlfriend of Wolper's research assistant, Boris. After witnessing Boris's extreme and ultimately successful efforts to bring Barbara out of her sleep, Wolper decides to forgo his cloning project and allow himself to fall in love with Meli, the young woman he recruited to carry his dead wife's fertilized egg. This transformation suggests that Wolper has learned this wisdom of tragedy: To obsess over the golem is to worship death as much as life; to release the dream of artificial vitality is to choose organic life but also inevitable demise. Either alternative leads to gentle sorrow. Both intimate the tense stillness in the suffering.

Transcendental Comedy

The loss of Aristotle's poetics of comedy is one of the great lacunae of Western aesthetics. I wonder what comic emotions parallel the tragic states, fear and pity. I am curious over how Joyce's Stephen would have revised Aristotle's comic theory. While I will never know what Aristotle or Stephen thought of comedy, I can guess that Aristotle's comic emotions would share the same polarity of his tragic states, the same mix of repulsion and attraction, and I can speculate that Stephen's theory of comedy would focus on arrest over motion, the constant over the ephemeral.

If tragedy arouses loathing and pity, then comedy inspires joy and sorrow. That the comic generates the former state is obvious. Laughter is foremost the goal of comedy, unbridled joy over ridiculous mishaps and tender reunions. The latter condition, sorrow, seems to be at odds with the comic mode. However, all great comedies—those of Aristophanes or Shakespeare, for instance, or even those of Howard Hawks or Woody Allen—are predicated on the idea that the world is always on the brink of chaos. In the Dionysian world of comedy, these are the ruling principles—really, non-principles. If something can go wrong, it will. Anything can happen, and it usually does. Mistaken identities, unpredictable accidents, slips of the tongue, dark misunderstandings, and nervous plots: These are the things of the comic world as much as happy endings. These troubling elements form the shaky grounds from which blissful unions arise. The comic ending gains its joy from relief as much as from happiness, from "sorrow averted" as much as from "joy achieved." This is the beauty of great comedy—the celebration of the unfathomable mystery by which the irons rails of tragedy suddenly and miraculously detour into the brief bliss of the wedding or the dance.

Beyond pornography, the fulfillment of transient desire, and beyond didacticism, the satisfaction of brief aversion, proper comedy, like proper tragedy, is a mode of transcendence. If tragedy reveals what is constant in loathing and pity and empowers one to move beyond ephemeral versions of these states and apprehend the "secret cause," then comedy shows what is ongoing in sorrow and joy and inspires one to transcend ephemeral instances of these conditions and likewise grasp the hidden origin. Both aesthetic modes, regardless of whether they explore suffering or happiness, open to a position untroubled by fear and desire. In doing so, these aesthetic forms disclose what is constant in beauty: *integritas, consonantia, claritas.*

Bergson and the Comic Golem

The golem is suited for the tragic vision. Is there a fruitful connection between proper comedy and the golem? If there is such a relationship, it would have to be found in Henri Bergson's theory of comedy, developed in *Laughter* (1900). In the essay, Bergson makes this startling claim: "The attitudes, gestures and movements of the human body are laughable in exact proportion as that body reminds us of a mere machine."[25] We laugh when we watch a human behave as if he were a machine—an automaton, a puppet. A mechanical man can't control his limbs; they continue their motions regardless of his intentions. The comedian runs to a ledge. His mind tells him to stop but his legs continue to churn. This same clown slips on a banana peel. He tries to maintain balance but his body falls to the pavement.

Even though the comedian suffers from his mishaps, he does not, as Bergson further argues, evoke pity. The "absence of feeling . . . usually accompanies laughter." "Indifference" is the "natural environment" for the comic. But of course the audience can only laugh at the mechanistic indifference of the comedian if its members are not indifferent. Though viewers of the comic are drawn to the automatic shenanigans of the comic actor, they are also repulsed by his inhumanity, his lack of sociability. Their laughter humiliates his nonconformity to human conventions as much as it celebrates his insouciant wit. This tension produces the "equivocal nature of the comic," a mode that hovers between "art" and "life." On the one hand, we laugh at someone when he appears to us as artificial, a player in a play, an android. On the other hand, we also laugh at this some person to correct his behavior, to return him to life, to human activity.[26]

In highlighting this duplicity of the comic mode, this tension between the automatic and the organic, Bergson's theory of laughter connects with Joyce's implied idea of the comic aesthetic. Bergson concludes that the comic grants us momentary freedom from mechanism because the comic allows us to separate ourselves, however briefly, from the mechanistic stiffness at which we laugh. However, this transcendence of determinism is predicated on the indifference of the comedian, the aloofness he displays in the face of gravity. This mechanistic grace under the pressure of causality—a transcendence of space and time—is precisely what inspires the temporary liberation of the human audience. If the audience is repulsed by the automatic limbs of the man-puppet, it is attracted by the unconcerned gaze of this same manikin. In laughing at this comic automaton, the audience wishes to humiliate him into joining them. But they also wish to enjoy his transcendence of the limitations of matter. This mutual embrace, if it could occur, would result in a condition in which the virtues of the human—sympathetic emotions—and the virtues of the machine—indifferent gestures—meet and marry. This state of being, a barely possibly ideal, would produce the aesthetic vision of the comic mode: a simultaneous attachment to and detachment from the joys and sorrows of the world, a human attunement to emotional vicissitudes liberated by a mechanistic aloofness to these same rises and falls. Standing between the tumult of the heart and the indifference of the circuit, one achieves the stasis of the third term: the gesture that remains still, the calm embracing everything.

Making Mr. Right

Though not as profound as *Blade Runner* and not as subtle as *Robocop*, Susan Seidelman's *Making Mr. Right* skillfully explores the comic possibilities of the golem.[27] Like *Robocop*, on the surface the film appears to be nothing more than a conventional Hollywood genre film, a light romantic comedy replete with the tired stereotypes of the culture industry. Surrounding the old formula of girl meets boy, girl loses boy, girl gets boy back, are a horde of boring and tasteless comic personae: the slimy politician playing the crowd; the sultry Latin lover from the wrong side of the tracks; the Jewish entertainment agents complaining in Yiddish accents; the over-sexed blonde bimbo; the ruggedly handsome, dumb brute; the neurotic mother; the nerdy Indian scientist. These Hollywood clichés move through a Miami landscape as superficial as a pasteboard mask—an environment composed of shopping malls, glitzy hotels, and shimmering freeways, all bathed in blinding sunlight and irradiating hot pink and lime green. The queen of this world is the film's protagonist, Frankie Stone, played by Anne Magnuson. Wearing garish two-toned dress suits and two-toned shoes to match, Frankie serves as the image consultant for the glitterati of the Miami scene. She polishes the surfaces of politicians, actresses, scientists, and celebrities at large. However, although at first Frankie resembles an extra in an eighties music video rather than a spiritual quester, she learns to penetrate appearances to reality. She achieves this insight through her interactions with a golem—an android named Ulysses, portrayed by John Malkovich.

In the opening of the film, Frankie's desire for the reality behind appearance is at war with her superficial vocation. The first scene of the movie depicts Frankie's main client and boyfriend, Congressman Steve Marcus (Ben Masters), on the morning news. He is shown at a Latin American beauty pageant, where he lustily kisses the contestants. The camera moves to Frankie, asleep in her apartment in front of her television set. Her first act in the film is to wake up and see her boyfriend for what he is: a hypocrite willing to deceive anyone to fulfill his greed for power. When Marcus knocks on her door seconds later, she locks him out. As Marcus slinks back to his car, Frankie throws from her window a life-size pasteboard picture of Marcus—a rejection not only of this master of surfaces but also of all appearances whatsoever. After waking up from drowsiness, locking out lies, and jettisoning the simulacrum, Frankie drives to work. During the trip—taken in a flashy red '64 Corvair convertible—Frankie applies makeup, showing that she is far from affirming authenticity. However, even as she applies a cosmetic mask in her showy car, the song playing as the opening credits roll, "Too Many Fish in the Sea," features this refrain: "No use crying forever / Too many fish in the sea." These lines, although they appear in a sugary pop song, point to this movement: from the shallow, predictable, landed male and toward the deep, tumultuous man of the ocean. This latter form of male recalls the fish—the Christ, *anthropos*. This connection is not too far-fetched: Frankie's name suggests "True Stone," the philosopher's stone, the elixir bringing spirit from matter and truth out of falsehood.

The opening, subtle for a light romantic comedy, casts an interesting light on the comic conventions that overrun the picture. The first scenes suggest that the realm of appearances is the world of death—people reduced to cardboard masks, shells without souls. In contrast, the habitat of truth is vital, characterized by alertness, discrimination, teeming oceans. Those who live for surfaces are little better than zombies, while those who delve below aspire to awareness. Stereotypical characters—people who enjoy no distinction between surface and depth—are blind machines. Characters pressing against cultural molds are complex beings negotiating between fate and freedom. Overwrought with stereotypes and featuring a protagonist trapped between conformity and rebellion, *Making Mr. Right*, despite its superficial ambience, is about a wasteland where people sacrifice spontaneity for performance. In the early sequences, the only living thing is Frankie, but barely so. Like her two-toned suits, Frankie is split. She is queen of automatons, engineer of conformist behavior; she is mistress of life, sounder of the sea.

Frankie begins to realize her potential for vitality when she meets Dr. Jeff Peters (also played by John Malkovich) and his recent creation, Ulysses, who looks exactly like his creator. Frankie encounters creator and creature when she takes a job as personal relations consultant for Chemtec, a scientific research corporation on the verge of losing its funding from Congress. Peters, the chief robotics engineer, has designed Ulysses to explore deep space. Peters and Chemtec hope that Ulysses will one day bring "space inside the American home" and "revolutionize the American way of life." These dreams are materialistic. As a promotional video for the research project suggests, Ulysses will map new areas in the universe suitable for capitalistic exploitation and translate raw materials of space into products to feed American greed. In undertaking tasks too dangerous for soft-shelled humans, Ulysses proves a modern-day golem: a robot who shields vulnerable men and women from the dangers of the fallen world.

Frankie recognizes in Peters and his golem her own split between appearance and depth, machine and organ. She realizes that Peters is aloof, misanthropic, a stereotypical "scientist" committed only to hard data, to what can be experienced with the senses. Stiffly unsympathetic to human nuances and emotions, he behaves more like a machine than a man. In contrast, the android Frankie has been hired to "humanize" for the grant foundations is more man than machine. As Frankie notices, Ulysses is warm and friendly, eager to learn about the human heart, and sensitive to suffering. If Peters is a human reducing himself to a machine—a paste-board mask—then Ulysses is a robot elevating himself to an organism—a creature from the deep.

Frankie can't realize her depths without Ulysses; Ulysses can't explore his humanity without Frankie. Each character is a spiritual catalyst for the other. Frankie the image consultant subjects the robot to a course in love. The machine masters the subject immediately. After learning how to listen to a woman, Ulysses quickly sees beyond Frankie's surfaces to her inmost interiors. In his childish, unassuming way, he understands Frankie's needs better than any man before. With this knowledge comes love—simple, direct, and unselfish. While Frankie helps Ulysses birth human emotion, Ulysses opens Frankie to an understanding of innocence. She discovers in his charitable sensitivity and indifference to social conformity a grace and sweetness lacking in organic men. In him is synthesized what in her is asunder—mechanistic detachment from complexity and organic embrace of nuance. Ulysses falls in love with her human conflicts; she develops affection for his mechanical harmonies.

Ulysses' love for Frankie transforms him from cute android to a mature *anthropos*. Through his courtship, he changes from a farcically comic automaton unable to control his limbs to a noble exemplar of the comic aesthetic, both attached to the earthly rhythm of joy and sorrow and detached from these same rises and falls. Ulysses' first appearance is purely comic. When he meets Frankie at Chemtec, he walks up to her, grabs her breasts, and asks, "What do you call these?" He then short-circuits and collapses. The inability to manage his urges and ignorance of societal conventions—perfect instances of Bergsonian comedy—organize Ulysses' behavior through much of the film. Later, when Frankie leaves him alone with her purse, he becomes fascinated by her diaphragm, which he blows up as if it were a balloon, and her lipstick, which he smears all over his mouth. Still later, during a sequence in which he escapes from Chemtec and explores a shopping mall, Ulysses walks naked from a dressing room in a men's clothing store, dons a tuxedo two sizes too small, and tries to have a conversation with a crude robot chanting advertising slogans.

In the midst of these and other shenanigans, Ulysses, blessed, as Peters claims, with a "retinal resolution" ten times greater than that of humans, develops increasingly profound insights into the human condition. After Frankie has suffered through a difficult day, without asking he knows exactly what she needs: a foot massage. Later, after hearing a speech from Frankie on the hopeless confusions of human love, he suggests that she is making an immediate matter of the heart far too complicated. He says, "If I were human, it would be simple. I would be in love with you."

By the end of the film, this innocent view remains, although it has been tempered by his suffering over his troubled love for Frankie. In a speech to the media just before he is to be launched into space, Ulysses, now mature and dignified, admits that being in space is far less frightening to him than are human beings: "People are frightening. They walk around hurt, confused, and are more alone than I will ever be in space. People can build an incredibly sophisticated space program and yet they can't solve their most basic problem: how to love and care for those who love them. Someday, when people have figured that out, they might be more than just machines." Ulysses reveals this light film's depths. No matter how seemingly civilized, beings attached to their own images and unable to love others outside their skins are automatons creaking through a wasteland. No matter how ostensibly mechanistic, creatures open to their hearts' mysteries and bent on connecting with the strange interiors of others are organisms making the world alive. Ulysses has become the fallen *anthropos*—totally aware of the world's pain but sufficiently aloof from the wounds to analyze their causes and remedies.

As Ulysses is transformed from a naïve child to an experienced man who retains his innocence, Frankie changes from a jaded adult to a love-smitten girl who can keep her wits about her. Initially, Frankie sees Ulysses as nothing more than a job— a machine she must educate in the ways of humans. Though she is amused by his antics, she never entertains romance with a robot. She is still hopeful that a human male can fulfill her needs. However, after Frankie witnesses Ulysses' nude body, endowed with a formidable male member, she admits to him that she can no longer think of him simply as a child. She begins to see him as a sexual being. Hours later, he reminds her that love need not be a labyrinth of deceit and suffering. It can be honest and joyful.

Beginning to fall for Ulysses but still hesitant to love a machine, Frankie takes his proxy, Peters, to her sister's wedding. Desperate to see Frankie, Ulysses hitchhikes to the wedding reception in his tuxedo. There he tells Frankie he loves her and gives her a long kiss. Tense at first, Frankie relaxes in his arms and gives herself over to her feelings. Even though Peters forbids Ulysses to have any contact with Frankie before his launching, Frankie stays faithful to her android love. Her cynical friend Trish tells her to return to Marcus—at least he has a good career and some man is better than none. But Frankie chooses not to go back to her old ways. Though aware of the problems of the fallen world, she holds true to her naïve dream of love with a robot.

Ulysses and Frankie are mirror images of one another, a child-adult and an adult-child. These two characters are homologous in other ways as well. Ulysses is a man who can behave like a woman. He puts on lipstick, wears his hair long, and embodies traditionally "feminine" values. Frankie is a woman who acts like a man. She possesses a man's name, wears her hair short, and runs her own business with traditional "masculine" power. Not only is each character androgynous, each is also committed to the work of redemption. Ulysses does not go into space. At the last minute, he trades places with his misanthropic double, Peters, who happily launches into seven years of solitude. Like Christ, Ulysses forsakes the heavens so that he can teach the earth to love. Likewise, Frankie rejects the easy solution of the cynic: the loveless marriage valuable only as a stay against loneliness. Renouncing Marcus, the cardboard man, Frankie opens herself to the deepest wounds of the fallen world and retains a hope for healing them.

In embracing life's painful depths over the smooth surfaces, its hard conflicts over tepid concords, Frankie becomes whole. This wholeness is signaled symbolically by the attire she wears to Ulysses' pre-launch press conference. After wearing two-toned dress suits for the course of the film, in this scene she dons three colors for the first time. This tripartite color scheme represents the synthesis of opposites by a third term. Like Ulysses, her spiritual double, by this point Frankie is attached to life's enduring rhythm between joy and sorrow and is detached from the flitting images born of fear and desire. Through the agency of the golem, she has experienced the comic vision. At the world's core is a mysterious stillness more alive than the meaningless motions whirling around it.

At the film's conclusion, space really does enter the home to revolutionize the American way of life, but this expansion and this transformation have nothing to do with financial security and material convenience. As Frankie tearfully watches the spaceship blast off on her television set, she hears a knock on her door. In a reversal of the film's opening, she opens the door. A man appearing to be Peters stands before her. She hugs him, saying she misses Ulysses already. The man then kisses her passionately. She realizes that this is not Peters at all. It is Ulysses. When she returns his kiss, he short-circuits and collapses to the ground. Desperate to revive him, she slaps his face. He comes back to life and says, fittingly, "I always fall apart at the wrong time. Nobody's perfect." He is the *anthropos* dismembered, fallen and imperfect. At the same time, he recalls the *anthropos* whole, unlapsed and pristine. Caught between the comic awkwardness of a physical plane where limbs run out of control and the joyful indifference of a spiritual plane where bodies moved unconcerned, Ulysses—the eternal wanderer and the lover who stays put—realizes the golem as comic genius.

Making Mr. Right is one of the only interesting comic golem films. I really can't come up with any others. Most comedies focusing on artificial life reduce the conscious machine to harmless cuteness. No doubt influenced by the adorable androids in the *Star Wars* trilogy and the irresistible alien in *E.T.*, comedies containing robots are not interested in mechanical transcendence at all but rather in normalizing intelligent machines, making them safe, attractive, innocuously human. Such films, like *Bicentennial Man* and *Iron Giant*, valorize stereotypical human behavior as the standard for nobility. In doing so, they express our collective human fear of machines usurping our alleged centrality in this solar system. But these films also are out to make a buck by seducing us with treacly machines whose primary purpose is to be man's best friend.

Two such films were released at about the same time as *Making Mr. Right*. The first, John Badham's *Short Circuit*, features Number 5, a military robot that gains human consciousness after it is struck by lightning. Unfortunately, this android expresses its humanity in tired comic clichés. Its tries at comic cuteness are unbearable. One wonders why the "good" scientists work so hard to save this cuddly bunch of circuits from the "bad" military men who wish to use this machine for some undoubtedly nefarious purpose. Simon Wincer's *D.A.R.Y.L.* is equally unwatchable. It features as its hero a "Data Analyzing Robot: Youth Lifeform," otherwise known as Daryl. Like Number 5, this robot is designed as a military weapon. But unlike the robot in *Short Circuit*, this machine looks just like a human, a small boy. After a military mishap leaves the artificial boy abandoned on a roadside, he is taken in by a family who believes he is a real boy. Many predictable comic clashes between human and machine ensue. Daryl learns the value of human life. Eventually, evil soldiers who wish to reclaim him as military property pursue him. Luckily, the humanized machine triumphs over the mechanized humans. Smarmy emotion overcomes cool efficiency. Familiar warmth outdoes strange distance.

These films are especially disappointing because of the potential they never even begin to fulfill. With more nerve, both would have explored the conscious machine as a duplicitous creature, a marriage of transcendental indifference and immanent concern. Playing it safe, both pictures prove especially crass products of the culture industry, commodities reinforcing the comfortable status quo. At best, they are failed golem movies. At worst, they are exploitations of the sacred for purposes of the profane.

Now that I think of it, *Making Mr. Right* is not very different from *Short Circuit* and *D.A.R.Y.L.* Like those cinematic trifles, this film was mainly meant to entertain audiences and make a sum of money. The same can probably be said of the other, more serious golem films discussed here, *Blade Runner* and *Robocop*. But then, rather quickly, I remember. Regardless of their crass designs—their primary statuses as commodities—something exquisite irradiates from each of these pictures: a vision of human perfection. Impossible to depict on the screen, this ideal can exist only in the mind. I have suggested that one failed representation of perfection is the film projector—a machine with consciousness. Obviously, one cannot take such an image seriously. It is comical. But perhaps in its very inappropriateness it points to this possibility: all things in space and time, generated by unending fear and desire, are, from the angle of eternity, silly. But from the perspective of the fallen world itself, each of these things, no matter how trifling, is a shard of the first and enduring human beyond the stars.

Chapter Three

Alchemical Cinema: The Dark Theater

The Oceanic Movie House

On still another day, one goes to the movies with this desire. Like Keats in his nightingale ode, he wants to dissolve into the gloom and there in the dimness forget the weariness and the fever and the fret. He does not hope to escape his painful life to a realm of blissful light. Nor does he imagine that he will merge with an ideal form above the flickering shadows. He yearns only for the black space into which he can disappear. Weary of the habits of his existence, the cold events that organize his day—the morning egg, the walk to the car, the evening drive, the dishes to wash—he dreams of a warm cave or a tepid ocean in which he can sink free of the carapace that has become his life. Once liberated from his skin, he will rejoin the darkness from which he arose. Distributed in this night, he will coalesce into a new form, supple and mercurial.

Holding in his psyche this dream of demise and rebirth, he can think of nothing better to do of a Sunday afternoon than go to the cinema. He prefers films of science fiction or fantasy or horror, pictures in which logic is suspended, causality effaced. But he is mostly drawn to the dark space where he can fade into anonymity.

He enters the half-lit theater and finds a seat in the middle. He likes being surrounded by unseen bodies, warm and breathing. Relaxing, he looks not at the blank screen in front or the recessed projector behind. He gazes around at the nebulous atmosphere and imagines that he inhabits a world under the sea. There, to the side, he glimpses an eel. Above hovers a porpoise. Somewhere there must be a grampus.

Suddenly, as if a treasure chest has exploded open and illuminated the depths, the screen overhead shines. Images shimmer and disappear in the frame. Men transmute into dolphins, and back again into silver men. Women turn mermaids and then again to women in sequins. A child grows wings and flies from the water into the clouds.

The curtain falls. Blackness covers the room. For the lover of shade, this is the most intense moment. He quivers in hope that something new will arise when the lights go up. He flutters in fear that the same man will still be there. The darkness vanishes. There he still sits. Is he different? Is he the same person he was?

These are the questions of alchemical cinema, films exploring the possibility of transmutation through dissolution of the old and new resolution. Drawing on alchemical imagery, these movies encourage meditation on the power of blackness, chaos, death, on how these traditionally negative elements are really positive: catalysts for fresh illuminations, orders, and lives. To behold the alchemical opus on the screen—to watch *Excalibur* or *Altered States* or *Blue Velvet*—is to feel the shadowy theater turn into an alembic, a retort in which leaden histories are boiled away before golden potencies.

But the situation is not simple. These commercial films depict alchemical transmutations through the conventions of Hollywood. Though an innovative fantasy film like *Excalibur* can freshly manipulate the outlandish imagery of medieval myth and lore, it nonetheless employs the well-worn formulas of the genre. The same is true of a science fiction picture like *Altered States* and a noir thriller like *Blue Velvet*. Both films, despite their startling originality, rely on time-tested narrative codes and image patterns. Bound by cinematic conventions of the Hollywood system, these alchemical movies only give the illusion of transformation. The ostensible conversions pictured in these films are really steps in an established sequence, transformations rendered in familiar images. These repeated structures not only foreclose the metamorphoses of the alchemical film. They also suggest that any change—not just cinematic change—is impossible: that all quick shifts are but examples of old habits. To view an alchemical film is to experience contradiction: a meditation on transmutation trapped in changeless convention.

The overtly Gnostic film erases itself. The Cabbalistic picture, influenced by the Gnostic *anthropos*, likewise consumes itself, with fate canceling freedom. In the same way, the alchemical movie, a quest for Gnostic spirit in the depths of matter, suffers a double bind. It proves both a disarming exploration of miraculous transmutations and an utterly expected marshalling of musty sequences and images. When stasis stops change, when change floods stability, what is left but chaos flickering briefly into orders that explode, orders that fall into turbulence only to reassert themselves with vigor? This is the dilemma of the alchemical film. It cancels its two poles—transmutation and stasis—and leaves its audiences extended into an ambiguous borderland. The question becomes: Is this crepuscular space mere confusion, a violent, nervous, edgy world where nothing comes of nothing; or is this shadowy land a fecund swamp out of which rare growths spring, beautiful forms in the muck?

The End of Gnosticism

In *Memories, Dreams, Reflections* (1961), Carl Jung sketches a history of esoteric thinking. For Jung, the occult current runs from classical Gnosticism, "remote" in its "neo-Platonic" desire to transcend the cosmos; through medieval and Renaissance alchemy, "grounded in the natural philosophy of the Middle Ages"; to modern psychology, which focuses on the concrete forms of the unconscious. What these elements of the esoteric tradition share is a belief that the human psyche or soul emerges from an ungraspable, androgynous abyss, falls into division and delusion when it forgets its origin and identifies with the discrete ego, and is redeemed only through an awareness of and re-identification with its unnamable, ineffable root.[1]

The Gnostic "god" is a trans-cosmic plenitude in which opposites thrive in harmony. Out of this original mystery emanates *aeons*. One of these aeons disrupts the concord. This turbulence produces our cosmos, where divisive events "rub and jostle one another."[2] This realm is material instead of spiritual, hierarchical instead of polarized, ruled by a dictator instead of a supple power. But there is hope. The eternals plant a spark into suffering humans. If this spark is ignited in gnosis, then its bearer realizes his origin in the plenitude, rejects the physical world, and liberates his soul to the abyss.

Medieval and Renaissance alchemists grounded their ideas on the Gnostic tradition. However, these scientifically minded men found the older model to be too otherworldly. While the ancient Gnostic wished to transcend matter, the medieval alchemist wanted to redeem it. The basic alchemical process involves dissolving elements into the chaos from which they arose, separating this indifferent mass into spirit and matter, and then reuniting these oppositions in a chemical marriage— from which springs the philosopher's stone. This alchemical dissolution and resolution reenacts the activities of God, who, alchemically interpreted, separates the chaos into distinctions only later to rejoin these antinomies during the marriage feast of the Revelation. Just as the cosmos emerges from a formless gulf, so the redeemed soul arises from the dissolution of worldly attachment. This latter transcendence is the purpose of alchemy. The chemical aspects of the art symbolize the interior process by which the adept refines his soul.[3]

The Gnostic plenitude, the fall, the return; the primal material, the division, the marriage: these terms and the circular journeys they suggest become for Jung the collective unconscious, the conscious ego, the individuated self. If alchemy is a more scientific Gnosticism, then Jungian psychoanalysis is a more psychological alchemy. The steps of psychological transformation run parallel to the sequences of alchemical transmutation. The neurotic's fixation on the ego at the expense of the collective unconscious is akin to the untrained alchemist's obsession with matter at the expense of spirit. The neurotic's becoming aware of his need to transcend ego to the unconscious is analogous to the alchemist's dissolving discrete matter

back into the boundless abyss. When the neurotic suffers conflict and reconcilia-
tion between egocentric desire and collective archetypes, he is experiencing the
alchemist's division of the primal chaos into spirit and matter and his effort to
marry these opposites. After the patient balances unconscious energy and conscious
form, he discovers his "individuation," a healthy state finally free of neurosis. This
"mandala" state of "multiety in unity" is similar to the alchemical achievement of
the philosopher's stone, the golden harmony.[4]

The Three Alchemical States

European alchemists of the Middle Ages and the Renaissance constituted an arcane,
complex, and heterogeneous tradition. However, they basically agreed that the
sacred marriage of opposites is best achieved in three interrelated steps marked by
three colors. The first step, the *nigredo*, the black stage, occurs when the alchemist
achieves the *prima materia*. This initial stage, reached when solid substances have been
boiled down to bubbling masses, is the first seed and the primal chaos, the original
abyss and the destructive monster. The primary symbols of this state are the ocean,
the dragon, and the serpent, especially the ouroboros and caduceus of Mercurius.
Mercurius—the spirit of life, the world soul, male and female at once—thrives at
every stage of the alchemical process. His presence in the primal soup as the circular viper or intertwined snakes ensures that even chaos and death contain potential
for organization and life. Although the *nigredo* is physical destruction or psychological pain, it is also the water of life, the womb.[5]

The psychological equivalent of the *nigredo* is melancholia.[6] Associated with the
influence of the planet Saturn, this psychic state is far from the sun, unhealthy, a
dark night of the soul. This mood is the interior equivalent to the goring of Adonis,
the dark forest journey of Dante, Hamlet's sable consciousness. Like these redemptive declines, the melancholia of the *nigredo* is remedy as much as disease, a marker
of spiritual genius as much as a symbol of material disorientation. In *The Book of Life*
(1489), Marsilio Ficino argues that melancholics tend to be brilliant philosophers.
Melancholy sympathy with gloomy Saturn and with the cold core of earth enables
one to persevere in confusion and nocturnal contemplation, to gaze within and
parse the heart's mysteries.[7]

In this night arises a moon, the second stage, the *albedo*, the white, the transition from gloom and dawn. This stage appears when the solution is blanched, no
color at all and the ground of all colors, both transparent spirit and opaque
body. It is the "good white snow"; it is also Luna, heavenly queen. During this
stage, the swells of the matrix are "congealed": Mercury as slivering snake is
"frozen," his quicksilver spirit transformed into a stable body. Mercury iced represents the world soul in a purified state. No longer boiling matter (his ouroboric

guise), he is matter and spirit at the same time. This new shape is innocence, the virgin waiting for marriage.[8]

Like the gloomy psychology of the *nigredo*, the moony one of the *albedo* is double. The whitened psyche, deep in dreams, forms a bridge between unconscious and consciousness. On the one hand, fantasies pose dangers, because sleeping visions can easily turn one "lunatic." On the other hand, the blanched mind enjoys glimpses of wisdom unavailable to the conscious ego. These oppositions are synthesized by the primary faculty of the *albedo*, the imagination, the borderland between understanding and intuition, matter and spirit.[9] From the underworld, Adonis imagines Venus; in the wood, Dante envisions Beatrice; returned from the deadly sea, Hamlet intones, "readiness is all." During his nocturnal lucubration, Ficino's melancholy thinker invokes the aid of the moon, a "procreative force" behind sweet dews and nourishing tides.[10]

The lunar stage is the precursor to the sun, the *rubedo*. Achieved by melting and recrystallizing the white, the *rubedo* figures the process by which the Red King marries the White Queen to produce the philosopher's stone. During this stage, the spiritual force of the red penetrates the purified body of the white, "sublimating" her from virgin to wife. The *rubedo* reveals Mercurius thriving as pure spirit, a fiery jewel capable of combining all oppositions into dynamic harmony—the philosopher's stone. In synthesizing life and death as well as chaos and order, this *rubedo* jewel is not simply life, the eternal infant; it is also death, the dying king.[11]

Psychologically, the *rubedo* signals that the archetypes of the collective unconscious have been realized by the conscious ego. The unconscious becomes conscious: the man understands his feminine energies; the woman apprehends her masculine side.[12] This is integration. The microcosm within realizes its connection to the macrocosm without, and both together become aware of their relationship to the trans-cosmic, the plenitude. Venus revives Adonis. Dante takes the hand of Beatrice. Hamlet dies to sweet angels singing. Ficino's philosopher, after a long night, achieves the awareness of the sun, close to Jupiter, the rational truth.[13]

The harmonies of the alchemical marriage and the psychological integration are not eternal but are moments in a perpetual dialectic: the philosopher's stone (the formed homunculus) is already the *prima materia* (putrid death); Jungian individuation (the inner *anthropos* redeemed) arises from and must return to the darkness of the unconscious (the *anthropos* lost). This is the key point about the alchemical process: the alchemical work is endless conflict and resolution. *Nigredo, albedo,* and *rubedo* are all temporary instances in the ongoing processes of life, concordant discords between chaos and order, death and birth. Figuring these polarities is Mercury, who generates, sustains, and alters each stage in the work. This hermaphroditic presence is the origin, the primary material; the means, the world soul; and the end, the philosopher's stone. Constant and changing, this "double" Mercury "consists of all conceivable opposites."[14] Hermes is the spirit of alchemy because he is a deity of *complete* being, revealing what many forget in their inhabitation of a half-world: chaos and ocean are the secret grounds of cosmos and city.

Mercury is the trickster, happiest when he is at *play*. Playing, he is able to achieve the double consciousness of the comic mode: the world is serious and not serious at the same time, a meaningful pattern of eternity and a filmy veil blocking the beyond. While immersed in the turbulence of the *nigredo*, Mercury can go with the flow and rise above the current. Resolving into the crystal of the *albedo*, Mercury stiffens into transparent geometry without forgetting the opaque flickers. He remains attuned throughout to the *rubedo*, the third term harmonizing matter and spirit. Embodying this *tertium quid*, Mercury never dissolves into fecund material, nor does he stiffen into spiritual rectitude. He enriches one pole with the other without becoming attached to either. This balance is akin to Schlegel's irony and Schiller's play. It is transcendence and failure to transcend. It is annihilating darkness and the light that forms anew.

Mercurius in the Cinema

Three films released in the eighties explore the shifts of Mercurius, his chaotic descents and cosmic risings. But while *Blue Velvet*, *Altered States*, and *Excalibur* all invoke the structures and images of the alchemical opus, each focuses on a specific stage of the conversion. Lynch's *Blue Velvet* lives primarily in the *nigredo*; it mediates on how aberrant nocturnal behavior might shock a young man out of his spiritual lassitude. Russell's *Altered States* likewise spends many scenes in turmoil but is finally more interested in the redemptive relationships of the *albedo* stage—between male and female, spirit and matter. Boorman's film on the perils of kingship focuses on the *rubedo*, on how easily the ruler purified by the magic stone can dissolve to the death from which he arose.

In spreading its gaze over the entire work—chaos, order arising from chaos, order, order returning to chaos only to arise again—Boorman's *Excalibur* exemplifies the main virtue and primary problem of all three pictures. Each movie is keenly conscious of the interactions among the various stages and how easily a character can become paralyzed in one state or another—how the road to redemption can so quickly turn static hell. In exploring the psychological dimensions of alchemical conversion, these movies also exhibit an awareness of the difficulty inherent in their project: how to represent mercurial transmutation in well-worn, predictable plots and conventions. These films, like their questing characters, risk at almost every instant an effacement of their conversions, an annihilation of change with stasis, of stillness with motion.

Gnostic cinema focuses on the relationship between absence and presence. Cabbalistic film meditates on the connection between transcendence and immanence. Alchemical cinema turns on the impossible marriage required for individual wholeness: between the potential of the unconscious for transformation and the ego's bent toward stability. In *The Origins and History of Consciousness* (1954), Erich Neumann illuminates the difficulty of alchemy's hero. Unlike the "extraverted" hero who tries to change the shape of the world, and unlike the "introverted" hero who through contemplation cultivates a culture's inner values, the hero of alchemical cinema practices "centroversion." He does not look to alter the world through inner or outer struggle alone but seeks to find a harmony between unconscious energy and conscious form.[15] Like the film reel itself, he wants to balance the frozen frame before the eyes and kinetic whirling behind the gaze. As the theatrical space, he vacillates between darkness annihilating difference and flickering light fixing subjects into objects.

The mythological prototype of this contest between indifference and differentiation is the fertility god, the Osiris or the Adonis who struggles to find permanence in impermanence. He quests for organic generation and inorganic stasis. The fertility god participates in the rhythms of biology. He falls dismembered to the underworld; he rises healed to the sun. He belongs to the matriarchal realm of the moon that waxes and wanes and the serpent that sheds skin. But the fertility god is above winter and summer. He never really dies but merely plays with forms of death. He is untouched by transience. He is one with the patriarchal region of light and order.[16]

This fertility god, like the alchemical Mercurius and the hero of alchemical cinema, is the principle by which the self enjoys resurrection and the power by which the resurrected self achieves indestructibility.[17] As god of resurrection, he represents the plight of the material body, its inevitable decline toward death, and the virtue of this same body, its ability to recover health. As god of permanence, he symbolizes the potential of the eternal spirit to overcome the body and the static vessel required for housing this spirit.[18]

Centroversion attunes to the unconscious, the origin from which the ego arises but also the abyss that this same ego must overcome. Centroversion defends against the unconscious, develops carapaces that reject the turbulent source. The instability of the unconscious is death to the ego; the rigidity of the ego kills the oceanic unconscious. The life of one is death to the other, and the demise of the other is vitality for the one.

In *Beyond the Pleasure Principle* (1920), Freud takes us deeper into this conflict. The compulsion to repeat traumatic experiences suggests that the unconscious possesses a death drive as well as a sex instinct. The repetition compulsion grows from an urge to return to the "inertia" that preceded the "pressure of external disturbing forces."[19] Resembling Neumann, Freud initially likens this drive to ego. He conjectures that "ego-instincts" "exercise pressure towards death," or cessation of desire, while "sexual instincts" push towards a "prolongation of life," or fulfillment of desire. However, after realizing that the ego possesses instincts other than self-preservation, Freud claims that the primary opposition is not between ego and sex but between life and death.[20]

Humans are driven by death as much as by life. This dualism is complex. If this death drive generates destruction, it also pushes toward the "Nirvana principle," the desire to "reduce, to keep constant or to remove internal tension due to stimuli."[21] Likewise, if the life drive cultivates satisfaction, then it also dissolves into strife, because "union with living substance of a different individual increases . . . tensions."[22]

We are destined to experience timelessness—eternal life—as stasis: as death. We are fated to experience pleasure—temporal vitality—as decay: also as death. The quest for nirvana, for eternal life, ends in a divorce from life, a lethargic numbness or an ascetic detachment. The descent into neurosis, the decline into moribund repetition, participates in the agitated rhythm of the organic world. The mystic longing for vitality enervates into a corpse; the control freak bent on stasis falls into fervid struggle.

These are the conundrums of the alchemical hero, of the alchemical film. They consume the hero. They erase his story. In the end, the student of Mercurius is left staring at the darkness—the somber alembic, the gloomy theater. But at least he has learned one thing: the blackness is not simply nothing; nothing might be everything.

Nigredo in *Blue Velvet*

Blue Velvet begins with a beautiful image of the *albedo* state, an ideal toward which the film strives.[23] Waving sinuously behind the opening credits, almost moving in rhythm with Angelo Badalamenti's haunting score, is a curtain of blue velvet. As it oscillates with the music, the cloth reflects light into an exquisite dance of colors: white and silver, sky blue, royal blue, navy blue, and then again the silver and white. The curtain seems actually to breathe, to live. Gathering pattern and turbulence, darkness and light, it represents the crystallization of chaos into pattern, the freezing of the ocean into rolling floes. Beginning the film with this image, Lynch places the audience in tense anticipation, ready for the ice to melt back into the slop or coagulate the waves into jewels. Will the *albedo* slouch back to the *nigredo*, or will it rise to the *rubedo*?

Lynch addresses this question in his favorite mode: parody. The film proper opens on red roses wavering in front of a white picket fence—*rubedo* emerging from *albedo*. However, the rose and fence are a little too perfect. They look artificial. The next shot heightens the unreality. A red fire truck moves down a quaint neighborhood street in slow motion; a fireman smiles and waves. This shot is followed by a return to the white fence. Yellow tulips blow in the foreground. We then see children crossing a quiet street under the guidance of a crossing guard, again in slow motion. These luminous reveries unfold to the music of Bobby Vinton singing his 1963 hit, "Blue Velvet." His voice recalls the popular crooners of the forties and fifties, the sentimental music of ideal America: small-town neighborhoods manicured by responsible citizens and protected by benevolent governments. The camera then focuses on a man watering a well-kept backyard. He wears clothes of the forties or the fifties. Inside, a woman who is apparently his wife sips coffee in a living room whose decor recalls mid-century America. The expression on her face is complacent. She and her husband are at ease in their artificial habitat. They resemble characters from a Capra film idealizing small-town America or a saccharine sitcom like *Father Knows Best*. These characters and their environment constitute a pastiche of the "good life," suggesting that most envision happiness merely as banal comfort, a condition from which all messiness has been expunged, all evil. This sort of Hollywood Eden, a repression of the *nigredo*, is a pale copy of the true *rubedo*, which originates in the gloomy deeps.

Because the people of this world are unaware of the interdependent relationship between chaos and order, darkness and light, they are stunned when turbulence erupts into their studio existence. Crime and death to these ciphers of Hollywood are fictional, remote dreams. While serenely sipping, the wife watches a black-and-white crime drama, likely an old film noir. The pistol glimmering on the screen does not affect her in the least. The husband contentedly watering his lawn becomes irate when his hose gets tangled. Unused to accidents, he becomes so angry that he suffers a stroke. He falls to the ground and writhes in the mud created by the flow of hose water. As he loses consciousness, a neighborhood dog repeatedly jumps up to bite the geyser. The camera slowly moves from this absurd scene to the grass and then under the green surface. Hundreds of squirming black beetles appear. They produce a terrifying sound, a mix of flowing lava and ravenous crunching. Because the Hollywood Eden represses and demonizes this subterranean realm, when it does erupt, it appears as hellish brutality.

This is what happens when one divides a bipolar cosmos of mutually inclusive oppositions into a hierarchical universe of mutually exclusive antinomies. What is in reality a thriving rhythm of interdependent polarity, a crepuscular dance of darkness and light, becomes in perception a dualistic battle between good and evil. To sever energy from form and favor form over energy is to create a world in which form is valued as the good and energy is demeaned to evil. Repressing turbulence, the Hollywood Eden turns into a static husk opposed to all that is dynamic and unpredictable. When the darker forces break into this banal shell, they appear not as vigorous currents but as devilish pollutions. "Good" society dooms itself to vague paranoia and quiet desperation. To live a vital existence, one must shatter the shells of Hollywood and descend to the ground. Then the beetles will not be frightening at all, but mirrors of the soul's hidden core.

Unlike his father, Jeffrey Beaumont, played by Kyle MacLachlan, is open to the darkness, eager to gain knowledge and experience beyond the codes that have shaped his life. His name—a combination of "peace" and "beautiful mountain"—expresses his quest: to transcend the comfort of the status quo to the heights of vision. Aptly, the first shot of Jeffrey features him walking through a vacant lot on which stands an abandoned shack. The lot serves as a path between Jeffrey's manicured neighborhood and the hospital where his father recovers. This *mise en scene* symbolizes Jeffrey's hunger for spaces forgotten by the mainstream. When Jeffrey reaches his father at the hospital, he is awakened to a new way of seeing. Hooked to numerous monitoring devices, his father looks less like a human and more like a thing. When the older man attempts to speak, he is unable to move his mouth. An expression of horror wrenches his face. Jeffrey's lawgiver and role model is now moribund, mute, and terrified. This fall of the father forces him to find his own path. Jeffrey does not flinch before this bracing possibility. On his way home, he again crosses the vacant lot. As he idly picks up pebbles, he finds a severed ear, rotted and teeming with ants. Instead of recoiling, Jeffrey gathers the ear in a bag and takes it to police headquarters. This is the first of many instances in which Jeffrey seizes opportunities for experiences far beyond those of his father.

This ear, true to its anatomy, serves as a threshold, a portal between apparent and hidden. From the minute Jeffrey encounters this detached organ, he is pulled into the *nigredo*, both a psychological disposition attuned to turbulence and an actual world fraught with violence. If Jeffrey's world before he discovers the ear resembles the cinematic environs of Capra, then the world he inhabits after finding this detached organ is close to the brutal noir cityscapes of forties cinema. The scene following the one in which Jeffrey deposits the ear with the detective is a telling modern instance of the noir genre. The camera shows a dark stairwell leading up to a single room. The door to the room opens. Standing at the threshold is the shadow of a man. The shadow moves out of the lighted portal and descends into the darkness. When this dark figure reaches the bottom of the stairs and returns to the light, its identity is revealed. It is Jeffrey. He tells his mother and aunt that he wishes to go for a walk, even though it's dark outside. He makes his way down familiar sidewalks—the same byways that glimmered earlier in the tawdry light of the American dream—but he experiences these paths in a different way. He first notices not a smiling fireman but a sullen fat man standing with a small dog. The man glowers at Jeffrey through dark glasses. Making his way past, Jeffrey looks down the tree-lined lane. The trees are gnarled and dark. They wave eerily in the wind. Unsettled, Jeffrey remembers the ear. As the organ moves closer to his mind's eye, a sinister hum pervades his head, as if a vast chasm echoes under the ear's opening. His inner eye then goes through the portal into the darkness. Jeffrey has entered into an abysmal realm beyond visual representation. He has found the boiling retort that kills to reanimate. A new identity is required for negotiating this darkness.

The Teenybopper and the Femme Fatale

Throughout the film, Jeffrey vacillates between the old world of soda pop complacency and a new one filled with violent obsessions. These two poles are represented by the two women in his life, Sandy Williams (Laura Dern) and Dorothy Vallens (Isabelli Rossellini). Jeffrey's goal is to find a rapprochement between the bright world of Sandy and the dark one of Dorothy. If he can overcome the dualism of the status quo, he might be able to discover how Sandy's world of law and spirit is dependent upon matter (Sandy, after all, means "sand") and how Dorothy's environment of criminality and lust requires spirit (Dorothy, of course, signifies "gift of god"). If Jeffrey finds this interpenetration, then the orders of daytime Lumberton will convert to the *rubedo*, spirit rising from matter, and the nighttime broil will turn to *nigredo*, matter originating spirit. In between will be the *albedo*, Sandy and Dorothy as thresholds between matter and spirit.

Sandy first appears during Jeffrey's nocturnal walk. After envisioning the ear dissolve into an abyss, Jeffrey visits Williams to ask more about the ear. Williams sends Jeffrey home with no answers. As Jeffrey crosses the Williams's yard, he hears a disembodied voice asking, "Are you the one who found the ear?" He looks toward the voice and sees only a dark willow rustling in the wind. Out of the blackness emerges a shadow that slowly coheres into a blond woman. Jeffrey asks her how she knows about the ear. She cryptically responds, "I just know." But this noirish apparition quickly transforms into a wholesome teenybopper hungry for a zany caper. As she and Jeffrey meander down the sidewalk, they move back and forth between teenage flirtation and discussion about the ear. Sandy confesses that she has overheard her father talking about the ear and has learned that a woman named Dorothy Vallens is involved. She leads Jeffrey to Dorothy's apartment. Standing outside, Jeffrey asks, "It's a strange world, isn't it?"

This initial conversation between Jeffrey and Sandy epitomizes their relationship. On the one hand, Sandy is the "girl next door," the "prom queen." She spends her days mooning over boys, giggling with her girlfriends, and hanging out at the soda shop. Jeffrey, a graduate from Sandy's high school who is home from college to tend the family hardware store during his dad's illness, easily enters into this teenybopper scene. He speaks with Sandy in a "gee-whiz" high school lingo and courts her in a large red fifties convertible. But on the other hand, Sandy, despite her wholesome appearance, is Jeffrey's guide into the noir world. Appearing from the sinister darkness, she provides Jeffrey the first clue to his investigation of the ear. Drawn to gloom as much as to brightness, she leads Jeffrey to the "bad" side of town to see Dorothy's apartment. These dark qualities of Sandy attract Jeffrey as much as her bright ones. Her invitation to real crime prompts Jeffrey's realization of the world's strangeness and starts him on a quest to solve the riddle of the ear alone. His outward journey toward factual knowledge corresponds to his inward pilgrimage toward self-awareness.

Sandy is complicit in Jeffrey's investigation. The day after their first meeting, Jeffrey picks up Sandy from high school and takes her to the soda shop. In the midst of banter reminiscent of *Happy Days*, Jeffrey tells Sandy that there exist "opportunities in life for gaining knowledge and experience." In seizing these opportunities, he continues, "it's sometimes necessary to take a risk." In this case, Jeffrey concludes, he must "break the law" to gain these fresh experiences and insights. Sandy reluctantly agrees to hear his plan. Jeffrey will disguise himself as an exterminator to achieve entry to Dorothy's apartment. While he sprays, Sandy will distract Dorothy by knocking on her door and pretending to be a Jehovah's Witness. Jeffrey will jimmy a window so that he can later break into the apartment. Once inside, he will "hide and observe." Sandy says that this plan is a "good day dream" but in reality is dangerous and weird.

Sandy's words detail the nature of Jeffrey's scheme. Measured against the conventions of small-town "reality," Jeffrey's plan is dreamy, a suspension of logic, an entry into an outland. To realize this reverie, Jeffrey must turn dangerous, weird. He must impersonate an exterminator, break into a private residence, and voyeuristically watch the movements of a stranger. But as Jeffrey is beginning to realize, these are the sacrifices required by the *nigredo* realm. Complicit in the plan, Sandy senses this as well.

In undertaking this plan, Jeffrey first meets Dorothy. To reach her apartment, he must enter into a building called "Deep River Apartments," a name suggesting the depths of the retort. But as Jeffrey descends, he rises. Dorothy's apartment is on the seventh floor. As Jeffrey climbs, we recall that seven represents completeness—seven planets in the solar system, seven days in a week. This is the logic of the *nigredo*—the darkness is the light. The interiors of Dorothy's apartment embody this duplicity. Her living room is carpeted and furnished in dark purple. This room ends abruptly at the kitchen, tiled and painted in bright white. While Jeffrey moves through this two-fold realm spraying, he steals a key to the apartment. When he returns later, he finds that Dorothy, too, is a mixture of matter and spirit—violent desire and charitable longing.

While Dorothy is singing at a nightclub, Jeffrey enters the apartment. He finds a child's conical party hat. He hides in a closet. Dorothy arrives. He watches her talk on the phone with someone who ostensibly holds her husband, Don, and child, Donnie, captive. She speaks to Don and then to the apparent kidnapper. When she hangs up, she weeps on the floor before retiring to the bathroom. She comes back to the living room wearing a blue velvet robe that recalls the shimmering blue cloth from the film's beginning. Her double garb—dark cloth and white reflection—provides a fitting transition to her subsequent gestures, radical departures from the maternal concern that she has shown for her kidnapped child. She hears Jeffrey in the closet. She grabs a knife, opens the closet door, and forces Jeffrey to emerge. She makes him undress and nicks his face with her knife, all the while commanding him not to look at her. She begins kissing Jeffrey near his penis, asking him what he wants and if he likes what she is doing.

Dorothy's vacillation between traditional family values and aberrant sexual desire continues. Someone knocks on the door. Dorothy sends Jeffrey back to the closet before letting Frank Booth (Dennis Hopper) into her apartment. Dressed in black, Frank takes on the violently dictatorial persona that Dorothy used toward Jeffrey. Dorothy plays the submissive role Jeffrey enacted toward her. Frank insists that she call him "Daddy." He orders her to get him bourbon. He turns down the electric lights and fires a candle. With satisfied resignation, he says, "Now it's dark." He demands that Dorothy sit in a chair. He directs her to spread her legs. He commands her not to look at him. He inhales vigorously from a small nitrous oxide cylinder attached to his belt. Intoxicated, he intones, "Baby wants to fuck." Dorothy responds, "Mommy loves you." Frank hits Dorothy in the face, again ordering her not to look at him. Dorothy moans with pleasure. Frank says, "Baby wants blue velvet." Dorothy places part of her robe in his mouth. He puts another part in hers. He throws her on the floor and brutally rams his fingers into her crotch. He crawls on top of her and simulates intercourse until he reaches orgasm. Dorothy seems to experience keen pleasure. Frank again hits Dorothy and tells her not to look at him. Then he blows out the candle, and once more says, "Now it's dark." He reminds Dorothy that she must stay alive for "Van Gogh," and then leaves.

From the closet, Jeffrey has witnessed this bizarre scene of sadistic, masochistic sex mixed with incestuous role-playing—Dorothy pretending to be mother and daughter, Frank acting out son and father. Though Dorothy and Frank are consumed by perverted lusts, they are also hungry for traditional family values. After Frank leaves, Dorothy tries to bring Jeffrey into this strange domestic configuration. She at first tenderly seduces him. While he is caressing her exposed breast, Dorothy requests that he hit her. She wants him to play Frank, to become father, husband, and son so that she can turn into daughter, wife, and mother. She is inviting him to join a new family, the family of the *nigredo*, the dark counter to his daytime domestic situation. Jeffrey recoils and leaves.

Frank Mercurius

At this point, for the first time, Jeffrey faces the terror of the *nigredo*. He encounters in Frank the unbridled chaos of the black stage, turbulence untinctured with Sandy's ambiguous wholesomeness and Dorothy's misplaced love. Beyond the oppositions embodied by these *albedo* figures—conflicts between matter and spirit, lust and love—Frank blurs all distinctions. Like the black he wears and the darkness with which he is obsessed, he creates a realm in which one cannot tell *this* from *that*. In his incestuous role-playing with Dorothy, he annihilates the differences among father, husband, and son. As the kidnapper of her husband and son, he repulses Dorothy; as her sadist lover, he attracts her. He plays a violent adult but also a vulnerable child. He wants total control over Dorothy's behavior yet he gives over the control of his mind to nitrous oxide.

Frank dominates the rest of the film. Jeffrey becomes obsessed with him. Because he assumes that Frank is behind the ear, he secretly shadows him wherever he goes and photographs his activities. He also imitates Frank with regard to Dorothy. Aroused by his initial encounter with her, he starts visiting her. At first, he makes love to her tenderly. However, she soon urges him to hit her just like Frank does. Jeffrey's mirroring of Frank becomes more intimate during a wild night in which Frank abducts him. After discovering Jeffrey leaving Dorothy's apartment, Frank forces the two into his car for a "joy ride." In the course of the night, Frank takes the boy to a lumberyard. After sniffing nitrous oxide, he smears his face with lipstick and does the same to Jeffrey. With Roy Orbison's "In Dreams" blaring on his stereo, he beats his double with the same intensity with which he earlier raped Dorothy. Frank thoroughly incorporates Jeffrey into his world. He marks Jeffrey with lipstick that has been on his own mouth, penetrates the boy with his fists, and annihilates the young man's pride. When Jeffrey wakes the next morning in the lumberyard, battered and alone, he is changed forever.

Frank's fixation on Orbison's song reveals his alchemical identity. Despite his terrifying crimes—he is a kidnapper, a rapist, and a drug dealer in league with a corrupt cop—he serves as a guide to the mystery that Jeffrey so fervently desires. Like the "Sandman" in the song who leads sleepers to their most desired dreams, Frank empowers Jeffrey to fulfill his dream of discovering the riddle of existence. Merging man and woman, adult and child, lover and murderer, nightmare and fantasy, Frank shows Jeffrey the complicity between opposites and offers the young man a vision of the wholeness that the bright neighborhood idyll precludes. But Frank not only unearths for Jeffrey the *nigredo*, the chaos where all conflicts blur into indifference. He also points the way out, the ascent to *albedo* and *rubedo*. His obsession with the songs "In Dreams" and "Blue Velvet" suggests the relationships of the white stage, the moon world where one can envision his ideal beloved, the white queen merging matter and spirit. Likewise, his connection with the police, with order, hints at the red stage, the sun realm in which one marries the beloved, the infant is conceived, and spirit rises from matter.

Led by Frank to the nadir, Jeffrey can now rise from the tomb to be reborn. To do this, he must consciously acknowledge and incorporate Frank's noir world and carry it over, refined, into the sunny lanes of his neighborhood. He begins this process. First, he reveals to Detective Williams the data he has gathered on Frank. This information, he hopes, will lead to Frank's arrest, the liberation of Dorothy's husband and child, and the cleansing of the corruption in the police department. He wishes to cleanse the *nigredo* world of its pollution, to whiten it. Second, he publicly owns his amorous relationship with Dorothy. Soon after vowing his love to

Sandy, he finds a deranged and naked Dorothy in his neighborhood. She has been driven mad with grief and terror and seeks Jeffrey's aid. Jeffrey helps her to the white world of the hospital, where she might be healed of her perversions and restored to an appropriate maternal identity. He also confesses to Sandy that he has been Dorothy's lover and asks forgiveness. She grants it, preparing the way for the *rubedo* marriage between two beings instructed by darkness.

After Jeffrey reports to Williams and helps Dorothy, he faces Frank in a death match. If he can kill Frank, he will find himself in a position to master and transcend the *nigredo*—to prove himself a man of violence and to purge this same violence. Jeffrey is up to the task. With Dorothy installed in the hospital, Jeffrey calls Sandy to tell her to have her father meet him at Dorothy's apartment. He assumes that he will find Don and possibly Donnie. When Jeffrey reaches Dorothy's place, the police are not yet there. He finds two dead men, both shot in the head: a man with only one ear, ostensibly Don, and another in a yellow suit, the corrupt cop. Saddened by this scene, Jeffrey prepares to leave, but he hears Frank coming up the stairs. Jeffrey takes the police radio from the dead cop and puts it in Dorothy's bedroom. He hides in the closet. Frank enters the apartment. He hears the radio and suspects that Jeffrey is in the bedroom. He fires several bullets into the room. Jeffrey rushes from the closet, grabs the dead cop's gun, and returns to hiding. When Frank discovers that Jeffrey is not in the room, he begins to fire into all the rooms until he settles on the closet. But when he opens the closet door, Jeffrey shoots him in the forehead. Sandy and her father rush in. All is well. Sandy and Jeffrey kiss outside of Dorothy's apartment as the bodies are being rolled out.

The Death of Life

But all is really *too* well. The final scenes of the film show that Jeffrey has regressed to his former self—the college kid happy in the artificial fields of the Hollywood Eden. The film moves from the dark and deadly night in front of Dorothy's building to a brightly lighted ear. In the background is the same syrupy, church-like tune that accompanied Sandy's earlier description of a gorgeous dream of robins spreading love over the evil land. To the tune, a woman sings these words: "Sometimes a wind blows / and you and I / float / in love / and kiss forever / in a darkness / and the mysteries / of love / come clear / and dance / in light / in you / in me / and show / that we / are Love." The camera moves slowly in on the ear and then out again to reveal that the ear is Jeffrey's. He is lounging in his well-manicured backyard in the bright sun. He is stirred by Sandy calling him for lunch. As he goes in, he greets his healed father and Detective Williams standing in the corner of his lawn. They are engaged in pleasant conversation. Walking through his house to his kitchen, Jeffrey sees his mother and Mrs. Williams cordially chatting in the living room. In the kitchen, he joins Sandy and his aunt gazing at a robin perched on the windowsill. The bird, which looks artificial, holds a writhing beetle in its mouth. Jeffrey looks at Sandy and says, "Maybe the robins are here." He means the robins of Sandy's allegorical dream. The aunt, however, is disgusted by the bird's eating of the beetle. Sandy and Jeffrey smile complacently before Sandy smarmily asks Jeffrey's earlier question, no longer unsettling: "A strange world, isn't it?" Jeffrey smiles knowingly. The camera then returns to the images that opened the film: the roses blowing before the white fence, the fire truck rolling by, the fireman waving.

This recapitulation of the opening scene shows that Jeffrey has not achieved transmutation. Instead of merging with, while transcending, Frank Mercurius, he has become one with his father. He embraces the well-kept lawn and represses the beetles underneath. Even when faced with the brutality of nature—the robin biting the writhing beetle—he acts as if he is beholding a cute spectacle. Too weak to incorporate Frank's polarized currents, idyll and nightmare, into his soul, Jeffrey settles for vapid hierarchy, pastoral exclusive of wilderness. But what he has not learned is this: order devoid of chaos is dead. Though he thinks that he has won life over death, he has fallen into death-in-life, a predictable and scripted existence, as mechanical as a clock.

If the mechanical robin and smarmy dialogue are not enough to convince us that Jeffrey has missed the meaning of his experience, the very last scene of the film certainly does. In a park, a small boy runs in slow motion. The sentimental song about the mystery of love continues to play. The child is wearing the conical party hat that Jeffrey earlier found in Dorothy's house. The camera moves outward to reveal the goal of the boy's sprint—his mother, Dorothy. She sits on a park bench wearing a brown blouse, no longer garbed in velvet robes. Donnie leaps into her arms. She hugs him happily. However, as she is hugging him, the expression on her face changes to wistful sadness. Her melancholy gaze is matched by an abrupt alteration in the soundtrack. The "Mystery of Love" changes to the final lines of "Blue Velvet," rendered in Dorothy's heartbreaking voice: "And I still can see blue velvet / Through my tears." During this transition, the camera moves away from Dorothy and into the blue sky. This shot fades into the image that opened the movie: a blue velvet curtain shimmering and waving.

These final sequences point to a world far more troubled and beautiful than Jeffrey's environment. Only through embracing the hard, sad reality of loss can one ascend to the boundless sky. Gathering depth and height, one grasps the mystery of polarity, the breathing velvet. In recoiling from these insights and fleeing back to the flatland, Jeffrey succumbs to the primary temptation of the *nigredo*. Before the eyes of the authentic spiritual seeker, the *nigredo*, though initially horrifying, appears as the creative chaos generating all order. However, for the weak seeker, the bored conformist on a lark, the dark stage, while at first exciting, manifests itself as consuming evil. Encountering this horror, the conformist runs scared, returns to the status quo. Only now he holds the conventions with even more intensity than before. He fixates on rules as safeguards against the darkness. Jeffrey, craven in the end, falls to this temptation.

Like Jeffrey, *Blue Velvet* annuls its brief marriage to Mercurius. Though Lynch, unlike his protagonist, is certainly aware of his erasures, he nonetheless leaves his audiences hovering in a limbo between seemingly irreconcilable oppositions. On the one hand, his film suggests that dismemberment of conventions generates new forms of life. On the other hand, the movie claims that societal conventions always contain and control disruptions. This latter current is illustrated by the film's endless citations of two cinematic genres: the small-town idyll and the urban film noir. By pitting these two worlds against one another, the picture suggests that both the good of the day and dark evil are performances, manifestations of existing scripts, lock steps in which no transformation is possible. Even if the film opens and closes with the unpredictable wavering of blue cloth, it intimates that unscripted transmutations are impossible.

Hopeful paean to alchemical transformation and cynical treatise on conformity, *Blue Velvet* forces meditation on a concept or image that merges and transcends change and stasis. This *tertium quid* would not be the white screen, gathering of finite and infinite, because Lynch's picture is a descent into the underworld, the dark swamp where one hungers for familiar things. Likewise, this synthesizing element would not be the lighted projector, blend of fate and freedom, because the movie is a meditation on darkness devoid of guiding beams, the chasm from which unconscious energies control conscious motions. Not the Gnostic blankness, not the Cabbalistic artifice, the third term in *Blue Velvet* is the dimmed auditorium itself, a retort in which one is forced to contemplate the potentially transforming powers of darkness and the complicity between shadow and light. Inviting viewers into this gloom, Lynch's film puts them in a position similar to that of Jeffrey. This position is characterized by a choice. One can sink into the blackness and learn to swim to the light; or one can recoil before descending and flee back to the tawdry gleams. A viewer taking the first path will watch the film again and again, repeatedly turning with Mercurius, more deeply sounding his soul in each revolution. An audience member bent on the second way will vow never again to watch such trash.

The Horror Show

In addition to invoking the forms of forties film noir and fifties situation comedies, *Blue Velvet* draws on a convention of sophisticated horror films: a protagonist finding the real monster not outside but within his interiors. Most horror movies are rather immature reinforcements of dualism, suggesting that good and evil are mutually exclusive opposites. However, the rare horror film blurs the boundaries between oppositions and explores secret interpenetrations between powers the world generally puts asunder. Like *Blue Velvet*, these literate horror flicks intimate the troubling conclusion of the *nigredo* world: to know oneself, one must acknowledge his own darkness.

The few horror films bold enough to depict this threshold between darkness and light mostly come from the classical movie age. One quickly thinks in this regard of James Whale's *Frankenstein* (1931) and George Waggner's *The Wolf Man* (1941). However, a few more recent horror films have also embraced the complicity between blindness and insight. Obviously, Polanski *Rosemary's Baby* (1968) comes to mind, as does Romero's *Night of the Living Dead* (1968). In this tradition of sophisticated horror are two even more contemporary films, Alan Parker's *Angel Heart* (1987) and Adrian Lyne's *Jacob's Ladder* (1990). The latter two films are fully aware of what is implicit in the earlier four movies: horror, properly seen, is not aberration but transcendence. This is the difficult wisdom of the *nigredo*. It is the sullen light of the left-hand path.

On the surface, *Angel Heart* is another dualistic horror film that exploits and then condemns the ills of devil worship. But the movie actually possesses hidden alchemical depths. Recalling the rich *The Heart of Darkness* more than the vapid *Exorcist*, the film features Harry Angel, a private investigator who embarks on an increasingly dark quest to discover the whereabouts of Johnny Favorite, a fifties crooner. Harry has been hired by Louis Cyphre, a refined man who claims that Johnny owes him money. Seeking Johnny's trail, Harry travels to Poughkeepsie, Coney Island, and New Orleans. Each person he questions about Johnny ends up brutally murdered. As Harry moves deeper into the occult world in which Johnny moved, he increasingly suffers flashbacks of a New Year's Eve celebration in Times Square just at the end of the Second World War.

Finally, after much psychological and physical duress, Harry finds out who Johnny is. In a final dialogue with Cyphre, Harry realizes that Johnny was a student of the occult. Years earlier, before the war, Johnny made a Faustian deal with Cyphre, who is actually Lucifer. Johnny agreed to give his soul in exchange for knowledge of the dark arts. However, before Satan could collect his debt, Johnny found a way to hide his soul in the body of a young soldier named Harry Angel. Harry remembers what he had been repressing: he killed those who knew Johnny. In solving the riddle of Johnny, he solves the mystery of his own identity. He now can acknowledge the chaos in his own being, the destructive powers of his heart. By doing so, he might be able to synthesize turbulence and pattern, demon and angel. If he can, he will realize that Cyphre is merely Mercurius in his black form—the dragon, the serpent.

But Parker's film, like Lynch's, does not conclude in the clarity of the *albedo*. After apprehending his identity, Harry is bewildered, terrified. The film cuts to an old wire cage elevator in a luridly lighted building. The door screeches and then slams closed. The sinister car descends to the depths. Throughout the film, this image has suggested hell. Ending with this scene, Parker's movie makes audiences wonder. Is Harry/Johnny merely depraved and thus doomed to suffer in the stasis of the Christian hell, or is this split being now aware of his dual powers and ready to achieve synthesis? Is *Angel Heart* a Christian allegory or an alchemical symbol? Or, more troublingly, is it both at once, a dogmatic system and a dynamic conversion? If it is both, it would aptly embody the mystery of the *nigredo*, itself both everything and nothing, death and life.

Jacob's Ladder, also known as *Dante's Inferno*, is consumed in a similar duplicity. It features a protagonist, Jacob Singer, very similar to Harry Angel. Like Harry, Jacob undergoes painful flashbacks possibly connected to horrific evils. Only in understanding and owning these flashbacks will Jacob be able to understand his identity. But what comes with this apprehension? Will Jacob suffer a hell of retribution in acknowledging his darker energies, or will he transmute his black forces into redemptive powers? Fittingly, this alchemical film never answers these questions.

Jacob, a philosophy student turned postman, suffers visions of demonic beings. He sees these monstrous figures in subways and hospitals, at parties and at his house. He is unsure as to the reality of these creatures. Are they from a real place or from his dreams? Things get worse when he begins to undergo flashbacks of his former wife, who left him, and his son, who was tragically killed. Jacob has a difficult time telling the difference between these fantasies of his family and the facts of his current sad existence. His situation becomes even more difficult when he starts to have violent recollections of the Vietnam War. Jacob suspects that his experiences of demons, his flashbacks of his family, and his recollections of the war are all related, but he doesn't know how.

Then one of Jacob's squad members reports that he suffers flashbacks and visions as well. Jacob and his old friend seek other squad members. They, too, have undergone the same terrors. The men discover a conspiracy. During the war, Jacob's squad was secretly given an experimental drug known as the "ladder." This drug induced hyper-aggressive rage that caused the squad members to turn on one another. Jacob recalls that he killed members of his own squad, but before he can publicize the conspiracy, the government begins a harassment campaign. Jacob realizes that he will never be able to bring the scandal to light. He is doomed to struggle alone with the demons arising from his guilt. It appears that Jacob will founder in the *nigredo*, will cede to the chaos.

Then Jacob visits his Mercurius, a chiropractor named Louis. While Louis straightens his spine (aligning him with the world axis), Jacob tells the angelic doctor of his visions. Louis tells Jacob of the medieval German mystic, Meister Eckhart. According to Eckhart, the "only thing that burns in Hell is the part of [us] that won't let go of life, [our] memories, [our] attachments." The demons burn these things away, but not in order to punish. They burn to free our souls. The lesson is this: If we're scared of dying, if we're holding on too tightly to life, then we'll see devils everywhere tearing our lives away. Life will be hell. However, if we've made peace, if we're no longer clinging to guilt and remorse, then the devils will turn angels. They will free us from earth.

Louis beautifully and succinctly describes how the hell of *nigredo* can become the purgatory and the heaven of the *albedo* and the *rubedo*. Sadly, we never know if Jacob successfully achieves this transmutation. The film ends with Jacob alone in his home. He sees another devilish being and again feels sorrowful fear. But then he witnesses his dead son. The boy looks at his father and then walks toward blinding light. Jacob follows. It appears that he is letting go of life and making his way heaven. But this appearance is simply that—an apparition. The film closes in serious epistemological crisis. We don't know if Jacob is alive or dead. We don't know if he's perceiving or dreaming. We don't know if he's in the present or the past. The movie's form meshes with its content. The audience faces the same conundrum as the protagonist: can one transmute horrific turbulence to blissful pattern, or is one doomed to chronic stasis?

Albedo in *Altered States*

Russell's *Altered States* is a more overt alchemical picture than *Blue Velvet*.[24] This clarity of alchemical vision is appropriate, because *Altered States* is a film about the *albedo* stage. Unlike the *nigredo* stage, in which bewildering riddles undo the psyche, the *albedo* level enjoys lucidity. Conundrums seem solvable and the mind begins to rest. If Lynch's *nigredo* picture shrouds its alchemical imagery, Russell's *albedo* movie makes its alchemical elements clear. Where Lynch's nervous midnight requires strenuous mapping, Russell's calmer depiction of the dawn provides guideposts and directions.

The first two sequences of *Altered States* establish the poles of the film—the danger of sinking too deeply into the chaos of the unconscious and the relative safety of floating between the turbulence of instinct and the order of domesticity. The opening scene features the vehicle by which the protagonist, Eddie Jessup (William Hurt), descends into his unconscious. Before the credits run, the camera lingers on a man floating in a vertical isolation tank. Near the top of the tank is a small glass portal. Through this portal appears a man's head in a glass helmet. The head is illuminated. The tank itself seems to be made of gold. This image recalls the alchemical alembic in which the immersed element might ascend to the condition of gold. The camera then moves to another man in a booth located outside the room in which the tank rests. He is studying readouts generated by the electrodes attached to the man in the tank. Like the alchemical adept, he meditates on the changes produced in the retort. This opening scene concludes with the observer, Arthur Rosenberg (Bob Balaban), helping the man from the tank. This man turns out to be Jessup, professor of medicine at Columbia. He and Arthur are conducting tests on what mental and physical transformations occur in the flotation tank. They are interested in how sense deprivation changes one's psychological constitution and how this mental condition alters the physical condition. Eddie confesses that his first time in the tank produced "mystical" states replete with allegorical images, mostly from Revelation. He also notes that he reexperienced the death of his father. Devoid of consciousness in the retort, Eddie descended into the *nigredo*, where he watched with his mind's eye the dissolution of the world and the death of the father.

In the film's next sequence, Eddie appears in another light. A party is taking place at Arthur's apartment. Several revelers await Eddie's arrival. Emily (Blair Brown), an anthropologist, is especially eager to meet Eddie, a notoriously unconventional genius. When Eddie does appear, the effect is startling. Sensing his presence, Emily looks to the door of Arthur's apartment. There in the threshold, surrounded by white light, is the silhouette of a man. Although the figure is Eddie, he seems to be more than human, an ideal man. This presentation is appropriate. In the preceding sequence, Eddie underwent the dissolution of the *nigredo*. Now he is refined into a material being organized by spiritual pattern. In this form, he is prepared for the union of the *albedo*, a merger with his female counterpart. Ideally, this meeting will result in the marriage of the *rubedo*. As soon as Eddie enters the party, he flirts with Emily. The two enjoy immediate rapport. Both have been labeled geniuses, have finished their doctorates early, and are obsessed with their research. Moreover, they appear to complement one another perfectly. Already briefed by Arthur, Emily believes that Eddie is a weird, shy genius who needs to be drawn out. She is suited to do this; though scientifically brilliant, she is also attuned to the pleasures of companionship. While Emily can reflect Eddie's hidden desire to connect with others, Eddie can mirror Emily's covert hunger for original scientific achievement. He is an eccentrically brilliant seeker, driven to discover great truths—the origin of consciousness, the connection between mind and body. This potentially selfish quality attracts the ambitious Emily.

The following sequence shows Eddie trying to reconcile the poles of his existence—the dangerous quest for individual identity and the safer urge to marry a compatible woman. After the party, Eddie and Emily make love. During a torrid session, Eddie looks from Emily to a circular light in her apartment. Ecstatic with desire, he fixates on the circle, as if it might reveal God or self. He stops having sex with a bewildered Emily. His effort to merge his hunger for self with his lust for another has failed. In the aftermath, he confesses to Emily that he began to see God when he was nine. These visions lasted until he was sixteen, when he witnessed the terrible death of his father and became skeptical toward spirit. However, he believes the tank might have reawakened his visionary capacity. Hopeful for eternity, he can turn away from a beautiful woman entwined around his body and stare longingly at a circular light.

The Lapsed Eve or the Virgin Mary

The remainder of the movie features Eddie's struggle to understand his relationship to Emily, to grasp the mysteries of the *albedo* state. For much of the narrative, he believes that Emily blocks his essential self, that she is Eve in the garden ruining his Adam within.

Right after his confession to Emily, he returns to the isolation tank. He experiences an extended allegorical vision of the fall and failed redemption. He first envisions himself as a young man, probably around sixteen. He sees the tank around him turn into a blue sky. Fish fly in the clouds. This is a picture of his innocent time, when heaven and earth were inseparable, when Jesus the fisher of men hovered visibly in the horizon.

The next part of the vision fractures this concord. Eddie's father lies in a hospital bed. A large black Bible falls to the floor. A shroud bearing the face of the crucified Jesus also flutters down. On the father's chest, a cross burns. A man with the head of a ram with seven horns and seven eyes hangs from a cross. This is an image of Jesus in two forms—in his Gospel role as lamb sacrificed for the sins of the world and in his Revelation guise as judge of the quick and the dead. Like the Bible and the shroud, this cross also falls, not to the floor but through what seems to be an abyss.

This complex sequence suggests the following connections. The death of Eddie's father signals the demise of innocence—of redemption, of Jesus as savior. But the father's Christlike death also offers hope—the man's dissolution, his crucifixion, might issue new life. The father not only represents Jesus—symbol of and liberator from sin. He also represents God—stern tyrant and gentle guide. As tyrant, he subjects his lamblike son to the terror of existence—he crucifies him. As guide, he leads his boy through the suffering necessary for an understanding of salvation. In his role as lamb, both victim and visionary, the son becomes one with his dying father.

The next cluster elaborates these themes, all associated with the *nigredo*, redemptive dismemberment. In a vast desert stands a ruined temple. Three crosses loom in the background. Near the temple, on a large stone, rests a large Bible, plated in gold and silver. The initials INRI are engraved in the metal. Below this acronym for "Jesus of Nazareth, King of the Jews" is an engraving of Jesus on the cross. Above the letters is an image of the seven-eyed ram. A hand unsuccessfully attempts to open the Bible. The ram with seven eyes and seven horns stands beside the Bible. A hand holding a knife stabs the ram. Blood splatters over the Bible. The hand opens the book. The book disappears and in its place emerges a cell-like sphere suspended in space. The globe pulses before exploding. The scene shifts to Eddie as an adult having intercourse with a woman on a stone. They are inside a dark room. Outside, the sky is lurid orange. Interspersed with this orgiastic sex are flashes of a haunting moon and the skull of a ram.

These concluding events of the vision explore the results of the fall. From this decline emerge rituals that might lead back to the garden—not only the practices in the temple but also, more significantly, the disciplines of alchemy, represented by the stone resting in front of the temple. A dark block of matter supporting the silver and gold of a sacred book, this rock symbolizes the steps of the alchemical work and the philosopher's stone itself. The arm that attempts to open the book to finds its secret belongs to Eddie as alchemist. He realizes that the only way to penetrate the mystery of the sacred book is through suffering and death. He slays the ram, a figure of his spiritual self, the Christ within. The book opens on what could be the origin of the universe, a bright sphere exploding into chaos. Of course, this same ballistic orb could signal the angry end of the cosmos, Armageddon. The sexual encounter between Eddie and the woman is equally ambiguous. Taking place on the stone, it could symbolize the *albedo* state, in which male and female crystallize out of the chaos. However, violence also suggests that this sex is criminal, a rape that will be punished come doomsday.

The duplicitous nature of these final images shows Eddie's twofold confusion. First, he is unsure about the nature of the *nigredo*. He thinks that this decline is an injustice perpetrated by a cruel God; but he also senses that fragmentation is required for higher resolution. Second, he is unclear about the meaning of the *albedo*. He appears to believe that sex with a female is a sin. At the same time, he intimates that this union marks an ascent from chaos to order. Eddie's agitation over these alchemical conditions keeps him from achieving wholeness and clarity.

The Essential Self

Eddie spends the rest of the film attempting to understand these visions. Though he agrees to marry Emily and even has two children with her, he is consumed with his quest for identity. After the allegorical vision in the tank, the film moves forward several years to show Eddie and Emily living in Boston—both teach at Harvard—and on the brink of divorce. Eddie is dissatisfied with his domestic life. He yearns for a major scientific breakthrough, a discovery that will reveal the "original self." He believes that each person bears within his physiology six billion years of memory, spanning from the first atom to the developed human being. He thinks that he can access this "immortal" self by sounding his own limbic system. If he can discover this essential wholeness, he will find, so he hopes, the only significance, the only solace, in this "meaningless horror of life."

Fed up with being a respectable professor at Harvard and a responsible husband at home, Eddie renews his quest for the primal self in Mexico. There he joins some Hinchi Indians located near San Luis Potosi. This tribe continues to practice ancient Toltec rituals centered on mushroom ingestion. The Indians mix the mushrooms into a hallucinogen that apparently evokes a "common experience" in everyone who takes the drug. Eddie meets with the chief of the tribe and arranges to participate in the ritual. Immediately after he takes the drug—significantly tinctured with a few drops of his own blood—he falls into a visionary trance. This vision appears to be a continuation of his last one, which ended with Eddie having sex with a woman on a stone while images of a bloody moon and a ram's skull flashed in the background. This sequence begins with Eddie and Emily sitting together in a beautiful garden, dressed in immaculately white clothes from the nineteenth century. They are Adam and Eve enjoying paradise. However, with a lascivious look in her eye, Emily eats a scoop of soft cream from a silver bowl. She then offers the cream to Eddie, who also partakes. This food is the forbidden fruit. Eddie and Emily are next shown leaving the garden, now wearing red formal clothes. Soon after, Eddie finds himself lying on his side in a vast, dark desert. He is now in modern garb. He is staring at Emily, who lies before him naked. She is on her belly, with her head arched backward. Her posture resembles that of the Egyptian sphinx. A dust storm rages, covering them with sand. Both are reduced to sandstone statues, which are after a time erased by the howling wind. Nothing remains but the wasteland.

As with his earlier vision, Eddie is trapped in Judeo-Christian imagery. If he is regressing to earlier forms of consciousness, he is getting no further than the myths of the ancient Near East. Although this paradigm offers the possibility that suffering and dismemberment might reveal the unfallen Adam or the spiritual Christ within, it also casts the feminine in a negative light, as a seductress who tempts man away from his innocence, from his identity. In his hallucination, Eddie inflects these old myths through his personal experience, translating the collective into the personal. He envisions Emily as a force pulling him from his origin and into the fallen world. Not only is she Eve casting him east of Eden, she is also the sphinx, devouring men unable to solve riddles.

When Eddie returns to Boston, he experiments with the drug in an isolation booth. His trances are filled with Christian images of sinners suffering in fire. What differentiates these sequences from the earlier ones is their impersonality. Neither Eddie nor Emily appears in these scenes. Eddie is moving from personal unconscious to collective unconscious. Significantly, the pictures of this transformation show individuals consumed by molten lava, egos dissolved into liquid. Eddie's own ego is undergoing similar erasure. He enters more deeply into the *nigredo*. He is on the verge of descending beneath individuality, language, and myth. He will soon reach the primitive.

This progression is ironic. The man in search of his essential self is undergoing visions that increasingly blur his individuality into collective energy. This problem persists in his next and most startling experience. In a new isolation tank aptly located in the bowels of a basement at Harvard Medical School, Eddie sinks into a vision so profound that it begins to change his physiology. He becomes what he sees. This time we do not see Eddie's vision. We hear about it through microphones in tank. This absence of visual data suggests that Eddie is now experiencing events beyond representation, forces too indistinct to be captured by images. To Arthur and Mason, a colleague from Harvard Medical School, Eddie details a prehistoric scene: grasslands, savannahs, newly born mountains still smoking, trees quivering with strange life, small and furry proto-humans stalking a goat. Eddie claims that he is becoming one of these humanoids. In an intense voice, he describes how wonderful it feels to hunt and kill a goat, to have blood in his mouth. He then makes a gorilla sound and falls silent. After several hours, Eddie finally stirs. When Arthur and Mason open the tank, they find Eddie with blood all over his mouth and unable to speak. Tests reveal a changed skull structure and altered DNA. Eddie has regressed beyond civilization to the most primitive human state. His inner visions are now manifesting themselves in outward phenomena.

The Mad Scientist

No longer simply an alchemist observing changes in his soul, Eddie is also an alchemical element undergoing physical changes. Blinded by his quest for the primal self, he is unable to register the bare fact that he is journeying back to a time when the idea of self did not exist, when barely conscious animals killed or were killed. He is mistaking the material energy of the *nigredo* for the spiritual end of his quest. Instead of accepting the *nigredo* for what it is—the unconscious turbulence giving rise to order—he perceives this condition as the goal of his inquiry. The cause of this interpretive mistake is Eddie's narcissism. Uninterested in the affection of Emily and obsessed with his quest, he wants only to sink into self. What he doesn't realize is that the depths of his psyche have nothing to do with his identity. These profundities pull him into a world where species take precedence over individuals. If he were not so intensely in love with himself, he would realize that the essential self is never a self-contained monad but a relationship between unconscious energy and conscious form. Increasingly rejecting consciousness in hopes of plunging deeper into his own being, he risks becoming a mere cell or atom.

Eddie's misguided quest to discover his discrete being by plunging into an indifferent sea results in monstrosity. From the moment that his shifting states of consciousness produce changed bodily conditions, his story becomes pure genre: the horror film. This move is fitting. As Eddie converts from a man to a monomaniac, the movie itself changes from "biopic"—a depiction of the life of John Lilly—to monster flick—a version of *The Wolf Man*. To stay too long in the *nigredo* without grasping its transformative virtues is to become stuck in the chaos, to ossify into a category mistake.

Only hours after his initial experience of an "altered state," Eddie suffers a bizarre transformation outside of the tank. Now uninterested in Emily's mature, intelligent, and challenging affection, he lies in bed naked with a student, a mere reflection of his egomania. He awakes from a postcoital slumber to find that his smooth arm is metamorphosing into a knotty, primitive appendage. The same occurs to his belly, which also tightens into hard knots. Thinking that he might be hallucinating and hoping to clear his head, he goes to the bathroom and gets under the shower. He looks to his feet. He is shocked to discover that both are covered in tough hair and expanded with a sixth digit.

Like a mad scientist, Eddie very soon after returns to the isolation tank alone. This time, he transforms fully into a prehistoric humanoid, an ape-man covered from head to toe in thick fur. He escapes from the tank and runs wildly through the basement of the medical school. He terrifies a custodian and almost beats a security guard to death. Fleeing from the building, he runs for a while with a pack of wild dogs. Eventually, he finds his way to a zoo. There, he kills and eats a goat. Bloated on blood, he falls asleep. When he awakens some hours later, he has resumed his normal state. He is again Eddie.

With the help of Mason, Eddie, naked and slightly bewildered, is returned to Emily, now living with the kids in a house outside of Boston. She has only recently returned from a research trip to Africa and is understandably very concerned about Eddie. She fears that he is going insane and that he is putting his body in danger. By the time Eddie makes it to her house after his transformation, she has been trying to find him for hours and is beside herself with worry. Mostly indifferent to her agitation, Eddie exultantly describes his time as an ape-man. He tells her that he became a primitive man driven only by a will to survive, an instinct only to eat and drink and sleep. He confesses that he had the "most supremely satisfying time" of his life. As an afterthought, he rather whimsically adds that he might have killed a man, the security guard. Even in his human form, Eddie is beginning to behave like an amoral animal, a monster.

Love Supreme

From the time that Eddie first experiences biological change, Emily tries to pull him out of his monomania. She attempts to convince Eddie that love is more important than truth. Like a muse of the *albedo*, she essays to elevate her estranged lover from the monstrous tomb he has built for himself. When Eddie comes home after his ape-man fiasco, he admits that he wonders how she "puts up" with him. She simply says that she loves him, revealing her understanding of a mystery beyond Eddie's scope. For Eddie, one must have a selfish reason for undergoing pain. In contrast, Emily knows that love inspires one to suffer charitably. While Eddie is controlled by a selfish theory of causal justice—if I feel pain, then I must gain recompense—Emily is buoyed by an unselfish sense of causeless mercy: I suffer offering solace where it is not deserved. Eddie, although he quests for an eternity beyond domestic cares, is bound by a temporal theory of narcissistic causality, of sequence: first this happens to me, then that will happen to me. Emily, although she is attuned to the temporal requirements of family life, is released into an eternal state unconcerned with the causal rigors of time: loving charity breaks the connection between "if" and "then," cause and effect.

Emily's and Eddie's opposing notions of human interaction produce two different environments. Eddie's narcissistic theory of causality leads not to justice, unbiased application of reward and punishment, but to anarchy, selfish will reducing difference to the same. Pushed to an extreme, his vision would generate a Hobbesian nightmare—a brutal world ruled by egocentric materialists little different from animals. Emily's practice of affectionate mercy strikes a balance between anarchy on the one hand and justice on the other. Flying in the face of the unbiased causality behind justice—this action causes this reward or punishment—mercy is beyond logic and unpredictable, a matter of the turbulent heart. However, although it is outside the categories of causality, mercy is not simply chaotic, a blurring of difference to the same. It is based on the mysterious discriminations of love, the cryptic rhythms that push a heart this way instead of that. Between the will of the anarchist and the reason of the judge, Emily's mercy if sufficiently pervasive would fashion a crepuscular, contingent world in which moods and inclinations, attractions and aversions would organize experience. This languorous universe would be conducive more to dreaming than to doing, more affable to the artist than to the scientist. If Eddie's anarchy suggests a habitat of darkness, Emily's intimates moonlight. Where Eddie ends in violence, Emily inspires sentimentality.

Energized by his transformation to an ape-man, Eddie wants to go back into the tank. This time he wants Emily, Arthur, and Mason to observe him. Emily is hesitant to agree to this. She fears that Eddie's conclusions concerning alteration are correct and that his genetic structure might be permanently changed. However, her affection prevails, and she does decide to study Eddie in the tank, but not before one final effort to instruct him in the mysteries of love. On the eve of his immersion, she asks Eddie for what he should give willingly. She asks him for love. Though he puts his arms around her as she sinks into his breast, his expression remains aloof. His mind is elsewhere, in the tank. If he is ever to rise to Emily's level of insight, he is obviously going to have to suffer a breakdown of DNA much more horrifying than the ones he has thus far suffered.

This is precisely what occurs. Eddie screams as he devolves into a blob containing only the outlines of face. This blob sinks into an abyss and then disappears into a bewildering array of lights, colors, and explosions. Eddie is moving backward in time, from organism, to cell, to atom, to primal soup, to the mindless galactic energy hovering before the big bang. Finally, though, there is nothing but a cold mist. Meanwhile, Arthur, Mason, and Emily have been stunned by the rays of energy irradiating from the tank. Emily awakens from her shock to notice that the room formerly containing the tank has become a whirlpool of gassy liquid. She walks into the soup searching for Eddie. When she gently reaches into the void, she magically metamorphoses. No longer a distressed woman in soggy clothes, she becomes totally calm and dry, wearing nothing at all. She hovers in luminous space, a goddess as much as a woman. She scoops her hands into the emptiness and pulls out a small sphere—an egg, the first atom. This seed turns into Eddie reformed, likewise naked and unconstrained by gravity. Emily tenderly holds the sides of his face and eases him out of the abyss. A full representative of the *albedo* power, an avatar of Isis or Venus, she has literally revived and reconstituted the mangled denizen of the *nigredo*, the dead Osiris, Adonis torn.

Eddie's ego has been shattered, and he has been reborn into a new being who understands the virtues of relationship, of love. Back in Emily's house after his annihilation, he confesses to her that she "redeemed" him. He descended into the "terror" and found only a "hideous nothing." After she rescued him from this nadir of the *nigredo*, he realized that "truth is transitory" and only "human life is real." However, even though he understands that human connections are the only meaningful element in the universe, he is hollowed by the truth he apprehended, the inhuman horror at the core of the physical world. If not for Emily's love, he says, he would be utterly consumed by this terror. Eager to translate Eddie fully to her level of being, Emily optimistically tells him that the two of them can resume their marriage, that his terror will be assuaged.

He tells her, though, that it is too late for him. He is wasted by his ordeal. As he turns to walk away from her, he begins to metamorphose again into the void. Emily screams to him: If "you love me, defy it!" She runs to help him. This time, however, the void is too powerful. When Emily touches the devolving Eddie, she too is transmuted into a pattern of blind energy. Eddie begins to bang against the wall, attempting to will his discrete self back into being. Meanwhile, Emily slowly fades. Eventually, Eddie reconstitutes. He rushes to the dwindling Emily and hugs her. Both disappear in a flash of light and reappear transformed: they are clean, naked, and beautiful, hugging affectionately in the half-light of the hallway. For the first time in the film, Eddie says, "I love you, Emily."

In this way, the movie concludes, leaving us with a perfect image of the *albedo*. Eddie and Emily are now once again mirror images of one another. Both have descended into the horrors of violent matter and have been refined by the spirit of love. Both have grasped the redemptive virtue of relationship and the hell of narcissism. They have realized the potential that they enjoyed earlier in the film, when they first met. Newly initiated into this *albedo* stage, they embrace in a threshold environment—in a partially lit hallway connecting a dark room and an illuminated one. This is the crepuscular, moony quality of the *albedo*, a halfway point between midnight and noon. Their psychological dispositions match this external situation. Emily and Eddie can now embody the loose "logic" of mercy, the ability to overlook the codes of reward and punishment, the talent for discriminating between authentic and inauthentic affection.

Now resting in this inward and outward state, Eddie and Emily can enjoy the shadowy Eden of the white stage. But they cannot languish long in this solace. The dangers of resting too long in the *albedo* are the same as stopping too long in the *nigredo*. One can become overly soft in the warm currents of unquestioning love, can take the pleasures of free affection for granted and once more turn selfish. To avoid this regression, one must transform the courtship of the *albedo* into the marriage of the *rubedo*—the ritualized partnership designed to produce a child, the philosopher's stone.

This is not the only danger suggested by the film. In pervading its second half with images and motifs from Hollywood genre films—not only horror pictures but also science fiction movies—*Altered States* unpleasantly hints at this possibility: all ostensible transmutations are really just predictable fulfillments of prefabricated plans, the strict logic of the genre plot. From the time that *Altered States* begins to draw on the wolf-man motif, we know that the picture is limited to two options: the "tragedy" of the beast being killed along with the man or the "comedy" of the man overcoming the beast with the help of his female beloved. Similar boundaries appear when the picture begins to draw on the "mad" scientist science fiction motif. The scientist can destroy himself and those he loves or he can overcome his monomania with the help, again, of his beloved. Genre mechanizes Emily as well. In spite of the power of her love, she is for the last third of the film the long-suffering woman of commercial cinema, the good wife who stands by her troubled beloved. These genre elements consume the film and reduce the characters to stable commodities. Their transformations are rehearsals of tired scripts, clichés designed to give paying audiences what they think they want.

In this way, *Altered States*, like *Blue Velvet*, counters its alchemical transmutations with genre clichés. In doing so, however, the film does not merely erase the metamorphoses that it depicts. Russell's picture leaves its audiences in the same limbo in which the characters find themselves. We are left in a dimly lit, transitional position, caught between visions of salubrious conversion and registers of the same old stuff. We resemble the element in the alembic, always tottering between what it is and what it is becoming. We become one with the fecund gloom in the theatrical space.

The Hold of Patriarchy

Reinforcing the patriarchal culture industry, Hollywood studios have produced very few films exploring the disruptive *albedo* state—a state in which woman are wiser and stronger than men. Hollywood films generally ignore alchemical agitations altogether, content to reinforce the standard (and marketable) dualisms of orthodox Christianity: man is better than woman; order is superior to chaos. Still, a few rare films have joined *Altered States* in espousing the virtues of the white goddess. Two such movies stand out: Roman Polanski's *Ninth Gate* (1999) and Norman Jewison's *Agnes of God* (1985).

Polanski's film appears to have nothing to do with salvation. The movie is a portrait of Satanists in quest of copies of a seventeenth-century book apparently written by the devil, *The Nine Gates of the Kingdom of Darkness*. These devil worshippers believe that if they can combine all three copies of the book, they will be able to pass from earth to hell, from human to devil. Satanist Boris Balkan owns one copy of the book. He hires Corso, a feckless rare book dealer, to find the other two copies. Corso travels all over Europe in search of the volumes. Other ambitious Satanists hound him. Former owners of the book die in bizarre ways. A beautiful young woman also follows Corso. He cannot tell if she is out to harm or help him. Eventually, with Corso's help, Balkan secures all three copies. In an abandoned old castle, he uses the volumes in a demonic ritual. Before he can achieve transformation from the temporal to the eternal, he burns up and dies. The next day, Corso returns to the castle with the charred volumes. There he and the young woman make love in front of the ruined castle. In doing so, they perfectly mimic one of the photographs in *The Nine Gates*. Realizing this, Corso understands that he has discovered the key to the gate. The film ends with him walking into the burnt castle and disappearing into the light, passing from matter to spirit.

If we simply treat the film as a horror story along the lines of *Rosemary's Baby* or *Angel Heart*, we end up with a rather silly movie. However, if we grasp the film as an alchemical allegory, the picture becomes an interesting exploration of the *albedo* state. In an alchemical light, Corso is the initiate in search of transformation, and the young woman is the white goddess translating the adept from dark chaos to organized energy. Throughout the film, the alchemical Corso struggles through the darkness of the *nigredo*. He believes that this is all the world is—a cesspool of evil. However, through the agency of the young woman, he understands that the evil is really chaos leaning toward order. After merging with the young woman, he sees that *The Nine Gates* is not a demonic book but an alchemical treatise; the author of the book is not Satan but Mercurius; the gate is a portal not from earth to hell but from energy to pattern—to waves of light.

But this movie, regardless of these alchemical meanings, remains silly. Like *Altered States*, it is both a profound analysis of the *albedo* condition and a trifling mixture of predictable cinematic genres. The same can be said of *Agnes of God*. On the surface the movie is a rather clichéd murder mystery tinged with hints of the supernatural. The picture explores the case of Agnes, a nun who apparently gave birth to and then murdered a child. Dr. Martha Livingstone, a court-appointed psychiatrist, soon learns that Agnes possesses no recollection of having sex, giving birth, or killing the child. The situation is made more complex by the fact that no virile males could have possibly come into contact with Agnes. Aware of Agnes's extreme naiveté and open to the possibility that the young nun miraculously conceived the child, Mother Miriam Ruth, the mother superior of the convent, diligently tries to defend Agnes from Livingstone's probing questions. The film centers on the conflict between Martha and Miriam, with Martha representing secular humanism and Miriam espousing Christian faith. In the end, neither is satisfied. Martha continues to struggle with the possibility that Agnes miraculously conceived the child and then killed it through divine agency in order to symbolize Christ's death. Miriam persists in battling the possibility that Agnes biologically conceived the baby and then brutally murdered it to hide the evidence of sin.

The mystery is never solved. Agnes, often dressed totally in white, is both an innocent vessel of holy miracle and a psychotic agent of horrendous murder, a symbol of the virginal Mary and a figure of evil Eve, a creator and a destroyer. She embodies the duplicities of the *albedo* stage, both life threatened by death and death rising to life. Aptly, her ambiguity fosters spiritual growth in the two adepts who study her mysteries. She shocks the agnostic Martha into questioning her reductive empiricism and entertaining miracles. She forces the faithful Miriam to doubt her long-held beliefs and face sordid possibilities. In encouraging both women to counter their positions, she inspires spiritual growth—an apprehension of the secret marriage of opposites.

Rubedo in *Excalibur*

The alchemical elements in *Excalibur* are even more apparent than they are in *Altered States*.[25] If the latter film draws heavily on esoteric art, the former one is an alchemical allegory. The film's main character is not Arthur but Merlin the magician. From the beginning of the picture to the end, Merlin tries to refine the violent world of the Dark Ages into an orderly kingdom. Knights to him are principles more than people, forces to be harnessed and arranged. Under Merlin's guidance, Arthur, the bastard son of a brutal marauder, becomes a gentle knight and a noble king. While *Excalibur* pauses on the vitality of the *nigredo* and the elegance of the *albedo*, it is mainly a meditation on kingship, the discipline of the *rubedo*. This focus provides the impetus for the film's allegorical rendering of the alchemical opus. Unlike the *nigredo*, suitable for the ambiguities of *Blue Velvet*, and unlike the *albedo*, appropriate for the reveries of *Altered States*, the *rubedo* is the daylight world of reason. The form of its message should be as translucent as its content.

Merlin, portrayed by Nicol Williamson, reveals his alchemical orientation at the film's climax, when Arthur discovers Guinevere and Lancelot committing adultery in the forest and suffers the sickness that wastes his kingdom. Weary of trying to elevate men from violence to civilization, Merlin has decided to leave earth and return to the other world from which he came. As he is leaving, he bids farewell to Morgana (Helen Mirren), Arthur's stepsister and an aspiring sorceress. She convinces Merlin to show her the "charm of making." He leads her down into a hidden cavern covered in luridly lighted ice. Amidst the shimmering crystals, Merlin tells Morgana that this subterranean cave houses the "coils of the dragon." In these coils, he confesses, his "power is born." This realm is pure potential, an undifferentiated reservoir of energy. Here "all things are possible" and "all things meet their opposites." Past and future, desire and regret, knowledge and oblivion, love and violence all blend and blur, waiting to be directed into actuality, separated into antinomies. This cavern is the *nigredo*.

Throughout the tale, Merlin tries to organize this vitality into law. The film opens in terrifying darkness. On a fiery hill in the night, knights engage in brutal combat. Their armored helmets resemble the heads of wild animals. Through the bloody smoke Merlin appears. He bears a staff topped with dragons of coiled gold. He telepathically communicates with the most violent knight, Uther Pendragon (Gabriel Byrne). Uther wants the "sword of power," Excalibur, a weapon that would enable him to become king. Merlin realizes that Uther wants the sword only so that he can enhance his military power. He knows that he must teach this barbaric chieftain that Excalibur should be used to "heal," not to "hack." He agrees to grant Uther the sword only for purposes of peace.

In the next scene, Merlin enacts in miniature his effort to direct Uther's turbulence. He stands before a murky lake in the dawn. He wordlessly conjures. A silver blade rises from the water, pushed upward by a woman's arm. This is Excalibur, guarded for centuries by the Lady of the Lake. Having elevated this weapon from the ooze to the sun, Merlin hopes to inspire the same transcendence in Uther. He knows, however, that this ascent will be difficult, because this sword of power is double, implement of Mercurius, always on the verge of hacking the world to chaos or healing its rifts.

Merlin arranges a parley between Uther, who holds the sword, and Cornwall (Colin Redgrave), Uther's enemy. The magician tells the knights that the sword was "forged when the world was young," when "bird and beast and flower were one with man," when "death was but a dream." Hypnotized by this artifact, a reminder of eternity, unity, and immortality, the barbarians agree to peace: "one king," "one land."

However, as Merlin soon sadly discovers, Uther is incapable of purging the animal. During a feast, he gazes lasciviously on Cornwall's wife, Igrayne (Katrine Boorman), and breaks the fragile concord. While he lays siege to Cornwall's castle, Uther begs Merlin to enable him to have Igrayne. Realizing that Uther is not the man to set the lands in order, Merlin agrees, with the stipulation that he will take possession of the child issuing from the king's lust. Once again, Merlin invokes chaos in hopes of fostering new order. While Cornwall and his knights are out attacking Uther's armies, Merlin raises the "dragon's breath" to propel Uther over Cornwall's moat. As Uther flies over the waters, he takes on the appearance of Cornwall. He makes love to

Igrayne. The issue is Arthur. Merlin takes charge of the babe only minutes after it is born. He hopes that this infant will develop into a king who can transform brutal material into salubrious spirit.

The next time Merlin appears, Arthur (Nigel Terry) has grown into a teenager under the guidance of Ector and his son Kay, both honorable knights. Unaware of his parentage, Arthur believes that Ector is his father and Kay is his brother. Kay is preparing to joust for the right to try to pull Excalibur from the stone into which Uther drove it just before he was killed by Cornwall's men. Ever since, ambitious knights have struggled to remove the sword from the stone, an act akin to extracting gold from lead, spirit from matter. A rather absent-minded squire to Kay, Arthur allows a thief to steal his knight's sword. As he runs after the culprit, he sees the sword glimmering in the stone. He easily removes it and proves himself worthy of being king. While the knights present divide into warring camps, those for the "boy king" and those against, the young Arthur retires to the forest with Merlin. In the nocturnal wood, Merlin teaches Arthur the secrets of the alchemical vision. Merlin tells him that the dragon is "everywhere" and "everything." It is spirit in matter, the spark of life going to the womb of the earth to be born. One should not fear this reptile of chaos but "rest" in the "arms of the dragon." Enlightened, Arthur awakes from a restful sleep to announce that Excalibur, too, is part of the dragon. He has learned the lesson—pristine handiwork originates in the slime.

Under Merlin's guidance, Arthur conquers all of England and unites the warring barbarians. At the end of the battles, the magician urges Arthur to commemorate this peace, because, as Merlin wearily points out, "it is the doom of men that they forget." This admonishment encourages Arthur to build a round table in the center of a circular castle. The warning also inspires the king to marry, so that he might produce an heir to keep the peace for years to come. These two events—the building of Camelot and the marriage between Arthur and Guinevere (Cherie Lunghi)—elevate the kingdom from the *nigredo* to the *albedo*. The knights no longer wear gray armor and helmets resembling beasts. They don silver carapaces and headdresses ornamented with wings. Likewise, these same knights forgo the dank fortresses of their warring days. They dwell in a luminous castle warm with scientific pursuit, decorous music, and well-coiffed women. These new outer coverings are perfectly suited for the Arthur's marriage to Guinevere, a melding not only of male and female but also of violence and love, reason and emotion. From this marriage might issue the golden child of eternal concord.

But the transition from the *albedo*—opposites coexisting in harmony—to the *rubedo*—opposites melded into one—is difficult, perhaps impossible. As Merlin confesses to Morgana during the wedding, the way of the alchemist is hard and lonely. Even as the magician tries to heal, his foresight shows him that he will fail. This melancholy condition presses Merlin more than ever during the marriage because he knows that this inauguration of the *albedo* will sadly result in a greedy child who will waste the land. As Merlin later admits, "Good and evil—there never is one without the other."

This is the morose truth haunting the alchemist: the chaos out of which order arises, the evil that originates good, are never absent. These unsettling powers are always lurking. The brutal turbulence of the *nigredo* can realistically be transformed into the elegant forms of the *albedo*: violence can be converted into law and lust into love. However, to transmute law into a happy commonwealth and love into domestic bliss—these alterations are perhaps ideal, occurring only in dreams and myths. The *rubedo* might emerge after numerous dissolutions. However, the more likely scenario is that the *rubedo* is only a dream that instills hope in a desolate world.

The Broken King

From the time of Arthur's wedding, Merlin becomes less prominent as he watches his hard-won orders dissolve back into the chaos. Ironically, the demise of spiritual refinement is caused by the man who elevated barbarism to civilization. When Arthur's knights first encounter Lancelot (Nicholas Clay), they wear gray armor and crude tusks. Lancelot, however, is covered in silver armor and elegant wings. He is in search of a king worthy of his service. After Lancelot easily defeats all of Arthur's knights, he takes on the king. Unable to defeat the master knight through ordinary means, an enraged Arthur draws on the powers of Excalibur to stun Lancelot into submission. Arthur's unseemly violence—his use of the sword to hack instead of to heal—brings the beautiful Lancelot into his service. Under the influence of this knight, Arthur's troops don elegant armor and defeat all enemies. Without Lancelot, secured with Arthur's barbarism, the decorum of Camelot and the marriage to Guinevere would never have come to pass.

However, as if tainted by the Arthurian lust for power that secured him in the first place, Lancelot destroys the order he built. From the instant Lancelot and Guinevere set eyes on one another, they fall desperately in love. Before the royal wedding takes place and before Camelot is completed, the seed of destruction is already present. The downfall of marriage and castle alike are inevitable.

Afraid that he will not be able to control his feelings for Guinevere, Lancelot absents himself from Camelot. Without his influence, the knights soon falter. Still angry over Uther's deception of her mother and slaughter of her father, Morgana spreads rumors among the idle knights of Guinevere's passion for Lancelot. With no wars to occupy their energies, the knights begin to suspect their queen and their champion. One night Gawain claims that Guinevere and Lancelot are no longer true. An angry Arthur demands that a champion step forth to defend Guinevere's honor. The night before the joust that will prove his beloved's guilt or innocence, Lancelot sleeps alone in the forest. During a nightmare grown from guilt, he stabs himself. Though wounded, he defeats Gawain to preserve the queen's honor. As Lancelot lies dying after the joust, Merlin claims that only Guinevere can save him. She places her hand on his wound. He springs to life. He retires to the forest to avoid being near his beloved. However, in the night, Guinevere arrives and makes love to him. Merlin informs Arthur of this assignation. The king rides into woods with Excalibur. Unable to slay his wife and his friend, he stabs the blade in the ground and leaves. When Lancelot finds the sword, he screams, "The king without a sword; the land without a king!" He flees. Guinevere sobs.

The kingdom decays. As Arthur discovers Guinevere and Lancelot, Merlin is showing Morgana the cavern of the dragon. The moment Arthur stabs the ground with Excalibur and relinquishes his power, a blade runs through the breast of Merlin. Weakened, he falls under Morgana's spell. She forces him to recite the charm of making. Armed with this power, she repeats history. She takes on the appearance of Guinevere, visits Arthur in the night, places him under a spell, and makes love to him. As Arthur nears climax, she reveals herself as his sister and tells him that she will now produce a son who will usurp his father. This infant grows into Mordred (Robert Addie), a cruel parody of the philosopher's stone. Though he wears golden armor and a helmet that resembles the sun, this progeny is a prod- uct of incest, a monstrous blurring of opposites, and a brutal tyrant, a warlord commanding his rebel knights to lay waste to the land. Bereft of his sword of power—physically and psychically castrated—Arthur is impotent and ill. He can only watch in silence as his kingdom is returned to chaos.

The agents of the interconnected vitalities of Merlin and Arthur are the caus- es of these men's respective demises. Merlin's charm of making empowers him to arrange for Uther to produce Arthur. His ability to conjure from the waters enables him to attain the sword that ensures Arthur's kingship. However, his charm betrays Morgana's father and gives rise to her violent grudge. Likewise, his retrieval of Excalibur allows Arthur to subdue into his service the knight who will commit adultery with his wife. Arthur suffers from his virtues in the same way. His ability to extract Excalibur from the stone elevates him to noble kingship. His skill in wielding the sword secures the lance of the greatest knight. But Lancelot's infideli- ty causes Arthur to lose this sword and to wound Merlin.

These pictures of decline suggest two unsettling possibilities: either the *rubedo* is impossible, a dream of transcendence never to be realized, or the *rubedo* arises only after numerous annihilations school the soul in the rigors of the spiritual life. The former possibility seems the most logical. Thus far in Boorman's film, the turbu- lence of the *nigredo* always overruns the patterns of the *albedo*. Agitated with the material energies of the black stage, the white level can never push entirely beyond matter to spirit. However, the remainder of *Excalibur* explores the latter possibility: the white stage must be repeatedly broken before it can leap into the red. Only from the nadir of suffering can the healing gold emerge. Only in the wasteland can the knight discover the Holy Grail, the chalice containing the blood of the savior. This sacred cup is the philosopher's stone.

The Holy Grail

In the depths of physical and psychic disease, tired of watching his lands and people die, Arthur sends his knights on a quest for the Holy Grail. He hopes that the sacred vessel will restore health. Over a period of many years, his knights perish in search of this prize. Most are killed in a trap set by Morgana and Mordred.

After years of searching for the Grail, Perceval (Paul Geoffrey) encounters this snare. He ends up hanging by the neck from a tree from which the corpses of several other knights sway. Near death, he goes into a trance. He imagines himself washed clean and wearing only a white sheet around his waist. He stands before a castle door. The door opens. Before him hovers a golden chalice. A disembodied voice asks, "Whom does the Grail serve?" Perceval cannot answer. The door closes. He comes out of his trance to find that his rope has been cut by the spur on the foot of one of the dead knights. He falls to the ground. He realizes that he has failed to grasp the Grail.

Perceval learns from this failure. Years later, Perceval once more beholds the Grail. After watching the last of the knights die, he encounters a bearded, haggard Lancelot, now a prophet of doom. Lancelot criticizes Perceval and all of Arthur's knights for their pride. A band of Lancelot's followers push Perceval into a stream. Unable to swim because of his armor, Perceval sinks in a deep part of the current. As he descends, he removes his armor, the last remnants of his knightly ego. He reaches bottom and fully accepts his death. The trance again comes. This time he knows the answer. The Grail serves the bearer of the voice: the Lord. A next question follows: "What is the secret of the Grail?" Perceval answers: "The king and the land are one." The Grail appears in his hands. He finds himself at Arthur's side. The king drinks and revives.

Perceval discovers within his own depths the secrets of the Grail. The chalice is a visible pattern of God's invisible being, a material vehicle in the service of spirit. The secret of this cup is the relationship between king and land—microcosm and macrocosm, part and whole. The king with the pure soul irradiates his virtues onto his environment. Inward and outward, spirit and matter, correspond. Suffering the nadir of the *nigredo*—laceration of ego—Perceval has moved through the *albedo*—verbal intercourse with the divine—and achieved the goal of his quest: the perfect synthesis of spirit and matter. His interior vision of the Grail's secret manifests itself in an actual Grail. Like the philosopher's stone, this chalice transforms Arthur's decaying matter into vibrant life.

Arthur sets about reviving his lands. He calls his remaining knights to arms and sets out to face the armies of his son. As he rides through the land with his knights, stalks and buds rise from the mud and blossoms shower down from the limbs of trees. Amidst the colors, he makes his way to the nunnery to which Guinevere has retired. No longer troubled by pride, he forgives her. In return, she reunites him with Excalibur, which she has kept hidden since the day he relinquished it. The *rubedo* state, it appears, has finally been achieved. Arthur's excruciating experiences in the underworlds of his malaise have yielded the spiritual prize that comes only to those blessed with capacious charity.

But the verdure quickly returns to muck. With the help of Merlin—who returns as a dream image at Arthur's revival—Arthur and his aged knights gain an advantage over Mordred's stronger army. As Morgana sleeps the night before the battle, Merlin visits her in a dream and makes her recite the charm of making. From her mouth issues a dense fog. The voicing of this spell drains Morgana of her beauty. She is reduced to an old hag. Bereft of Morgana's magic and forced to fight in a mist, Mordred's army cannot defeat Arthur. By the end of the day, almost all soldiers are dead. Their bloody corpses sink into mud under the gloom. Of the handful of knights still alive are Arthur and Mordred. The two meet in the center of the field. As Mordred mortally wounds his father with his lance, Arthur slays his son with Excalibur. Arthur retires to the margins of the field to nurse his wound. A blood-red sea roils in the distance and a portentous orange sky lowers. Arthur calls Perceval to his side. The two are the only living souls on the plain. Arthur tells Perceval to carry Excalibur to the lake and throw it in the water. When he hurls the blade, a hand rises from the water's surface, catches the blade, and sinks into the deep. When the stunned Perceval returns to report to Arthur what he has seen, he finds that Arthur is on a funeral barge floating on the waves. Around his body are three tall maidens. This is the last scene in the film.

Before Arthur takes the field one last time, he tells Kay that now, "once more," he "must ride with [his] knights to defend what was, and the dream of what could be." These lines suggest that the condition of spiritual perfection exists only in wishes and reveries. Although one might die to the body to attain the elixir of eternal life, this manna is impotent before the decaying matter to which it is subjected. The Grail can resuscitate the king and the land for only a brief season before both ruler and flower again descend into the cold earth. The perfect Camelot probably never existed. If it did, it did only for a sliver of time before it disappeared.

In focusing on the difficulties of achieving the end of the alchemical opus, in *Excalibur* Boorman shows an awareness of the double binds of his cinematic medium. Even if his picture depicts sweet conversions of chaos to order, his narrative remains a dream, a series of flickering illusions. The dreamy qualities of his movie emphasize the tenuousness of his harmonies. A lurid green light plays over the stones, and the water shimmers in an unworldly brightness. Arthur and Mordred alike are conceived in hypnagogic trysts hovering somewhere between empirical reality and magical reverie. Merlin fades into the precinct of dreams, and from that outlandish zone translates the landscape into a creepy mist blurring men to ghosts. Arthur admits that his political utopia exists only in the half reality of nostalgic vision and unreal dreams. What else can Boorman's own film be, but such a dream? At the conclusion of this ravishing tale, we are left in a shadowy limbo, inflated with hope, but bereft of faith. Out of this state, a psychology akin to the murky retort, something new might come, but likely not.

Red Never Lasts

Two other recent films have likewise explored the tenuousness of the *rubedo* stage. Chris Columbus's *Harry Potter and the Sorcerer's Stone* (2001) and Sam Mendes's *American Beauty* (1999) focus on the difficulty of achieving and sustaining the complex, dynamic order of the red stage. As much as *Excalibur*, the films show the ultimately tragic nature of existence. Chaos ordered soon explodes back to turbulence. Order energized breaks into stiff fragments. All one can do is dream of the stone or the rose.

The first cinematic installment of the *Harry Potter* book series was bound to be an alchemical allegory. Rowling's six books so far have brilliantly explored the physical and psychological states of the alchemical sequence, mainly, the impossible interactions of the *rubedo*. Harry Potter is an initiate attempting to awaken his own chaotic powers, represented by Voldemort, and channel them into healthy order, symbolized by Dumbeldore. *The Sorcerer's Stone* depicts Harry's first struggle to achieve this transformation.

Columbus's picture features Harry's efforts to save the philosopher's stone from Voldemort, the dark wizard who tried to murder Harry when he was an infant. Since Harry bears Voldemort's powers—he took on the energies when he survived Voldemort's murderous spell—he is the only wizard capable of defeating the formidable black magician. Harry's affinity with Voldemort allows him to uncover Voldemort's plot to seize the stone. Through breaking numerous house rules of Hogwarts' School of Witchcraft and Wizardry (through invoking chaos), Harry discovers Voldemort trying to extract the stone from the magical mirror in which Dumbledore has hidden it. Because Harry can channel his dark powers into charitable energies, he is able to draw the stone from the glass. Knowing he cannot defeat the boy holding the elixir, Voldemort flees in agony. Harry is knocked unconscious by the efflux of Voldemort's pain.

When Harry awakens, he finds that Dumbledore has destroyed the stone. The tumultuous world will not allow the sweet order of the stone to persist. After clutching the stone for a moment, Harry is left with nothing but his struggle with the chaos.

The overall structure of *American Beauty*, a film on mid-life crisis and suburban angst, is almost exactly the same as that of *Harry Potter*, a movie on childish wonder and fantastical magic. The alchemical initiate of this film is Lester Burnham, a man in middle age who hates the predictability of his life. He rejects the static order and descends into chaos. He quits his job, takes to smoking grass, and develops a crush on his teenage daughter's friend. His decline is not deadly but generative. He enjoys visions of gorgeous red roses. He discovers salubrious vitalities. He becomes a full, complex, capacious human being, a king of his domain.

This largesse is exemplified at the film's end. After lustily pursuing his daughter's friend, Lester finds himself in a position to seduce her. But as he begins to remove her clothes, he realizes that this seemingly brash teenager is really a scared girl. Rather than take advantage of her vulnerability, he charitably transforms his lust to compassion. He treats the girl as a kind father would a disturbed daughter. He feels deep satisfaction. He has consummated his development not in selfish *eros* but in generous *caritas*. This affirmation reveals his true marriage of affection and rectitude, heart and head, soul and body. It shows his achievement of the spirit of the philosopher's stone.

This harmony is brief. Within minutes of Lester's epiphany, he is murdered by a psychotic neighbor ashamed of having made a homosexual pass at Lester hours earlier. The blood flooding from his blasted skull marks the gap between the rosy red of the *rubedo* and the lurid crimson of the *nigredo*. But at the same time, this blood suggests that the *nigredo* contains the seeds of the *rubedo*. The vision of wholeness remains even in the midst of decay, although this harmony might be nothing but an ideal.

Perhaps we continually swarm movie theaters because all movies, regardless of subject matter, possess on some level the qualities overtly on display in *Excalibur*—the attractive twilight of the dream, in which anything can metamorphose into anything else. While the seed requires months to birth a stalk and then a rose, the gloomy auditorium can in an instant warm bare commons into apple blossoms, or scientists into simians. Witnessing the quick cuts and blurring images on the screen, we ourselves dream of defying the constraints of time—its slow successions and constraining chains. We envision ourselves exploding violently into something unimagined and new or more gently fading into a porous form open to unseen currents. Though we feel our thighs hard on the seat and a rumble in our belly, for two hours we are not contained in our bag of skin. Returning to this old sack in the concluding darkness, we wonder if we have enjoyed an experience that has altered us forever or if we have merely been diverted for a time before coming home to the boxes in which we were born.

Epilogue:
The Gnostic Romance

In *A Natural Perspective* (1965), Northrop Frye wrote that interest in literature tends "to center either in the area of tragedy, realism, and irony, or in the area of comedy and romance." Those attuned to the former sort of literature hope that the text will yield a serious truth, a useful criticism of life, or an ennobling moral. Readers interested in the latter type are keen on uncritical enjoyment of a story—the pleasurable conventions of set forms, the joy of aesthetic closure. If enjoyment of the first literary form requires a sophisticated, somewhat jaded outlook on life, a sense of fragmentation, then appreciation of the second kind of literature emerges from a primitive hope that concord wins out over discord, that boy and girl will always fall into each other's arms.[1]

Readers in the camp of comedy and romance are likely to be moviegoers enamored of the soothing stories projected onto the screen. Even when commercial cinema ventures into tragedy, realism, or irony—narrative modes beyond the favored romantic and comic structures—it often attenuates these modes into comforting conventions, harmless plots driven by clichéd acting. Though some commercial films transcend the financial requirements of the picture house and achieve the status of high art, the majority of popular movies produced by Hollywood fall, regardless of subject matter, into the category of romance—the unrealistic tale told for the sake of giving pleasure.

Most commercial cinema is romantic in this way because most big studio pictures are driven by genre. Of course, all works of art, literary or otherwise, are delimited by genre. However, while "high" arts such as serious literature tend to deploy elements of genre in fresh ways, "popular" arts like commercial cinema often follow the conventions of genre in a predictable manner. If sophisticated revisions of genre unsettle artifice with "reality" and disrupt the audience's expectations, then uncritical embraces of genre exclude messy "reality" in favor of stereotype and fulfill viewers' desires for simplicity. Commercial cinema wants to give the people what they want: love stories, detective stories, horror tales, narratives of war, science fictions. These and other predominant cinematic genres serve as self-contained commodities. Audiences purchase them in hopes of getting immediate satisfaction—the "good" feeling, the "shocking" spectacle, the moral "uplift." When the rules of the genre are violated—when the ending is not happy, when the human "spirit" does not prevail—then viewers deem the product faulty. They are not interested in buying a contraption that does not properly function.

This is the romance of almost all commercial film. It gives men and women predictable and quick satisfaction. More concerned with meeting the requirements of popular genre than with revealing the rigors of the real, commercial movies, despite their extremely complex technologies, are primitive: rituals that demand not detached analysis but uncritical participation. Rejecting the nuanced contingencies of "lifelike" behavior, the popular cinema approaches the straightforward narratives and stock characters of folklore or myth. While this archetypal quality might interest a small contingency of thinkers, this ritualized quality of mainstream cinema is precisely what inspires most serious intellectuals to reject commercial cinema for encouraging, at best, decadent reveries of escape and, at worst, harmful dreams of unattainable perfection.

In his essay of 1935, "The Work of Art in the Age of Mechanical Reproduction," Walter Benjamin, a sometime friend of Adorno, highlights these superficialities of commercial cinema. For Benjamin, the cinema, along with photography, wrenches art away from its traditional "cult" values and reduces it to a commodity to be exhibited and consumed. In making images endlessly reproducible—not only traditional art images but also dramatic representations—modern cinema strips artworks and actors of their "aura." In earlier times, works of art could be seen only in one place, generally a temple or a museum. This uniqueness gave these works a sacred atmosphere. In the same way, a stage actor in any age presents his or her complete and mysterious being to the audience, the "whole living person." Film makes the work of art available at any place and at any time. It flattens the numinous density of the particular work to a thin abstraction contiguous with other thin abstractions. The vehicle of the film, the camera, attenuates the actor in the same fashion. In forcing the actor to perform in front of a machine instead of other humans and in shooting only parts of his body, the camera empties the actor of wholeness. It strips him of his corporeality. It fragments him into easily digestible bits. Transforming the richness of serious art and human gesture into tenuous flickers in exhibition houses, the cinema fosters an age in which contemplation becomes almost impossible. While the great painting or the stately play invited the spectator to unrushed contemplation of the great mysteries of life, the cinematic image moves too quickly to foster meditation. Its transitions distract the viewer from thinking, reducing him to a passive screen.[2]

To apply Frye's theory of romance to the genres of commercial cinema is gently to condemn commercial pictures as rather decadent trifles. To invoke Benjamin's ideas on modern film is to cast movies as obstacles to the numinous. These differences in degree, however, give way to similarities in kind. Film as ritualized romance and film as mechanical reproduction: both descriptions suggest that popular cinema operates on the level of daydream, divorced alike from empirical data and sacred powers. As immediate wish fulfillment, commercial cinema disables critical thinking. Metamorphosing minds into mirrors of flickering images, popular pictures further transform individual agents into ciphers of ideologies, the general dreams of the masses.

The commercial film as veil to reality, to thinking, to freedom—to the world, to reason, to morality: this is a bleak proposition, considering how wildly popular the cinema has become. However, one can examine this conjecture from another angle, one that casts cinematic genres in a more positive light. Frye and Benjamin offer the clues to this more optimistic interpretation. Frye claims that the action of the romance, in avoiding mimesis, can only be "archetypal." This suggests that the surfaces of the romance—be it a literary comedy or a commercial genre film—might open to the enduring patterns of the psyche, symbols emerging from a collective unconscious to organize individual thoughts. Likewise, Benjamin claims that the movie camera's ability to focus on events that escape conscious perception makes it a conduit to unconscious phenomena. Though for Benjamin this effect constitutes a surgical intrusion into reality, his remark contains a more positive hint: the cinema reveals visions unavailable to everyday sight.

The cinematic flight from empirical reality might open to an alternative reality beyond consciousness. The reveries of the popular screen could bloom into dreams of eternities beyond reason. The images overwhelming the individual mind could well usher one to a collective unconsciousness, a shared panorama of symbols. The commercial cinema's attenuation of realism, reason, and agency need not be a limitation but a virtue—an ability to transcend the boundaries of common sense. Film could be an eminently *spiritual* medium: a realization of invisible worlds, ungraspable thoughts, and immanent potencies. Unconstrained by space and time, the rules of logic, or the codes of conventional morality, the commercial genre film, despite its obvious role in a system of greed and exploitation, might serve as one of the last links to the palaces of the soul—those planes of vision where wishes come true and longing is unknown.

If films are spiritual events, then the Gnostic pictures discussed in this book are especially powerful revelations of the potential virtues of most all commercial films. These Gnostic movies both deploy and explode the elements of genre. They both offer and remove the pleasures of romance. In pointing to unsettling energies lurking beneath the surfaces of conventional narratives, these movies invite us to witness them as we would allegorical dreams, visible wish fulfillments of ungraspable yet enduring desires. As allegories of spirit—veils and revelations at the same time—these Gnostic films further urge us to envision all moving pictures in the same fashion, as vulgar surfaces that are yet perfectly designed to reveal pristine heights and depths.

These are unreasonable speculations concerning what so obviously seems to be an anti-spiritual medium. However, though these conjectures are likely untenable, we should not forget what Jung realized: healing archetypes can appear in strange places, in the music hall as well as in the museum, in pulp fiction as well as in Milton. It is all in the way of seeing. For the materialist, Harlequin romance as well as horror flick will be diversions from sordid life. However, for the spiritual seeker, perhaps insomniac and prone to drink, the images in the movie house—not even as real as ghosts—might open to the soul more seductively than the verse or the painting. If the world is a dream of some god, then the fevered reveries of the matinee are cries of the divine, intense and impossible.

Endnotes

Prologue

1. In the introduction especially but also throughout the book, I provide detailed expositions of each of these three movements. Along the way, I clearly lay out my definitions of "Gnostic" and "Gnosticism," two vague and slippery terms that run the risk of becoming almost meaningless if left undefined.

2. Of course Fritz Lang's *Metropolis* (1927) is another example of a heretical experiment gone wrong. It depicts the evils of technology gone unchecked. This overweening technological arrogance is figured by a female automaton bent on destroying the lives of the innocent masses. However, even if this film cautions against Gnostic arrogance, the film also espouses certain key Gnostic ideas: the world is controlled by an evil tyrant; this oppressed world might be liberated by a female figure of wisdom; liberation takes the form of rejecting the conventional laws of orthodox society. For an excellent study of how this and other German expressionist films influenced Nazi Germany, see Siegfried Kracauer's *From Caligari to Hitler: A Psychological History of the German Film*.

3. Other films from these same directors function similarly—as critiques of the human propensity to grasp, rather cravenly, illusion, and as calls for humans to risk the suffering of nonconformity. One thinks in this regard of Antonioni's *L'avventura* (1960), Fellini's *La Dolce Vita* (1960), and Visconti's *The Stranger* (1967). For a general discussion of these three Italian directors, see Peter E. Bondanella's *Italian Cinema: From Neorealism to the Present*.

4. Slava Tsukerman's *Liquid Sky* (1982) also fits into the category of the "cult" Gnostic film. In this movie, a tiny alien with a heroin addiction comes to earth and enlists a model who happens to be a drug addict to help him secure his narcotic fix. The only problem is that the alien and the model must kill humans in order to get a special heroin ingredient from their brains. Eventually, after killing matter in search of vision, the alien decides to leave earth. The model pleads for him not to leave. She then injects herself with a large dose of heroin and turns into a beam of light. She transcends matter for spirit. For an excellent discussion of this film and the three films mentioned above, see David Lavery's "Gnosticism and the Cult Film."

5. In locating spiritual virtues in commercial Gnostic cinema, my book pushes against the main arguments of Theodore Roszak's wonderful novel, *Flicker*. The book features a secret and violent Gnostic sect that uses occult film production techniques to breed in viewers a nihilistic, apocalyptic hatred of matter.

6. Some recent books exploring the spiritual possibilities of film from a Christian perspective are the following: Richard Walsh's *Reading the Gospels in the Dark*; Conrad Ostwalt's *Secular Steeples: Popular Culture and the Religious Imagination*; Craig Detweiler and Barry Taylor's *A Matrix of Meanings: Finding God in Pop Culture*; Robert Walsh's and George Aichele's *Screening Scripture: Intertextual Connections between Religion and*

149

Film; Robert K. Johnston's *Reel Spirituality: Theology and Film in Dialogue*; William D. Romanowski's *Eyes Wide Open: Looking for God in Popular Culture*; Bryan P. Stone's *Faith and Film: Theological Themes at the Cinema*; and Albert J. Bergsen and Andrew M. Greeley's *God in the Movies*. These books devoted to Judeo-Christian perspectives have been matched by book-length studies of religion in *The Matrix* that are more open to eclectic religion perspectives. Among the works on the religion or religiously inflected philosophy behind the film are Stephen Faller's *Beyond the Matrix: Revolutions and Revelations*; Matt Lawrence's *Like a Splinter in Your Mind: The Philosophy behind* The Matrix Trilogy; Chris Seay and Greg Garrett's *The Gospel Reloaded: Exploring Spirituality and Faith in* The Matrix; Glenn Yeffeth's *Taking the Red Pill: Science, Philosophy, and Religion in* The Matrix; Jake Horsley's *Matrix Warrior: Being the One*; and William Irwin's The Matrix *and Philosophy: Welcome to the Desert of the Real*.

7. For an account of how esoteric traditions informed the Age of Reason, see Joscelyn Godwin's *The Theosophical Enlightenment* (1994).

8. For a study of how Gnosticism and its esoteric offshoots influenced the Romantic age, see Kathleen Raine's *Blake and Tradition* and James Rieger's *The Mutiny Within: The Heresies of Percy Bysshe Shelley*.

9. See Arthur Versluis, *Esoteric Origins of the American Renaissance*.

10. Victoria Nelson illuminates the esoteric tendencies of Lovecraft and Dick in *The Secret Life of Puppets*.

Introduction

1. Carl Jung is the primary source of the idea that alchemy issues from Gnosticism. In his *Memories, Dreams, Reflections*, he argues that a current runs from ancient Gnosticism through medieval and Renaissance alchemy to twentieth-century depth psychology. The persistent characteristics of this current are the following: the origin of existence is an unfathomable abyss; this abyss descends into time in the form of conflicted oppositions; redemption from conflict comes in the figure of a savior reflecting the original abyss: the Gnostic savior from the hidden god; the philosopher's stone; the primal Self. The differences among these movements lie in emphasis on matter. Gnosticism wishes to escape matter; alchemy wishes to discover spirit in matter; depth psychology wants to find a purely materialistic redemption. These differences in focus on materiality have led some thinkers to draw a sharp dichotomy between Gnosticism and alchemy. For instance, Kathleen Raine in *Blake and Tradition* says, "The great difference between the Neoplatonic [and by extension, the Gnostic, even more anti-materialistic than Neoplatonism] and the alchemical philosophies lies in their opposed conceptions of the nature of matter. For Plotinus and his school, matter is mere mire, the dregs of the universe, a philosophic 'non-entity' because incapable of form except as it reflects intelligibles. To the alchemists spirit and matter, active and passive, light and darkness, above and below are, like the Chinese yin and yang, complementary principles, both alike rooted in the divine. The *deus absconditus* is hidden and operating in matter, no less than He is to be found in the spiritual order" (118).

2. Theodor Adorno and Max Horkheimer, "The Culture Industry: The Enlightenment as Mass Deception," 120–67.

3. Jean-Louis Baudry, "Ideological Effects of the Basic Cinematographic Apparatus," 345–55.

4. Laura Mulvey, "Visual Pleasure's and Narrative Cinema," 198–209.

5. Jean Baudrillard, *Simulacra and Simulation*, 1–42.

6. Herbert Marcuse, *One-Dimensional Man: Studies in the Ideology of Advanced-Industrial Society*, 1–18.

7. In this regard, see especially Michel Foucault's *The Order of Things: An Archaeology of the Human Sciences*.

8. Of course, here I could invoke other important theories of the conspiracy of the commercial film. One thinks in this context of David Bordwell's chapter on classical Hollywood cinema in *Narration in Fictional Film*. In this section, Bordwell discusses the basic structures of the commercial film—how it goes about representing the "real." Noel Carroll's entire body of critical work has been indispensa-

ble in helping me think through the relationship between film and insight, especially his chapter on ideology in *Theorizing the Moving Image*. Richard Allen offers an especially lucid account of cinema viewing and philosophical theories of perception in "Looking at Motion Pictures" (76–94). While each of these pieces—along with those of Adorno and Horkheimer, Baudry and Baudrillard—have helped me to articulate my position, none has focused on how cinematic perception might connect to esoteric transcendence.

9. *The Matrix* has already spawned a voluminous amount of criticism. Although no one has yet focused on the film's esoteric self-contradictions, several have noted the film's religious elements and its relationships to Baudrillard. See, for instance, Frances Flannery-Dailey and Richard Wagner's "Wake Up! Gnosticism and Buddhism in *The Matrix*"; James L. Ford's "Buddhism, Mythology, and *The Matrix*," 125–44; Dino Felluga's "*The Matrix*: Paradigm of Post-Modernism or Intellectual Poseur? (Part I)," 71–84; Andrew Gordon's "*The Matrix*: Paradigm of Post-Modernism or Intellectual Poseur? (Part II)," 85–102; Michael Brannigan's "There Is No Spoon: A Buddhist Mirror," 101–10; Gary Bassham's, "The Religion of *The Matrix* and the Problems of Pluralism," 11–25; Christopher Williams's "Mastering the Real: Trinity as the 'Real' Hero of *The Matrix*," 2–17; and David Lavery's "From Cinescape to Cyberspace: Zionists and Agents, Realists and Gamers in *The Matrix* and *eXistenZ*," 150–57. While these essays more or less track the ways in which *The Matrix* inflects either religious currents or Baudrillardian ideas, a few other pieces intelligently reveal the film's rich contradictions, even if these pieces do not relate the contradictions to the esoteric tradition. See Russell J. A. Kilbourn's "Re-Writing 'Reality': Reading *The Matrix*," 43–54; Thomas S. Hibbs's "Notes from the Underground: *The Matrix* and Nihilism," 155–65; and Sarah E. Worth's "The Paradox of Real Response to Neo-Fiction," 178–87.

10. Two recent essays on the ways in which *A.I.* explores relationships and reversal between humans and machines are John Tibbetts' "Robots Redux: *A.I. Artificial Intelligence* (2001)," 258–61; and Tim Kreider's "Review: *A.I. Artificial Intelligence*," 32–39. Though these essays meditate intelligently on the film's blurrings of the boundaries between mechanism and organism, neither focuses on how the movie inflects the golem tradition or urges, through paradox, transcendence of the rift between cog and consciousness.

11. The two most revealing pieces on *Dead Man* are Jonathan Rosenbaum's *Dead Man* and Mary Katherine Hall's "Now You Are a Killer of White Men: Jim Jarmusch's *Dead Man* and Traditions of Revisionism in the Western," 3–14. Although neither of these works explores the alchemical elements of *Dead Man*, both meditate on the ways in which Jarmusch's picture attempts to revise the traditional Western through its "mystical" commitments.

12. Paul Valéry, *Sea Shells*, 23. In this regard, see Philip Kuberski's chapter, "The Metaphor of the Shell," 78–93. Like Valéry, Kuberski finds that the shell is double—a familiar geometry and a strange involute: "The prophetic and the memorable, the future and the past are . . . conserved within the inward and outward whorls of a shell, as if within the covers of a book. And yet the pages of this book are themselves blank and nacreous, streaked by blues perhaps but without trace or inscription. Its form is thus apocalyptic in the sense that it speaks of destruction and revelation, and suggests how each can be the consequence of the other. More ancient, more marvelous, more unfathomable than the wonders of the ancient world . . . the seashell is, like them, a recollection of life's earliest architectures and enigmas" (80).

13. Michael Bird, "Film as Hierophany," 10–11.

14. Ibid., 11–13.

15. Ibid., 14–17. Paul Schrader's idea of the transcendental film, expressed in *Transcendental Style in Film*, as based on sparseness—as opposed to overabundance—is similar to Bird's notions. It is significant that Schrader uses Bresson and Dreyer—along with Ozu—to exemplify his ideas (1–15).

16. This idea runs counter to Schrader's notion that transcendental cinema is grounded on sparseness. I'm suggesting that overabundance can exhaust significance.

17. Friedrich Schlegel, *Philosophical Fragments*, 36.

18. Ibid., 45.

19. Samuel Taylor Coleridge, *Biographia Literaria*, 2:5–6.

20. Sigmund Freud, "The Uncanny," 217–52.

21. Tzvetan Todorov, *The Fantastic*, 33, 52.

22. Martin Heidegger, *Being and Time*, 176–77.

23. Victoria Nelson, *The Secret Life of Puppets*, 1–24.

24. William Blake, *The Complete Poetry and Prose*, 641. My remarks on Blake's senses of the concrete are largely informed by Northrop Frye's still brilliant study, *Fearful Symmetry: A Study of William Blake*, 3–30.

25. Blake, *Complete Poetry and Prose*, 647.

26. Ibid., 39.

27. Ibid., 2–3.

28. I am here also influenced by Frye, *Fearful Symmetry*, 45–48.

29. Of the many books on the Eleusinian mysteries, some of the most thorough and lucid are Carl Kerenyi's *Eleusis*, Marvin W. Meyer's *The Ancient Mysteries*, and S. Angus's *The Mystery Religions*.

30. Three excellent studies of the golden age of theater building are Edwin Heathcote's *Cinema Builders*, 11–23; David Naylor's *American Picture Palaces: The Architecture of Fantasy*, 31–140; and Dennis Sharp's *The Picture Palace and Other Buildings for the Movies*, 69–84.

Chapter One

1. I should be clear here that I'm using one of many specific interpretive modes in my description of Gnosticism, using a strain of interpretation inaugurated by Hans Jonas in *The Gnostic Religion* in the middle of the twentieth century. This strain is existentialist, deeply influenced by Heidegger. This way of reading Gnosticism is especially illuminating for cinema (and literary) studies. Books on Gnosticism that more or less partake of this existential current include: Kurt Rudolph, *Gnosis: The Nature and History of Gnosticism*; Jacques Lacarriere, *The Gnostics*; and Ioan P. Couliano, *The Tree of Gnosis*. Below I specify how certain of these scholars of gnosis bear on individual discussions of Basilides, Valentinus, and Mani. For a more historically based perspective on Gnosticism, see Elaine Pagels, *The Gnostic Gospels*. A more recent study that questions the validity of "Gnosticism" as a term is Michael Allen Williams's *Rethinking Gnosticism*.

2. *Secret Book According to John*, 23–51.

3. In my discussion of Basilides, I largely follow the informative and lyrical depiction of this Gnostic in Lacarriere, *The Gnostics*, 46–51.

4. Hippolytus, *The Refutation of All Heresies*, 103.

5. Ibid., 104, 106–8.

6. Irenaeus, *Against Heresies*, 349–50.

7. Ibid., 350.

8. Hippolytus, *The Refutation of All Heresies*, 108.

9. Lacarriere, *The Gnostics*, 50.

10. In my discussion of Valentinus, I draw largely from Jonas, *The Gnostic Religion*, 174–96.

11. Ibid., 174–75.

12. Ibid., 179–83.

13. Ibid., 188–90.

14. Ibid., 194–97.

15. My rendering of the system of Mani is mostly based on Rudolph, *Gnosis*, 85–86.

16. Ibid.

17. Ibid., 86.

18. Ibid., 66–67.

19. Of the little scholarship on *The Truman Show*, Michael Bliss's *Dreams within a Dream*, 200–222, is the most revealing. See also Kim Newman, "Rubber Reality," 8–9; and Kevin H. Martin, "*The Truman Show*," 53–56, 61–62. These studies highlight the blurring of appearance and reality in the film, and thus point to the Gnostic tradition. However, although these works were important guides for me, none of them explores the Gnostic melancholia of the film or the movie's esoteric double binds.

20. Quoted in Raymond Klibansky, Erwin Panofsky, and Fritz Saxl, *Saturn and Melancholy*, 18. Frances Yates, in *The Occult Philosophy in the Elizabethan Age*, 61, also discusses Ficino's relationship to Pseudo-Aristotle.

21. Klibansky, Panofsky, and Saxl. *Saturn and Melancholy*, 15–16; Yates, *Occult Philosophy*, 61–62.

22. Marsilio Ficino, *The Book of Life*, 6–7.

23. As with *The Truman Show*, very little scholarly work has yet been done on *Dark City*. Two revealing articles, however, are Jane Ryan's "*Dark City*," 95–109; and Estelle Shay's "*Dark City*," 71–72, 77. In *The Secret Life of Puppets*, Victoria Nelson notably illuminates the film's Lovecraftian collapses of reality and dream (135–42).

24. Sigmund Freud, *The Schreber Case*.

25. Jorge Luis Borges, *Labyrinths*, 8–18.

26. Ibid., 15, 17.

27. Ibid., 18.

28. Ibid.

29. I have gleaned from two essays in my meditations on *eXistenZ*: Mark Browning's "'Thou, The Player of the Game, Art God': Nabokovian Game-playing in Cronenberg's *eXistenZ*," 57–68; and David Lavery's "From Cinescape to Cyberspace," 150–57.

30. Martin Heidegger, *Being and Time*, 7–12. Of course, Heidegger's emphasis on generosity toward the strangeness of the particular thing is ironic in light of his ties to Nazism, a violently dictatorial system. Several recent books have explored Heidegger's complex, troubling relationship to the Nazis: Julian Young's *Heidegger, Philosophy, Nazism*; Tom Rockmore's *On Heidegger's Nazism and Philosophy*; Hugo Ott's *Heidegger*; Hans Sluga's *Heidegger's Crisis*; Tom Rockmore's and Joseph Margolis's collection, *The Heidegger Case*.

31. Heidegger, "What is Metaphysics?" 91–112.

Chapter Two

1. See Carl H. Kraeling, *Anthropos and Son of Man*, 38–53, for an excellent discussion of the figure of the *anthropos*. For a discussion of these three forms of declension, see Rudolph, *Gnosis*, 91.

2. Jean Dorresse, *The Secret Books of the Egyptian Gnostics*, 81–6.

3. *Secret Book according to John*, 23–51.

4. Gershom Scholem, *On the Kabbalah and Its Symbolism*, 197–98. Though Scholem remains the master of Cabbala explication even after fifty years, two more recent scholars have added mightily to our knowledge of Jewish mysticism. Moshe Idel's *Golem*, the definitive study of the android strain in Jewish mysticism, has been indispensable. In a more general way, Eliot R. Wolfson's *Through a Speculum That Shines* and *Language, Eros, Being* have inspired my thoughts on Cabbala. Both books are brilliantly eclectic works on Jewish literature and other strains of religious and philosophical thought.

5. Scholem, *Major Trends in Jewish Mysticism*, 208–17.

6. Ibid., 215–17.

7. Ibid., 230–35.

8. Ibid., 233–35.

9. Scholem, *On the Kabbalah*, 162.

10. Ibid., 176–82.

11. Ibid., 175.

12. Ibid., 190. In his novel *The Golem* (1915), Gustav Meyrink explores the golem of ecstatic magic. Though Meyrink is not entirely true to the Jewish traditions of the golem, he nonetheless captures the spirit of this creature in exploring its relationship to his protagonist, Athanasius Pernath, a cutter of fine jewels living in the Jewish ghetto of Prague in the early twentieth century. Because shock treatment has wiped out his memory, Pernath is trapped in a sordid present but haunted by dim recollections of a happier life. A modern-day Adam, he has been ripped from an Eden that he can now barely remember. He begins to have visions of a golem that stalks the streets of Prague every thirty-three years, apparently committing horrendous crimes. This is none other than the legendary creature of Rabbi Loew. Periodically coming to life and troubling the ghetto dwellers, this being reflects several currents of meaning: it is the microcosm of the ghetto's architecture, one with the enigmatic buildings that seem almost alive and sinister; it is the paradoxical population of the ghetto, comprised of mystical saints and murderous rogues; it is the spiritual potential of all men, inseparable from the *anthropos*. Embodying these levels—the material, the conflict between matter and spirit, and the spiritual—the golem gathers and transcends the three stages of the alchemical work: *nigredo*, *albebo*, *rubedo*. He doubles and inspires the spiritual quest of Pernath, who struggles through the chaos of the ghetto in hopes of reconciling the oppositions that tear his soul. In the end, he realizes the golem within, achieving a balance between past and present, matter and spirit. This union is figured by his union with a young woman who dreams of producing a hermaphrodite, symbol for the philosopher's stone.

13. According to Moshe Idel in *Golem*, Johann Reuchlin in *De Arte Cabalistica* (1517) was the first to mention the golem as a being created as a servant (177–79). As Idel points out elsewhere, the "blueprint" for the Loew legend is actually Rabbi Elijah of Chem. A Polish Cabbalist writing between 1630 and 1650 reports that Elijah fashioned a golem two generations before Loew. Elijah apparently "made a creature out of matter [*golem*] and form [*zurah*] and it was performing hard work for him, for a long period, and the name of truth ['*emet*] was hanging upon his neck, until he took, finally, for a certain reason, the name from his neck and it turned to dust." "The Golem in Jewish Magic and Mysticism," 30.

14. Elie Wiesel, *The Golem*, 32.

15. Though there have been excellent studies of the android in science fiction films—some of which actually make mention of the golem—no writer has yet explored in detail the overlap between golem and android in science fiction devoted to esoteric themes. The most profound work on androids in a science fiction film is J. P. Telotte's *Replications*. This fascinating, intelligent book has influenced my thinking in numerous ways. I have also drawn from Telotte's equally excellent, related study: *A Distant Technology*. Another useful study of this connection between android and science fiction cinema is Per Schelde's *Androids, Humanoids, and Other Science Fiction Monsters*.

16. No one has yet developed the golem motif in *Blade Runner*. Still, very good work on related subjects exists and has been very helpful. One of the best general discussions of the film in relation to the science fiction genre is Vivian Sobchack's *Screening Space*. See also Telotte, *Replications*, 150–54; Schelde, *Androids, Humanoids*, 231–38; Scott Bukatman, *Blade Runner*, 64–85; Sharon L. Gravett, "The Sacred and the Profane," 38–45; Joseph Francavilla, "The Android as *Doppelgänger*," 4–15; Judith B. Kerman, "Technology and Politics in the *Blade Runner* Dystopia," 16–24; Donald Desser, "The New Eve: The Influence of *Paradise Lost* and *Frankenstein* on *Blade Runner*," 53–65; and Jack Boozer Jr., "Crashing the Gates of Insight," 212–28.

17. I follow Scott Bukatman in my discussion on vision in *Blade Runner*. Bukatman aptly calls the film both a "drama about vision" and a "drama *of* vision" (10).

18. Blake, *Complete Poetry and Prose*, 122.

19. Friedrich Schiller, *Letters on the Aesthetic Education of Man*, 64–78.

20. Ibid., 74–77, 79–80.

21. James Joyce, *Portrait of the Artist as a Young Man*, 256–57.

22. Ibid., 256.

23. Ibid., 266–68.

24. There has been very little scholarship on *Robocop*, and none on the film's inflection of the golem motif. Still, in my discussion of the film, I found the following work especially helpful: Schelde, *Androids, Humanoids*, 208–12; Telotte, *Replications*, 150-4; Rob Van Scheers, *Paul Verhoeven*, 184–208; and J. P. Telotte, "Verhoeven, Virilio and 'Cinematic Derealization,'" 30–38.

25. Henri Bergson, *Laughter*, 4.

26. Ibid., 56–65.

27. I have located no significant critical work on *Making Mr. Right*, though Telotte, *Replications*, 224–27, and Schelde, *Androids, Humanoids*, 148, 203, mention the film. The reason is clear—the film appears to be rather a trifle. However, as I hope to show, Seidelman's film is surprisingly profound in certain ways.

Chapter Three

1. C. G. Jung, *Memories, Dreams, Reflections*, 201–7. My reading of alchemy is based on Jung's interpretation. I migrate toward Jung for an obvious reason. Jung's alchemy is psychological and thus a subtle vehicle for illuminating the dual journeys of cinematic characters, the outward dramas and corresponding inward vexations. There are other traditions for reading alchemy, however. For instance, the two leading exponents of the "traditionalist" school of alchemy, Titus Burckhardt (*Alchemy*) and Julius Evola (*The Hermetic Tradition*). Both believe, like Jung, that alchemy is foremost a spiritual technique but both also maintain that the physical components of the art are also important. A book with a strictly (and rich) historical emphasis is Stanislas Klossowski de Rola's *The Golden Game*. Two other general histories of alchemy—useful texts for reference—are E. J. Holmyard's *Alchemy* and John Read's *From Alchemy to Chemistry*.

2. Jung, *Psychology and Religion*, pars. 629–31.

3. Jung, *Alchemical Studies*, pars. 157–58, 168.

4. Jung, *Mysterium Coniunctionis*, par. 523.

5. Jung, *Psychology and Alchemy*, pars. 26, 334, 172.

6. Jung, *Mysterium Coniunctionis*, pars. 306, 446.

7. Ficino, *Book of Life*, 113–15.

8. Jung, *Psychology and Alchemy*, par. 334; *Mysterium Coniunctionis*, pars. 154–55, 158–59, 172–73; *Alchemical Studies*, par. 263.

9. Jung, *Mysterium Coniunctionis*, pars. 158–59, 172–73.

10. Ficino, *Book of Life*, 285–87.

11. Jung, *Psychology and Alchemy*, pars. 271–72, 325, 334–35; *Mysterium Coniunctionis*, pars. 498–500; 504–5, 642.

12. Jung, *Mysterium Coniunctionis*, pars. 498–500, 504–5.

13. Ficino, *Book of Life*, 265–67.

14. Jung, *Alchemical Studies*, pars. 282–303.

15. Neumann, *Origin and History of Consciousness*, 1:220–21.

16. Ibid, 1:225–27.

17. Ibid., 1:226.

18. Ibid., 1:227.

19. Freud, *Beyond the Pleasure Principle*, 76.

20. Ibid., 14–15.

21. Ibid., 43.

22. Ibid., 43.

23. I have found several pieces on Lynch to be helpful. I am especially indebted to John Alexander's *The Films of David Lynch*, which connects Lynch's *Evaserhead* to the alchemical *nisredo*. I was also assisted by Michael Atkinson's Freudian reading of the film in *Blue Velvet*. Michael Chion also helpfully invokes Freud in *David Lynch*, 83–99. Janet Preston's more theologically traditional study, "Dantean Imagery in *Blue Velvet*," *Literature/Film Quarterly* 18, no. 3 (1990): 167–72, was also very revealing. The best synoptic study of Lynch so far is Martha Nochimson's Jungian reading of him, *The Passion of David Lynch*. This remarkable book is a mine of insights on Lynch's consciousness. I should say that it seems to me that the canon of David Lynch is ripe for a full study of Lynch's religious modes.

24. Unfortunately, Ken Russell's underrated film has received almost no critical attention. The only significant essay I was able to find was Rebecca Bell-Metereau's "*Altered States* and the Popular Myth of Self-Discovery," 171–79. This piece intelligently discusses Jessup's quest for self in relationship to his limited view of women.

25. Boorman's *Excalibur* has been neglected by serious critics. This is very unfortunate. I hope my discussion works to bring the picture into a more flattering critical light.

Epilogue

1. Northrop Frye, *A Natural Perspective*, 3–33.

2. Walter Benjamin, *Illuminations*, 217–52.

Filmography

Agnes of God. Directed by Norman Jewison. Cast: Jane Fonda, Anne Bancroft, Meg Tilly. Columbia Pictures Corporation, Delphi IV Productions, 1985.

A.I. Directed by Steven Spielberg. Cast: Haley Joel Osment, Jude Law, William Hurt. Warner Brothers, Dreamworks SKG, Amblin Entertainment, Stanley Kubrick Productions, 2001.

Altered States. Directed by Ken Russell. Cast: William Hurt, Blair Brown. Warner Brothers, 1980.

American Beauty. Directed by Sam Mendes. Cast: Kevin Spacey, Annette Bening, Thora Birch, Wes Bentley. Dreamworks SKG, Jinks/Cohen Company, 1999.

Angel Heart. Directed by Alan Parker. Cast: Mickey Rourke, Lisa Bonet, Robert De Niro, Charlotte Rampling. Carolco Entertaiment, Union, Winkast Film Productions, Ltd., 1987.

Bicentennial Man. Directed by Chris Columbus. Cast: Robin Williams, Sam Neill, Embeth Davidtz, Oliver Platt. 1492 Pictures, Columbia Pictures Corporation, Laurence Mark Productions, Radiant Productions, Touchstone Pictures, 1999.

Blade Runner. Directed by Ridley Scott. Cast: Harrison Ford, Rutger Hauer, Darryl Hannah, Sean Young. Blade Runner Partnership, Ladd Company, 1982.

Blow Up. Directed by Michelangelo Antonioni. Cast: David Hemmings, Vanessa Redgrave, Sarah Miles. Bridge Films, 1966.

Blue Velvet. Directed by David Lynch. Cast: Kyle McLachlan, Dennis Hopper, Isabella Rossellini, Laura Dern. De Laurentiis Entertainment Group, 1986.

Creator. Directed by Ivan Passer. Cast: Peter O'Toole, Mariel Hemingway, Vincent Spano, Virginia Madsen. Kings Road Entertainment, Universal Pictures, 1985.

Dark City. Directed by Alex Proyas. Cast: Rufus Sewell, Jennifer Connelly, Kiefer Sutherland, William Hurt. Mystery Clock Cinema, New Line Cinema, 1998.

D.A.R.Y.L. Directed by Simon Wincer. Cast: Barret Oliver, Mary Beth Hurt, Michael McKean. Paramount Pictures, World Film Services, 1985.

Dead Man. Directed by Jim Jarmusch. Cast: Johnny Depp, Gary Farmer. Pandora Filmproduktion GmbH, JVC Entertainment, Newmarket Capital Group L.P., 12 Gauge Productions, 1995.

Death in Venice. Directed by Luchino Visconti. Cast: Dirk Bogarde, Romolovalli, Mark Bums. Alfa Cinematografica, 1971.

Donnie Darko. Directed by Richard Kelly. Cast: Jake Gyllenhaal, Holmes Osborne, Maggie Gyllenhaal, Mary McDonnell. Pandora Cinema, Flower Films, Adam Fields Productions, Gaylord Films, 2001.

EdTV. Directed by Ron Howard. Cast: Matthew McConaughy, Jenna Elfman, Woody Harrelson. Imagine Entertainment, Universal Pictures, 1998.

8 1/2. Directed by Frederica Fellini. Cast: Marcello Mastroianni, Claudi Cardinale, Anouk Aimée. Cineriz, Francinex, 1963.

Excalibur. Directed by John Boorman. Cast: Nigel Terry, Helen Mirren, Nicholas Clay, Cheri Lunghi, Nicol Williamson. Warner Brothers, 1981.

eXistenZ. Directed by David Cronenberg. Cast: Jennifer Jason Leigh, Jude Law, Ian Holm. Alliance Atlantis Communications, Canadian Television Fund, Natural Nylon Entertainment, Serendipity Point Films, The Harold Greenberg Fund, The Movie Network, Téléfilm Canada, Union Générale Cinématographique, 1999.

The Fifth Element. Directed by Luc Besson. Cast: Bruce Willis, Milla Jovovich, Ian Holm. Gaumont, 1997.

Frankenstein. Directed by James Whale. Cast: Colin Clive, Mae Clanke, Bons Karlott. Universal Pictures, 1931.

Gattaca. Directed by Andrew Niccol. Cast: Ethan Hawke, Uma Thurman, Jude Law. Columbia Pictures, Jersey Films, 1997.

Gods and Monsters. Directed by Bill Condon. Cast: Ian McKellen, Brendan Fraser, Lynn Redgrave. BBC, Lions Gate Films, Inc., Regent Entertainment, Showtime Networks, Spike Productions, 1998.

The Golem. Directed by Paul Wegener. Cast: Paul Wegener, Albert Steinrück, Lyda Salmonova. Projektion-AG Union, 1920.

Harry Potter and the Sorcerer's Stone. Directed by Chris Columbus. Cast: Daniel Radcliffe, Richard Harris, Maggie Smith. 1492 Pictures, Heyday Films, Warner Brothers, 2001.

Homonculus. Directed by Otlo Rippert. Cast: Olaf Fønss, Friedrichkühne, Sventriedland. Deutsche Biosup GmbH, 1916.

Iron Giant. Directed by Brad Bird. Cast: Jennifer Aniston, Vin Diesel, Harry Connick, Jr., Christopher McDonald. Warner Brothers Animation, Warner Brothers, 1999.

Jacob's Ladder. Directed by Adrian Lyne. Cast: Tim Robbins, Elizabeth Peña, Danny Aiello. Carolco Pictures, Inc., 1990.

Making Mr. Right. Directed by Susan Seidelman. Cast: Ann Magnuson, John Malkovich. Barry & Enright Productions, Orion Pictures Corporation, 1997.

Man Facing Southeast. Directed by Elisea Subiela. Cast: Lorenzo Quinteros, Hugo Soto, Inés Vernengo. Cinequanon, Transeuropa S. A. Cinematogratica, 1987.

The Man Who Fell to Earth. Directed by Nicholas Roeg. Cast: David Bowie, Kip Tarn, Candy Clark. British Lion Films Corporation, 1976.

The Matrix. Directed by Andy and Larry Wachowski. Cast: Keanu Reeves, Carrie-Anne Moss, Laurence Fishburne, Hugo Weaving. Groucho II Film Partnership, Silver Pictures, Village Roadshow Pictures, 1999.

The Ninth Gate. Directed by Roman Polanski. Cast: Johnny Depp, Frank Langella, Lena Olin, Emmanuelle Seigner. Araba Films, Bac Films, Kino Vision, Le Studio Canal+, Live Entertainment, Origen Producciones Cinematografias S.A., Orly Films, R.P. Productions, TF1 Film Productions, Vía Digital, 1999.

Pi. Directed by Daren Aronofsky. Cast: Sean Gullette, Mark Margolis, Ben Shenkman. Harvest Filmworks, Truth and Soul Pictures, Plantain Films, Protozoa Pictures, 1998.

Pleasantville. Directed by Gary Ross. Cast: Tobey Maguire, Reese Witherspoon, Joan Allen, William H. Macy. Larger Than Life Productions, New Line Cinema, 1998.

Repo Man. Directed by Alex Cox. Cast: Emilio Estevez, Harry Dean Stanton, Tracey Walter. Edge City, 1984.

Robocop. Directed by Paul Verhoeven. Cast: Peter Weller, Nancy Allen, Ronny Cox, Kurtwood Smith. Orion Pictures, 1987.

Short Circuit. Directed by John Badham. Cast: Ally Sheedy, Steve Guttenberg. PSO, 1986.

Thirteenth Floor. Directed by Josef Rusnak. Cast: Craig Bierko, Armin Meuller-Stahl, Gretchen Mol. Centropolis Film Productions, 1999.

Total Recall. Directed by Paul Verhoeven. Cast: Arnold Schwarzenegger, Rachel Ticotin, Sharon Stone. Carolco International N.V., Carolco Pictures, Inc., Tristar Pictures, 1990.

The Truman Show. Directed by Peter Weir. Cast: Jim Carrey, Laura Linney, Ed Harris, Natascha McElhone. Paramount Pictures, Scott Rudin Productions, 1998.

Vanilla Sky. Directed by Cameron Crowe. Cast: Tom Cruise, Penélope Cruz, Cameron Diaz, Jason Lee. Artisan Entertainment, Cruise/Wagner Productions, Vinyl Films, Summit Entertainment, Sogecine, SA, 2001.

Bibliography

Adorno, Theodor, and Max Horkheimer. "The Culture Industry: The Enlightenment as Mass Deception." In *Dialectic of Enlightenment*, translated by John
Cumming. New York: Continuum, 1976.

Alexander, John. *The Films of David Lynch.* London: Charles Letts, 1993.

Allen, Richard. "Looking at Motion Pictures." In *Film Theory and Philosophy*, edited
by Richard Allen and Murray Smith, 76–94. Oxford and London: Oxford
Univ. Press, 1997.

Angus, S. *The Mystery Religions.* New York: Dover, 1975.

Atkinson, Michael. *Blue Velvet.* London: BFI Publishing, 1997.

Bassham, Gary. "The Religion of *The Matrix* and the Problems of Pluralism." In
The Matrix *and Philosophy: Welcome to the Desert of the Real*, edited by William Irwin,
11–25. Chicago: Open Court, 2002.

Baudrillard, Jean. *Simulacra and Simulation.* Translated by Sheila Faria Glaser. Ann
Arbor, MI: Univ. of Michigan Press, 1994.

Baudry, Jean-Louis. "Ideological Effects of the Basic Cinematographic Apparatus."
In *Film Theory and Criticism: Introductory Readings.* 5th ed. Edited by Leo Braudy and
Marshall Cohen, 345–55. Oxford and New York: Oxford Univ. Press, 1999.

Bell-Metereau, Rebecca. "*Altered States* and the Popular Myth of Self-Discovery." *The
Journal of Popular Film and Television* 9 (Winter 1982): 171–79.

Benjamin, Walter. *Illuminations.* Edited and with an introduction by Hannah Arendt.
New York: Shocken, 1969.

Bergsen, Albert J., and Andrew M. Greeley. *God in the Movies.* Piscataway, NJ:
Transaction Publishers, 2000.

Bergson, Henri. *Laughter: An Essay on the Meaning of the Comic.* Translated by Cloudsley
Brereton. New York: Macmillan, 1911.

Bird, Michael. "Film as Hierophany." In *Religion in Film*, edited by John R. May and
Michael Bird, 10–17. Knoxville: Univ. of Tennessee Press, 1982.

Blake, William. *The Complete Poetry and Prose of William Blake.* Edited by David V. Erdman with commentary by Harold Bloom. Berkeley and Los Angeles: Univ. of California Press, 1982.

Bliss, Michael. *Dreams within a Dream: The Films of Peter Weir.* Carbondale, IL: Southern Illinois Univ. Press, 2000.

Bondanella, Peter E. *Italian Cinema: From Neorealism to the Present.* 3rd ed. New York and London: Continuum International Publishing, 2001.

Boozer, Jack Jr., "Crashing the Gates of Insight: *Blade Runner.*" In *Retrofitting* Blade Runner: *Issues in Ridley Scott's* Blade Runner *and Philip K. Dick's* Do Androids Dream of Electric Sheep? Edited by Judith B. Kerman, 212–28. Bowling Green, OH: Bowling Green State Univ. Popular Press, 1997.

Bordwell, David. *Narration in Fictional Film.* Madison: Univ. of Wisconsin Press, 1985.

Borges, Jorge Luis. *Labyrinths: Selected Stories and Other Writings.* Edited by Donald A. Yages and James E. Irby. New York: New Directions, 1962.

Brannigan, Michael. "There Is No Spoon: A Buddhist Mirror." In The Matrix *and Philosophy: Welcome to the Desert of the Real,* edited by William Irwin, 101–10. Chicago: Open Court, 2002.

Browne, Sir Thomas. *Selected Writings.* Edited by Sir Geoffrey Keynes. Chicago and London: Univ. of Chicago Press.

Browning, Mark. "'Thou, The Player of the Game, Art God': Nabokovian Game-playing in Cronenberg's *eXistenZ.*" *Canadian Journal of Film Studies* 12 (Spring 2003): 57–68.

Bukatman, Scott. *Blade Runner.* London: BFI Publishing, 1999.

Burckhardt, Titus. *Alchemy: Science of the Cosmos, Science of the Soul.* Rev. ed. Louisville, KY: Fons Vitae, 1997.

Carroll, Noel. *Theorizing the Moving Image.* Cambridge: Cambridge Univ. Press, 1996.

Chion, Michael. *David Lynch.* Translated by Robert Julian. London: BFI Publishing, 1995.

Coleridge, Samuel Taylor. *Biographia Literaria.* 2 vols. Edited by J. Shawcross. Oxford: Oxford Univ. Press, 1907.

Couliano, Ioan P. *The Tree of Gnosis: Gnostic Mythology from Early Christianity to Modern Nihilism.* New York: Harper Collins, 1992.

De Rola, Stanislas Klossowki. *The Golden Game: Alchemical Engravings of the Seventeenth Century.* London: Thames & Hudson, 1997.

Desser, Donald. "The New Eve: The Influence of *Paradise Lost* and *Frankenstein* on *Blade Runner.*" In *Retrofitting* Blade Runner: *Issues in Ridley Scott's* Blade Runner *and Philip K. Dick's* Do Androids Dream of Electric Sheep? Edited by Judith B. Kerman, 53–65. Bowling Green, OH: Bowling Green State Univ. Popular Press, 1997.

Detweiler, Craig, and Barry Taylor. *A Matrix of Meanings: Finding God in Pop Culture.* Grand Rapids, MI: Baker Academic Publishing, 2003.

Dorresse, Jean. *The Secret Books of the Egyptian Gnostics: An Introduction to the Gnostic Coptic Manuscripts Discovered at Chenoboskion.* Translated by Philip Mairet. London: Hollis & Carter, 1960.

Gravett, Sharon L. "The Sacred and the Profane: Examining the Religious Subtext of Ridley Scott's *Blade Runner.*" *Literature / Film Quarterly* 26 (Jan. 1998): 38–45.

Faller, Stephen. *Beyond the Matrix: Revolutions and Revelations.* St. Louis: Chalice Press, 2004.

Felluga, Dino. "*The Matrix*: Paradigm of Post-Modernism or Intellectual Poseur? (Part I)." In *Taking the Red Pill: Science, Philosophy, and Religion in* The Matrix, edited by Glenn Yeffeth with an introduction by David Gerrold, 71–84. Dallas: BenBella Books, 2003.

Ficino, Marsilio. *The Book of Life.* Translated by Charles Boer. Dallas: Spring Publications, 1980.

Flannery-Dailey, Frances, and Richard Wagner. "Wake Up! Gnosticism and Buddhism in *The Matrix.*" *Journal of Religion and Film* 5 (October 2001). http:// www.unomaha.edu/ ~wwwjrf/ gnostic.htm (accessed March 23, 2004).

Ford, James L. "Buddhism, Mythology, and *The Matrix.*" In *Taking the Red Pill: Science, Philosophy, and Religion in* The Matrix, edited by Glenn Yeffeth with an introduction by David Gerrold, 125–44. Dallas: BenBella Books, 2003.

Foucault, Michel. *The Order of Things: An Archaeology of the Human Sciences.* New York: Vintage, 1994.

Francavilla, Joseph. "The Android as *Doppelgänger.*" In *Retrofitting* Blade Runner: *Issues in Ridley Scott's* Blade Runner *and Philip K. Dick's* Do Androids Dream of Electric Sheep? Edited by Judith B. Kerman, 4–15. Bowling Green, OH: Bowling Green State Univ. Popular Press, 1997.

Freud, Sigmund. *Beyond the Pleasure Principle.* Edited and translated by James Strachey with an introduction by Gregory Zilboorg and a biographical introduction by Peter Gay. New York and London: Norton, 1961.

———. *The Schreber Case.* Translated by Andrew Webber with an introduction by Colin McCabe. New York: Penguin, 2003.

———. "The Uncanny." In vol. 17 of *Standard Edition of the Complete Psychological Works of Sigmund Freud*, 217–52. London: Hogarth, 1959.

Frye, Northrop. *Fearful Symmetry: A Study of William Blake.* Princeton: Princeton Univ. Press, 1947.

———. *A Natural Perspective: The Development of Shakespearean Comedy and Romance.* New York: Harcourt, Brace, Jovanovich, 1965.

Godwin, Joscelyn. *The Theosophical Enlightenment.* Albany: State Univ. of New York Press, 1994.

Gordon, Andrew. "*The Matrix*: Paradigm of Post-Modernism or Intellectual Poseur? (Part II)." In *Taking the Red Pill: Philosophy, and Religion in* The Matrix, edited by Glenn Yeffeth with an introduction by David Gerrold, 85–102. Dallas: BenBella Books, 2003.

Hall, Mary Katherine. "Now You Are a Killer of White Men: Jim Jarmusch's *Dead Man* and Traditions of Revisionism in the Western." *Journal of Film and Video* 52 (Winter 2001): 3–14.

Heathcote, Edwin. *Cinema Builders*. West Sussex: Wiley-Academy, 2001.

Heidegger, Martin. *Being and Time*. Translated by John Macquarrie and Edward Robinson. New York: Harper, 1962.

———. *Discourse on Thinking*. Translated by John Anderson and E. Hans Freund. New York: Harper, 1966.

———. "What is Metaphysics?" in *Heidegger: Basic Writings*, edited and with an introduction by David Farrell Krell, 91–112. New York: Harper & Row, 1977.

Hibbs, Thomas S. "Notes from the Underground: *The Matrix* and Nihilism." In *The Matrix and Philosophy: Welcome to the Desert of the Real*, 155–65. Chicago: Open Court, 2002.

Hippolytus. *The Refutation of All Heresies*. Vol. 5 of *Anti-Nicene Fathers: The Writings of the Fathers Down to A.D. 325*, edited by Alexander Roberts and James Donaldson. Peabody, MA: Hendrickson Publishers, 1994.

Holmyard, E. J. *Alchemy*. New York: Dover, 1990.

Horsley, Jake. *Matrix Warrior: Being the One*. New York: St. Martin's/Griffin, 2003.

Idel, Moshe. "The Golem in Jewish Magic and Mysticism." In *Golem! Danger, Deliverance and Art*. New York: The Jewish Museum, 1988.

———. *Golem: Jewish Magical and Mystical Traditions on the Artificial Anthropoid*. Albany: State Univ. of New York Press, 1990.

Irenaeus. *Against Heresies*. Vol. 1 of *Anti-Nicene Fathers: The Writings of the Fathers Down to A.D. 325*, edited by Alexander Roberts and James Donaldson. Peabody, MA: Hendrickson Publishers, 1994.

Irwin, William. *The Matrix and Philosophy: Welcome to the Desert of the Real*. Chicago: Open Court, 2002.

Johnston, Robert K. *Reel Spirituality: Theology and Film in Dialogue*. Grand Rapids, MI: Baker Academic, 2001.

Jonas, Hans. *The Gnostic Religion: The Message of an Alien God and the Beginnings of Christianity*. 3rd ed. Boston: Beacon Press, 2001.

Joyce, James. *Portrait of the Artist as a Young Man*. New York: Everyman's Library, 1964.

Jung, Carl Gustav. *Alchemical Studies*. Vol. 13 of *Collected Works of C. G. Jung*. Edited by Sir Herbert Read et al. and translated by R. F. C. Hull. Princeton: Bollingen Press of Princeton Univ. Press, 1967– .

———. *Memories, Dreams, Reflections*. Reissue edited by Amiela Jaffe. Translated by Clara Winston and Richard Winston. New York: Vintage, 1989.

———. *Mysterium Coniunctionis*. Vol. 14 of *Collected Works of C. G. Jung*. Edited by Sir Herbert Read et al. and translated by R. F. C. Hull. Princeton: Bollingen Press of Princeton Univ. Press, 1967– .

―――. *Psychology and Alchemy.* Vol. 12 of *Collected Works Collected Works of C. G. Jung.* Edited by Sir Herbert Read et al. and translated by R. F. C. Hull. Princeton: Bollingen Press of Princeton Univ. Press, 1967– .

―――. *Psychology and Religion: West and East.* Vol. 11 of *Collected Works of C. G. Jung.* Edited by Sir Herbert Read et al. and translated by R. F. C. Hull. Princeton: Bollingen Press of Princeton Univ. Press, 1967– .

Kerenyi, Carl. *Eleusis.* Translated by Ralph Manheim. Princeton: Bollingen Press of Princeton Univ. Press, 1991.

Kerman, Judith B. "Technology and Politics in the *Blade Runner* Dystopia." In *Retrofitting* Blade Runner: *Issues in Ridley Scott's* Blade Runner *and Philip K. Dick's* Do Androids Dream of Electric Sheep? Edited by Judith B. Kerman, 16–24. Bowling Green, OH: Bowling Green State Univ. Popular Press, 1997.

Kilbourn, Russell J. A. "Re-Writing 'Reality': Reading *The Matrix.*" *Canadian Journal of Film Studies* 9 (Fall 2000): 43–54.

Klibansky, Raymond, Erwin Panofsky, and Friza Saxl. *Saturn and Melancholy: Studies in the History of Natural Philosophy, Religion, and Art.* New York: Basic Books, 1964.

Kracauer, Siegfried. *From Caligari to Hitler: A Psychological History of German Film.* Edited by Leonardo Quaeresima. Princeton: Princeton Univ. Press, 2004.

Kraeling, Carl H. *Anthropos and Son of Man: A Study in the Religious Syncretism of the Hellenistic Orient.* New York: AMS Press, 1966.

Kreider, Tim. "Review: *A.I. Artificial Intelligence.*" *Film Quarterly* 567 (Winter 2002–03): 32–39.

Kuberski, Philip. *The Persistence of Memory: Organism, Myth, Text.* Berkeley: Univ. of California Press, 1992.

Lacarriere, Jacques. *The Gnostics.* Translated by Nina Rootes. San Francisco: City Lights, 1989.

Lavery, David. "From Cinescape to Cyberspace: Zionists and Agents, Realists and Gamers in *The Matrix* and *eXistenZ.*" *Journal of Popular Film and Television* 28 (Winter 2001): 150–57.

―――. "Gnosticism and the Cult Film." In *The Cult Film Experience: Beyond All Reason,* edited by J. P. Telotte, 187–200. Austin: Univ. of Texas Press, 1991.

Lawrence, Matt. *Like a Splinter in Your Mind: The Philosophy behind* The Matrix Trilogy. Cambridge: Blackwell, 2004.

Marcuse, Herbert. *One-Dimensional Man: Studies in the Ideology of Advanced Industrial Society.* Boston: Beacon Press, 1991.

Martin, Kevin H. "*The Truman Show:* The Unreal World." *Cinefex* 75 (October 1998): 53–56, 61–62.

Meyer, Marvin W., ed. *The Ancient Mysteries: A Sourcebook: Sacred Texts of the Mystery Religions of the Ancient Mediterranean World.* Philadelphia: Univ. of Pennsylvania Press, 1999.

Meyrink, Gustav. *The Golem.* New York: Dover, 1985.

Mulvey, Laura, "Visual Pleasure and Narrative Cinema." *Narrative, Apparatus, Ideology: A Film Theory Reader*, edited by Philip Rosen, 198–209. New York: Columbia Univ. Press, 1986.

Naylor, David. *American Picture Palaces: The Architecture of Fantasy*. New York: Van Nostrand Reinhold, 1981.

Nelson, Victoria. *The Secret Life of Puppets*. Cambridge, MA, and London: Harvard Univ. Press, 2002.

Neumann, Erich. *The Origins and History of Consciousness: The Psychological Stages in the Development of Personality*. 2 vols. With a foreword by C. G. Jung. Translated by R. F. C. Hull. New York: Harper Torchbooks/The Bollingen Library, 1954.

Newman, Kim. "Rubber Reality: As in *The Truman Show* and *Dark City* Normal Life Proves an Illusion in *The Matrix*, But This Virtual World Has Better Special Effects." *Sight and Sound* 9 (June 1999): 8–9.

Nochimson, Martha. *The Passion of David Lynch: Wild at Heart in Hollywood*. Austin: Univ. of Texas Press, 1997.

Ostwalt, Conrad. *Secular Steeples: Popular Culture and the Religious Imagination*. New York and London: Trinity Press of Continuum Press International, 2003.

Ott, Hugo. *Heidegger: A Political Life*. Translated by Allan Blunden. New York: Basic Books, 1993.

Pagels, Elaine. *The Gnostic Gospels*. New York: Vintage, 1989.

Paracelsus. *Selected Writings*. Edited by Jolande Jacobi. Translated by Norbert Guterman. Princeton: Bollingen Press of Princeton Univ. Press, 1988.

Preston, Janet. "Dantean Imagery in *Blue Velvet*." *Literature / Film Quarterly* 18 (1990): 167–72.

Raine, Kathleen. *Blake and Tradition*. Princeton: Bollingen Press of Princeton Univ. Press, 1969.

Read, John. *From Alchemy to Chemistry*. New York: Dover, 1995.

Rieger, James. *The Mutiny Within: The Heresies of Percy Bysshe Shelley*. New York: George Braziller, 1967.

Rockmore, Tom, and Joseph Margolis, eds. *The Heidegger Case: On Philosophy and Politics*. Philadelphia: Temple Univ. Press, 1992.

———. *On Heidegger's Nazism and Philosophy*. Berkeley: Univ. of California Press, 1997.

Romanowski, William D. *Eyes Wide Open: Looking for God in Popular Culture*. Grand Rapids, MI: Brazos Press of Baker Academic, 2001.

Rosenbaum, Jonathan. *Dead Man*. London: British Film Institute, 2000.

Roszak, Theodore. *Flicker: A Novel*. New York: Summit, 1991.

Rudolph, Kurt. *Gnosis: The Nature and History of Gnosticism*. San Francisco: Harper SanFrancisco, 1987.

Ryan, Jane. "*Dark City*." In *Jung and Film: Post-Jungian Takes on the Moving Image*, edited by Christopher Hauke and Ian Alister, 95–109. London and New York: Routledge, 2001.

Schelde, Per. *Androids, Humanoids, and Other Science Fiction Monsters: Science and Soul in Science Fiction Films.* New York and London: New York Univ. Press, 1993.

Schiller, Friedrich. *Letters on the Aesthetic Education of Man.* Translated and with an introduction by Reginald Snell. New York: Frederick Ungar, 1965.

Schlegel, Friedrich. *Philosophical Fragments.* Translated by Peter Firchow. Minneapolis: Univ. of Minnesota Press, 1991.

Scholem, Gershon. *Major Trends in Jewish Mysticism.* Foreword by Robert Alter. New York: Schoken, 1995.

————. *On the Kabbalah and Its Symbolism.* Translated by Ralph Manheim. New York: Schocken, 1996.

Schrader, Paul. *Transcendental Style in Film: Ozu, Bresson, Dreyer.* New York: Da Capo, 1972.

Seay, Chris, and Greg Garrett. *The Gospel Reloaded: Exploring Spirituality and Faith in* The Matrix. Colorado Springs: Pinon Press of Navpress, 2003.

Secret Book according to John. In *The Gnostic Scriptures: A New Translation with Annotations and Introductions,* edited and translated by Bentley Layton, 23–51. Garden City, NY: Doubleday, 1987.

Sharp, Dennis. *The Picture Palace and Other Buildings for the Movies.* New York: Frederick A. Praeger, 1969.

Shay, Estelle. "*Dark City*: Masters of the Dark." *Cinefex* 74 (July 1998): 71–72, 77.

Sluga, Hans. *Heidegger's Crisis: Philosophy and the Politics of Nazi Germany.* Cambridge, MA, and London: Harvard Univ. Press, 1993.

Sobchack, Vivian. *Screening Space: The American Science Fiction Film.* New Brunswick, NJ: Rutgers Univ. Press, 1997.

Stone, Bryan P. *Faith and Film: Theological Themes at the Cinema.* St. Louis: Chalice Press, 2000.

Telotte, J. P. *A Distant Technology: Science Fiction Film and the Machine Age.* Hanover, NH, and London: Wesleyan Univ. Press, 1999.

————. *Replications: A Robotic History of the Science Fiction Film.* Urbana and Chicago: Univ. of Illinois Press, 1995.

————. "Verhoeven, Virilio and 'Cinematic Derealization.'" *Film Quarterly* 53 (Winter 1999–2000): 30–38.

Tibbetts, John. "Robots Redux: *A.I. Artificial Intelligence* (2001)." *Film and Literature Quarterly* 29, no. 4 (2001): 258–61.

Todorov, Tzvetan. *The Fantastic: A Structural Approach to a Literary Genre.* Ithaca, NY: Cornell Univ. Press, 1975.

Valéry, Paul. *Sea Shells.* Foreword by Mary Oliver. Translated by Ralph Manheim. Boston: Beacon, 1998.

Van Scheers, Rob. *Paul Verhoeven.* Translated by Aletta Stevens. New York: Faber & Faber, 1997.

Versluis, Arthur. *Esoteric Origins of the American Renaissance.* Oxford and New York: Oxford Univ. Press, 2001.

Walsh, Richard. *Reading the Gospels in the Dark: Portrayals of Jesus in Film*. New York and London: Trinity Press of Continuum Press International, 2003.

Walsh, Robert, and George Aichele, eds. *Screening Scripture: Intertextual Connections between Religion and Film*. New York and London: Trinity Press of Continuum Press International, 2002.

Wiesel, Elie. *The Golem: The Story of a Legend*. Illustrated by Mark Podwal. Translated by Anne Borchardt. New York: Summit, 1983.

Williams, Christopher. "Mastering the Real: Trinity as the 'Real' Hero of *The Matrix*." *Film Criticism* 27 (Spring 2003): 2–17.

Williams, Michael Allen. *Rethinking Gnosticism: An Argument for Dismantling a Dubious Category*. Princeton: Princeton Univ. Press, 1999.

Wolfson, Elliot R. *Language, Eros, and Being: Kabbalistic Hermeneutics and Poetic Imagination*. New York: Fordham Univ. Press, 2005.

———. *Through a Speculum That Shines: Vision and Imagination in Medieval Jewish Mysticism*. Princeton: Princeton Univ. Press, 1997.

Worth, Sarah E. "The Paradox of Real Response to Neo-Fiction." In The Matrix and Philosophy: Welcome to the Desert of the Real, edited by William Irwin, 178–87. Chicago: Open Court, 2002.

Yates, Frances. *The Occult Philosophy in the Elizabethan Age*. London and New York: Routledge, 1979.

Yeffeth, Glenn, ed. *Taking the Red Pill: Science, Philosophy, and Religion in* The Matrix. Dallas: Benbella Books, 2003.

Young, Julian. *Heidegger, Philosophy, Nazism*. Cambridge: Cambridge Univ. Press, 1997.

Index